Praise for *The Work Revolution*

"Dr. Clow makes a good case for why we must *revolutionize* work. Some will resist it (and she shows *why*), but those who embrace it (and she shows *how*) will be the ones who win in a world where things are turning upside down. Her book provides an inside look at Google's culture as an example of a positively designed workplace that has created phenomenal business success. She draws on her work there to show that companies managed by "old-school work systems" cannot compete with those who understand the power of a "grassroots" culture where empowerment is bottom-up rather than top-down. I am convinced that she accurately describes the future state of the successful organization."

—**Aubrey Daniels,** PhD, author of four best-selling books, including *OOPS!: 13 Management Practices That Waste Time and Money (and what to do instead)*

"Don't fight for work-life balance; fight for a work revolution! Julie Clow's new book, *The Work Revolution*, lays out the new rules for success. Packed with self-assessments, case studies, and expert contributions, this book shows all of us the new way to work—and live—for greater productivity and less stress. I've never had so much fun reading a book about work."

—**Kevin Kruse,** coauthor of the *New York Times* best-seller, *We: How to Increase Performance and Profits Through Full Engagement*

"Looking to massively change your workplace? Julie Clow wants to change all organizations and shows how the power to do so is in your hands. Do your part by following the practical strategies and examples in this book. Your current and future employees will be deeply engaged, results-driven, and happy—and, so will you!"

—**Tony Bingham,** President and CEO, American Society for Training and Development

"We can do it! Julie tackles today's biggest challenge—remaking our organizations for the knowledge economy—with pragmatic optimism. Filled with ideas and examples, *The Work Revolution* is a book that will inspire individuals and guide corporations on the critical journey ahead."

—**Tamara J. Erickson,** author of *What's Next, Gen X?: Keeping Up, Moving Ahead, and Getting the Career You Want*

"*The Work Revolution* is a crisp and actionable manifesto for designing workplaces and leadership models that will sustain innovation, talent, and learning in these radically changing times. Julie Clow has written a must-read for business leaders, employees, and talent managers worldwide!"

—**Elliott Masie,** Chair, The Learning CONSORTIUM

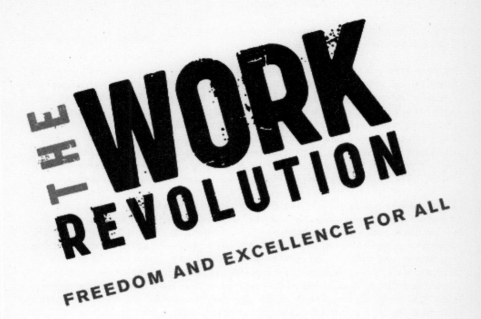

THE WORK REVOLUTION

FREEDOM AND EXCELLENCE FOR ALL

JULIE CLOW, PhD

WILEY

John Wiley & Sons, Inc.

Published by John Wiley & Sons, Inc., Hoboken, New Jersey.
Published simultaneously in Canada.

For general information on our other products and services or for technical support, please contact our Customer Care Department within the United States at (800) 762–2974, outside the United States at (317) 572-3993 or fax (317) 572-4002.

Wiley publishes in a variety of print and electronic formats and by print-on-demand. Some material included with standard print versions of this book may not be included in e-books or in print-on-demand. If this book refers to media such as a CD or DVD that is not included in the version you purchased, you may download this material at http://booksupport.wiley.com. For more information about Wiley products, visit www.wiley.com.

Library of Congress Cataloging-in-Publication Data:

Clow, Julie, 1974-
    The work revolution : freedom and excellence for all / Julie Clow.
      p.   cm.
    Includes bibliographical references and index.
    ISBN 978-1-118-17205-6 (cloth); ISBN 978-1-118-22681-0 (ebk);
    ISBN 978-1-118-23984-1 (ebk); ISBN 978-1-118-26454-6 (ebk)
      1. Corporate culture.   2. Organizational behavior.   3. Organizational change.
    4. Job satisfaction. I. Title.
    HD58.7.C56 2012
    306.3'6—dc23
                                                            2012003555

Printed in the United States of America
10 9 8 7 6 5 4 3 2 1

To my Dad and Mom, for teaching me positive thinking.

*To my awe-inspiring big (little) sister, Michele,
for being my best friend in life.*

*And to my beautiful daughter, Danielle, for being brave
enough and strong enough to ride the roller coasters
with me, and ultimately enjoying the ride.*

CONTENTS

Preface   xi

Chapter 1   This Thing We Call Work   1
Chapter 2   Signs We Have It Wrong   19
Chapter 3   The New Rules   39
Chapter 4   Impact, Not Activities   61
Chapter 5   Energy, Not Schedules   93
Chapter 6   Strengths, Not Job Slots   125
Chapter 7   The Right Things, Not Everything   157
Chapter 8   Grassroots, Not Top-Down   181
Chapter 9   Conclusion   207

Epilogue   217

Appendix   223

Notes   231

Acknowledgments   239

About the Author   243

Index   245

PREFACE

"Who is your book for?"

Whenever I revealed to people that I was writing *The Work Revolution*, they were curious about my target audience. And every single time they asked, I was caught off-guard.

"Well," I'd start to say, "everyone?"

Then I would second-guess myself and give them the answer I believed they were really waiting to hear: leaders and managers, entrepreneurs, organizational development consultants, and so on.

But, in fact, I stand by my original answer. We all work. Even if we don't have formal jobs, we do work of some kind, almost every day.

Self-help books are designed to teach people about themselves, and how to cope in their worlds. Interestingly, in most of these books, work is often a subchapter, or a tangent. In my life, however, work looms very large, both because it defines me and because I devote so much time to it. When I am happy at work, I tend to be happy in life. And when my work is a struggle, it negatively taints my entire outlook and existence. Anyone can relate to being miserable at work, and each of us can stand to improve his or her relationship with work.

Chalk it up to my positive-thinking childhood, but I believe we are capable of finding joy in both our work and play. Thus, I am hereby calling this a *work-help* book.

Although I might not have all of the answers, in *The Work Revolution* I share my philosophy and the principles that, cumulatively so far, have come closest to delivering joy in my work existence. This book is about reviving the humanity in our organizations. It's about tapping into the huge potential of these communities, of which we are already a part. If we can get *work* right, we can get anything right. Right?

CHAPTER 1

This Thing We Call Work

Once upon a time, long, long ago, we humans made our living working the land. We labored for ourselves, and the effort we put into our work was clearly tied to what we got out of it. If we planted seeds, we'd harvest a crop. But life then was tough, often grueling. When things went well, we could see our hard work pay off—though, too often it didn't; droughts and storms and unrelenting cold weather would come along more often than we could bear, wreaking havoc on our crops and destroying all we'd worked so hard to create.

As we evolved, we became more sophisticated. We designed massive production assembly lines to manufacture everything under the sun. By now, more often than not, we worked for someone else, earning wages by the hour, which dramatically improved our economic outlook and offered security and consistency. And we took pride in our work; we could see that the wheels we built or the chassis we helped to assemble produced a beautiful car down the line. It wasn't a rich life, but we were no longer impoverished.

But, alas, we evolved again. Rather than working with our hands, we started working with our minds. Our minds dreamed up a grand new reality, one in which the world was connected as never before. We built robots to assemble our cars, developed methods to modify the crops to become more weather resistant, and invented countless ways to automate our lives and make things profoundly easier. We organized the world's information, to make it accessible simply by typing a few words into a search box, or taking a picture of an object to learn more about it. Our economic lives tilted toward the prosperous, with ever more promise of abundance. And we began to live happily ever after.

Oh wait: No, we didn't.

WHAT IS THE PROBLEM?

You'd think we'd be happy working with our minds. We get to sit around and *think* for a living! Create ideas! Bring them to life! We have almost reached the promised land of perpetual contentment and happiness—except that we are still relegated to a dreary corporate world erected in the vast wasteland of the status quo, as so aptly illustrated and mocked in Dilbert cartoons, movies like *Office Space*, and the TV show *The Office*. Consequently, most of us now feel:

- *Overwhelmed*: We have far too much to do, too much information to process, and too many people to coordinate with. We can't keep up with it all, and we are drowning. Too-long to-do lists and overflowing e-mail inboxes are the causes of self-defeating guilt for many of us.

- *"Anonymized"*: The people who put in just enough effort to keep from getting fired are treated the same way as those who go all-out—those who truly care and want to succeed, and genuinely want to create value. But their efforts are rarely recognized, so what's the point? The result? Those of us who do care tend to get buried among the masses of the mediocre.

- *Disconnected*: Ironically, the very inventions that have given us such a profound sense of connectedness are incredibly complex, and thus require unimaginably esoteric work to make them happen. The work we do now is highly specialized, buried deep within the layers of our products, and the link between our contributions and the actual use of these products is too abstract for most of us to derive any strong sense of meaning from our work.

- *Mistrusted*: We work in companies fraught with rules and policies and dress codes and scheduled hours. It feels no different from when we were in high school, except the clothes we wear now are not nearly as fun, and food fights don't break out nearly as often.

We hear a lot about employee engagement and how it is abysmally lacking in today's workforce. For example, the 2011 Employee

Engagement Report from BlessingWhite (representing 11,000 respondents globally) found that only 31 percent of employees are fully engaged in their work, and 39 percent of all respondents plan to leave their current organization within the next year.[1] Business leaders wring their hands in despair, wishing they could find the answers to solve this problem. They roll out new strategies, hire new leaders. They search for reasons—it's the gen-Y age! The economy is terrible!—so they can conveniently shift the blame when they fail to figure it out.

Meanwhile, employees have no sense of empowerment; they feel like victims in a gigantic, tragically unmovable system. I was chatting recently with my dad just before he retired (or, more accurately, was laid off, which he took as a great reason to retire). He was relaying his frustrations about showing up to do garage-door repairs (my dad has always been adept at fixing things), only to discover once again that he didn't have the right parts. He knew exactly why: The person who ordered the parts was disconnected from the people who were taking the service calls, who were disconnected from the people who were ordering different equipment for original installation—you get the picture. He could trace the entire issue from one end of the organization to the other, and back again, with astounding details and insight. When I asked him, "Dad, why don't you just tell them how to fix it?" he quietly chuckled and shook his head. His wisdom was trapped in the tiny box representing his perceived influence on the organization. I realized at that moment how lucky I was to be working at Google at the time. Not because of The Perks (free lunches, massage program, parties, etc.), but because Google knows how to operate a sustainable, positive workplace in the new knowledge economy. As an employee of Google, I could have just gone and fixed a problem like the one my dad faced.

Why haven't other organizations figured this out? Why aren't they all clamoring to make big changes? The short answer is that we are too fixated on the symptoms of problems, rather than the problems themselves. For example, productivity gurus make a very good living teaching people how to manage their inboxes and task lists. One of the most popular productivity books, in print for 10 years, is selling as strongly as ever today. I would never argue that personal productivity isn't an important skill, but it will not solve the problem of information overload! Our ability to create and access data and information will continue to multiply exponentially, and no matter how many devices we carry and how religious we are about Inbox Zero (the philosophy and approach to processing e-mails each day to maintain an empty inbox),[2] we will never be able to keep up with the relevant (and not-so-relevant) flows of information. This is our new reality and we haven't yet figured out how to sustainably adjust to it.

Likewise, we hire young employees into our organizations and are shocked—shocked!!—at their level of dissatisfaction. How dare they insist on jobs that have "meaning"! We had to work hard to get where we are, and they act as if they should get it all on day one. Again, this is a symptom of the disconnect between our new global, always-on reality (which gen-Y folks know as their *only* reality) and our outdated work models. This clash isn't about gen Yers versus baby boomers and the lack of understanding in either direction; it's about the fact that we are blind to the deeper problems, and all too eager to deflect the blame.

Management fad after management fad is paraded throughout our organizations, promising the next-best fix for employee engagement and organizational productivity (though, most often, these fads can rarely be integrated into one solution). Everyone gets trained, processes are redesigned, and, then, about a year later, we revisit our problems only to realize that absolutely nothing has changed.

STARTING A WORK REVOLUTION

I am an optimist at heart, so I believe that we can fix this. Here is my Work Revolution Manifesto:

- I believe that it is possible to love your work, your workplace, and those you work with.

- I believe that it is possible to find your dream job and to excel at it, no matter how well (or badly) you did in school.

- I believe that every organization can thrive, generate more value for their customers and shareholders, and become wildly successful by sticking to the things they do the best and hiring people who belong.

- I believe the workplace isn't a zero-sum game, in which either the employees win or the organization wins, but not both; I believe that what is in the best interest of the employee is also in the best interest of the organization, and that getting this right is what leads to a thriving, profitable business.

In sum, I believe that freedom in the workplace is worth fighting for, and that every person and every organization can be excellent. When we unleash human potential, great things happen. But it's going to require loosening our death grip on control; we have to let go just a bit.

I posit that we can start the Work Revolution by implementing two, seemingly counterintuitive, strategies:

Strategy 1: Don't aim to change one organization. Change them all.

Strategy 2: Follow the easy path.

Strategy 1: Change All the Organizations

Starting a Work Revolution sounds daunting, even lofty, requiring a lucky confluence of factors. Changing any *one* organization, to swing it around from declining to thriving, is a wildly improbable prospect (as evidenced by the consultancy profession, which is booming and promises to be prosperous for a very long time). So far, few organizations have revolutionized the way they work. We have been regaled with stories of Google (which I will add to here), W.L. Gore, and IDEO, companies that have been so idealized it seems utterly impossible to replicate their successes.[3] But the fact is, these organizations *started out* with savvy and innovative management practices. They didn't have to turn around hundred-year-old legacies. That is why we see so many shining examples of start-ups that are able to launch with thriving, healthy, organizational cultures.

Consequently, what I'm proposing is *not* that we change at a rate of one organization at a time. It may seem counterintuitive, but if we aim big, if we try to change *every* organization, we just might be successful. How is that possible?

Jonni Kanerva is a software engineering manager at Google. He also happens to be one of the best managers I've ever worked for. He took me under his wing when I joined the Engineering Education (engEDU) team. During his tenure there, he carefully crafted a brilliant teaching methodology to delve deep into the core of this mysterious thing we call *innovation*. His innovation learning series, Ideas to Innovation (i2i), became wildly popular at Google. One of the concepts, in particular, stood out for me: It was a brainstorming exercise he facilitated with teams. He would start by having teams think about a big goal they were working toward. Articulating this goal was sometimes quite hard to do; but, he explained, it was important to boil it down to a simple problem statement. He would then ask the team to *multiply the problem by 100*. In other words, if they thought about solving the same problem, but 100 times bigger, what would they do? Of course, this little thought exercise required people to think about their problem in an entirely different way. It reframed it so that they were no longer obsessing about the details— the ins-and-outs, the minutiae of the work. It pulled them back and forced them to think at a completely different level and solve for the problem in truly novel ways. Now *that* is innovation.

That is our task at hand. If we shift from thinking about changing our current organizations to changing the entire *world of work*, what would that look like? It would *not* entail diving into organizational theory or organizational design. It would *not* involve changing out leaders or implementing a new training initiative. It *would* require a complete rewrite of the rules, a complete rethinking about the way we work, everywhere.

THE TALE OF THE START-UP

Jessica Lawrence, Managing Director of NY Tech Meetup,
Freelance Writer, and Speaker

At the start of a company's life, everything seems magical. The founders are best friends, the happy sound of employees playing Ping-Pong fills the air, and an office fridge well-stocked with beer purrs quietly in the corner. Start-ups are often looked to for inspiration; they seem to epitomize the ideal company, and provide a stark contrast to the old, slow, outdated, risk-averse, joyless large companies that many start-up founders quit in search of a better life.

The truth, though, is that every company in the world began as a start-up. At some point, all companies were staffed by a couple of people without much more than fresh ideas and a lot of passion, who were always smiling because they were exercising their autonomy in building something that was truly their own.

This image of the start-up is an idolized one. On the surface, start-ups look and feel different from older, larger companies: They are staffed by people who are more energetic, innovative, optimistic, open-minded, and willing to take risks. And while many of these attributes are accurate descriptors, much about how people actually work and are managed in start-ups is hardly different at all from mainstream companies.

A start-up typically begins with a couple of best friends who share a dream. As new employees are hired, new rules, habits, and structures are put in place, leading to a relatively quick regression into the type of management many people feel most comfortable with: "face time."

Although start-ups may have a culture of innovative thinking, their work and management practices do not necessarily reflect that. The start-up culture is largely based on face time—teams huddle together in an office space, hunch over computers, and often work long into the night and on weekends, to build their dream company. Working all the time is the only acceptable behavior at these companies, because at each stage in the start-up life cycle there is a perception of urgency that is driven by multiple forces.

Initially, a start-up faces the pressure of being first to market. It competes head-to-head with other companies working on the same idea, and first-to-market "wins." The start-up's employees work as many hours as humanly possible, in the same physical space, to make the collaboration process as quick and seamless as possible.

Once a start-up receives funding, the urgency comes from a different source—the investor wins or loses based on the success of the company.

(continued)

(*continued*)

The start-up founders now feel the pressure of pleasing an investor. I've heard tales of some venture capitalists calling or e-mailing start-ups at 10:00 or 11:00 o'clock at night as a test to see how quickly they respond.

During these phases of growth, start-up founders often face significant hurdles, and suffer depression and burnout, though very few openly admit it. They worry that revealing the toll that their unbalanced work life is taking on them will paint them as weak to current and/or future investors. They feel pressure to appear tough and be willing to brave anything to get the job done.

At first, working 80 hours a week in their own company feels different to entrepreneurs than working 80 hours a week for someone else. Many start-up founders seem to know what they are signing up for when they jump in, but that knowledge does not enable them to become superhuman overnight and continue to function well in the long term, in the high-pressure, high-demand environment of a start-up.

Although the habit of overworking in a start-up may feel different than overworking for a big, old company, its long-term effect is no different. Worse, it establishes habits of behavior that get passed on to new employees, and eventually become part of the new company's culture. Without intervention, start-ups are at risk of falling into the same patterns as the large companies they sought to counteract in the first place.

Strategy 2: Follow the Easy Path

Change is hard! It requires grit and determination! Blood, sweat, and tears! Right?

Wrong. My premise is that change is not only possible, but that it is easy. Think for a moment about doing something you love, something that comes easily to you but that may be hard for other people. Recall the feeling you get when you are in your groove—you might work long hours, but the time flies by, as you are swept along by the energy generated by the extreme satisfaction you get from what you are producing. This is called *flow* in positive psychology terms.[4] Martha

Beck lays this out brilliantly in her book *Finding Your Own North Star*,[5] as well as her follow-up *Steering by Starlight*,[6] and I believe these principles can readily be applied to organizations.

When you love what you do, and feel like you fit like a glove in your organization, *everything* becomes easy—in the sense that things come together almost magically, wins come fast, and energy remains high. When an organization focuses teams on the things that they are perfectly positioned to do, everything clicks! Customers come pouring in, and the results are far and away better than those of any competitors. Forcing things, pushing things along, making things happen by brute force—this all sounds noble, but in the end, it wastes energy and time, and is most often a signal that you are headed in the wrong direction.

We are so accustomed to the principle of hard work (especially in America, where we were founded on the Puritan ethic of noble suffering) that we have completely overlooked the notion that *easy* often points the way to *right*. Because I am a behavioral scientist by training, I am careful not to expect change when the desired behaviors are hard, unless you significantly alter the environment and put a lot of time investing in positive reinforcement of these behaviors. Fortunately, all the principles that underlie the Work Revolution are built around this notion of finding the "North Star"[7] both for individuals and organizations, pointing the way to the ultimate state of flow. It is appropriate then, that we embark by first making the change from work *force* to work *flow*.

Tying together strategies 1 and 2, the crux of the Work Revolution is thinking big and keeping it simple. The book *Influencer: The Power to Change Anything*, states that we often look at big problems and make the assumption that they require big solutions.[8] In fact, big problems sometimes can be solved very simply using small solutions that have powerful leverage. In *The Work Revolution: Freedom and Excellence for All*, I will stay true to the big ideas while religiously seeking ways to make change easy.

THE THREE CHANNELS OF CHANGE

Fred Kofman, author of the must-read book *Conscious Business*, defines the idea of *unconditional responsibility*.[9] If you say, "I can't be happy in my work because my organization is too bureaucratic," you are choosing to be a victim. To be a victim is to be a spectator and completely give up power. While it might be soothing to blame all of your ills, injustices, and bad results on external factors outside of your control, this renders you unable to make any changes and, thus, become part of the solution.

If, however, you choose to be a player (the opposite of victim) and claim "response-ability," then you focus 100 percent on the factors that are within your control. You are saying, "I can make a choice on what to do, given that the world has presented me with this situation."

If we all showed up at work taking 100 percent responsibility (not to be confused with *blame*), then we would all be empowered to be part of the solution. As a player, Kofman states, "There's always something I can do. I am free to choose how I respond to this. . . . When you are a player, there is no 'they'; if anything bothers you, then it's your problem."

So the first step—or, rather, the prerequisite—in the Work Revolution is that everyone, individuals and leaders alike, step up to respond to the problems of their organizations. Change can happen when individuals, leaders, and their teams line up to each take 100 percent responsibility. Some books are written *about* organizations— how to design an organization, create a vision for an organization, or merge two organizations. Other books are written to help leaders perform better at their jobs. Still other books are written for individuals to help them reach their full potential. *The Work Revolution* is written for all three audiences.

Individuals

When all is said and done, most of us devote 12 hours a day getting ready for work, getting to/from work, and, of course, doing the work itself. And this is assuming you don't spend additional time answering e-mails at night, reading work-related articles on the weekend, and putting in overtime at the office or at home. Why should we be okay with living a miserable work existence when it consumes so much of our time? And given that our identities are so closely aligned with what we do, why wouldn't we want to be glowing with pride about our work?

To go back to the commentary on generational differences, I've become fascinated with the growing community of gen Yers who refuse to succumb to subpar working lives. Here are a few examples:

Jenny Blake, author of *Life After College: The Complete Guide to Getting What You Want*,[10] writes a blog of the same name, serves as a life coach, and makes her living doing the very thing she was born on this planet to do, which is to help every other human on this planet find their true potential and *go after it*. She's 28 years old.

Charlie Hoehn, author of the e-book *Recession-Proof Graduate*,[11] assures graduates that companies that won't hire them because of their inexperience aren't worth working for. His premise is that graduates should volunteer, take on projects they love, and prove themselves as worthy hires to the innovative companies of the world that are using cutting-edge job-seeking strategies. He's a thriving entrepreneur at age 26.

Jamie Varon graduated from college, landed a great job (or so she thought), and had an "early-life" crisis after exactly two weeks of work. She quit, started her own business, Shatterboxx,[12] doing website design (she's self-taught), and moved first to Rome and then Paris, where she's living her dream life at the age of 26.

The list goes on and on . . .

How is it that each of these amazing, but quite young, individuals has figured it out in their twenties? Frankly, for whatever musings there might be about gen Yers being "entitled," that attitude has led to their having absolutely no patience for the ridiculousness of corporate lives, and they are opting out, in droves. They are optimistic that they can do the things they are passionate about, and can make money at it. Fortunately, what starts in the younger generations spreads upward to their elders, as evidenced by the former's immediate Facebook adoption, and the subsequent accelerated adoption by older age groups (Figure 1.1). We *all* need to become more entitled. We need to insist on a work life that is fulfilling and fun.

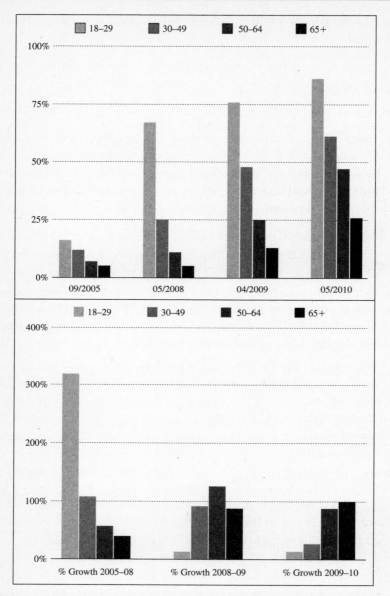

Figure 1.1   Adoption of social media by age. The top graph shows the percentage of the population using social media. The bottom one shows adoption growth year over year.

Data Source: Mary Madden, "Older Adults and Social Media," August 27, 2010; http://pewinternet.org/Reports/2010/Older-Adults-and-Social-Media.aspx. *Illustration*: Brian Lanier

As individuals, we might posit that we work for companies that are behind the times, inflexible, or impossibly conservative. You might even work for the government, in which case this is surely true. But you still have a choice. You can show up to work today and do everything in your power to create your own sense of freedom in that environment. Even if you can't knock down the inflexible pillars of organizational bureaucracy, you can stake tiny little tents of initiative and plant grassroots ideas throughout the organization.

Each of us, as individuals, can do things now, in our current roles, in whatever workplace we happen to be in, to make changes that will result in our own personal happiness.

Leaders

Leadership: This topic alone is responsible for a preposterous amount of shelf space at the few brick-and-mortar bookstores still in existence. Every organization grapples with developing its leaders. Leadership classes are chockful of information so "fluffy" it might as well be coming from horoscopes. Aubrey and Jamie Daniels, in their book *Measure of a Leader,* boil down leadership to my favorite definition: The most vital indicator of positive leadership is "the percentage of individuals volunteering discretionary effort" in the organization.[13] Simple as that. Put another way, how many people on your team go above and beyond their job responsibilities *just because they are inspired to do so*? If you were to create the perfect team, this is exactly what you would want from every member. But before this definition can be implemented, we have to make a few assumptions:

- Individuals have the freedom to initiate their own work.
- Individuals are inspired by work they believe is meaningful.
- Individuals see the impact of, and are rewarded by, the work they do.

So, of course, while the definition is simple, it is not trivial to carry it out. But that doesn't mean we shouldn't try. Wouldn't it be rewarding to know that you have contributed to the core happiness of individuals on your team, by making their working lives better? And wouldn't it feel even better to know that your efforts contributed significantly to the organization's bottom line? To quote again from *Measure of a Leader*, "The energy requirements of the leader increase in direct relationship to the decrease in the commitment of the followers." Simply put, your job gets easier, and requires less energy, as you become a better leader. Plus, the payoff is much more gratifying.

As a leader of a team—perhaps a manager or a supervisor—it is certainly valid to point out that you are literally caught in the middle between what Barry Oshry, in *Seeing Systems: Unlocking the Mysteries of Organizational Life*, refers to as the Tops in the organization, who want everything done, and the Bottoms, who want to do nothing.[14] But you are a *leader*, and you can fashion your team any way you want. When your team successes start becoming obvious, your approach will eventually meet with wide regard and appreciation, and eventually be copied with zeal.

Anyone who shows up as a leader in any context, whether as a temporary leader for a short-term project or the full-time head of a division, can, with new principles in mind, lead a team of engaged and excited employees.

Organizations

Do you want your company to survive? Fun fact: As of 2003, the average S&P 500 company had a lifespan of 25 years. Fast-forward to today: The average company lifespan is down to 10 to 15 years![15] Okay, that's not really a *fun* fact. But if your organization doesn't start creating a fun work environment, it will become one of those statistics. Note that when I say "fun" here, I don't mean that you should set up a carnival atmosphere and let people play all day. What I mean is, when individuals are tapping into their deepest potential and doing work that is meaningful to them, they will see their work, and the challenges at hand, as fun. I also mean that you should be working hard to create an environment where people can poke fun at themselves, share a laugh with each other, and play an occasional game of Ping-Pong, pool, or Foosball.

> "I've mentioned the idea of using the word *play* to replace the word work. If you have no way to feel playful doing your work, get different work."
> —*Martha Beck, "News from Martha Beck Inc.," April 2010*

When your employees can show up at work, know they have a voice, feel empowered to make things happen, and have fun doing it, you will have created an environment that fosters innovation and ensures that you stay agile to meet the constantly changing demands of the business environment.

Whether you are a unit leader, on the board of directors, the head of human resources, or even the CEO, you can plant the seeds for culture changes, sponsor initiatives that spawn grassroots contributions, and persist in moving the company in the right direction through the decisions that are in your span of control to make. If you have any influence on the design, culture, or operations of an organization, there are fundamental changes you can make in policies, processes, strategies, and culture, to create a better environment.

TYING IT ALL TOGETHER

Starting a Work Revolution requires that individuals, leaders, and organizations take action; all three groups are critical to its success. This book articulates the rules most of us are following today in our jobs, the reasons they no longer work, and what we can do instead. For each new rule, you'll find simple steps that every individual, leader, and organization can take to make those changes now.

But before I talk about the new rules, pause here to gauge the health of your organization today—to establish a baseline, if you will. After all, once you have fully realized the changes brought about by the Work Revolution, it'll be great fun to go back and have a laugh at the "before pictures."

GOOGLE: MY INSPIRATION AND MUSE

I finished graduate school in the summer of 1999 and entered the workforce naïve and optimistic. I expected to be as excited about work as I had been about school, which I always loved. It was quite a letdown, though I don't think I ever fully voiced this at the time. In the first seven years of my career, I sampled work life in a wide variety of organizations, since I served in a consultant-type role. I generally enjoyed my work, and I was far from miserable; but I did feel constrained and limited by the bounds of the corporate life. It was hard to spread my wings and feel like I could really make an impact.

In 2006, I made the big leap to move to California and join Google. I spent the first two weeks looking over my shoulder, waiting for someone to tell me to fill in a timecard, asking what work schedule I planned to keep, or putting other constraints around my time. This never happened. Consequently, I felt a complete sense of autonomy over my work and how I did it. It was pure magic.

During my tenure at Google, I continued to draw inspiration as I reflected on how the work environment at the company utterly changed me. I was free to pursue work that I believed would have the greatest impact. When the work actually did contribute value, I was rewarded with promotions and bonuses. I explored a variety of roles on different teams during the five years I spent there, and when I made the very difficult decision to leave Google in 2011, I left feeling enormous gratitude for the friends I had made and the rich perspective I gained about organizational culture.

I moved on to a wonderful opportunity to start up a learning and development function for a very cool nontraditional financial company in New York (my dream city). The new company is every bit as innovative as Google in its management approach, and so I felt completely at home there, from day one. I could never go back to a traditional corporate environment.

Throughout *The Work Revolution*, you will find plenty of examples from my years at Google, where I collected valuable experiences and illustrative stories. I have endeavored to deconstruct Google's management practices to make them accessible to everyone and every organization. I am not suggesting that all organizations can, or should, become another Google; what I am saying is that you can shape your organization to have Google-like qualities, which I have distilled in this book.

I admit, Google is my muse and inspiration, but even Google is not perfect. No organization is. Nevertheless, we can strive to make our organizations great places to work, and that requires nothing more than an insistence on optimism and a determination to do everything in our control to make it happen.

CHAPTER 2

Signs We Have It Wrong

I think it's safe to assume you know when you are miserable in your job, but let's start with a really quick test, anyway. On a scale of 1 to 10, how loudly and sincerely would you sing David Allan Coe's song, "Take This Job and Shove It" at a karaoke bar? If you said 10, let me suggest that there *might* be room for improvement at your organization. It's just a guess. If so, feel free to skip the rest of this chapter and move right to Chapter 3. I'd venture that most of you, however, fall somewhere in the middle of the Job-Shove-It scale: Some days you feel good, and generally like the role you play at work, while other days you feel stifled, frustrated, or even appalled about something that happened on the job, whether it is a new policy or some leadership maneuver that has everyone dumbfounded.

The objective of this chapter is to bring awareness to the various aspects of organizational culture that can either lift people up or drag them down, with, perhaps, a little more nuance than on the Job-Shove-It scale. As in any book on change, this one offers hundreds of ideas and suggestions; so the question is, where do you start? Which changes are most important? And how can you embark on a path of change without losing focus or taking on too much at a time?

The quiz in this chapter is designed to help you think about what is working now for you and your organization, and where you have the most room for improvement in the future. You may read some of these questions and think, "Oh, we're already on top of that!" That's wonderful. I expect that many organizations will have already started their journey to implement many of the principles in this book. The quiz is intended simply to give you foresight into the strong and weak points about your workplace. Ultimately, it is a tool to bring clarity and focus. You might decide to start with the weak points and make changes there. You might, alternatively, start with an area of strength and build on that success. In either case, use the results from the quiz to serve as a guide as you move through the rest of the book. It will help you decide which strategies to adopt and how and when to tackle the most important areas for you, your team, and your company.

THE DELUXE JOB-SHOVE-IT QUIZ

The Deluxe Job-Shove-It Quiz, which expands widely on the question I asked to begin this chapter, will help you assess the cultural health of your organization. It contains five sections to highlight different aspects of your organization—from its operating philosophy to your team and your individual role.

QUIZ INSTRUCTIONS

Select the answer that best describes your organization for the following questions in each of the five categories. Answer each item as honestly as you can—and with a sense of humor. There are no trick questions; each relates directly to concepts and strategies described throughout this book.

Your Organization's Philosophy

1. My organization has a mission statement:

    a. And I can recite it.

    b. And I would recognize it if I saw it.

    c. It is plastered on the wall somewhere. I might be able to find it.

    d. Mission statement? What mission statement?

2. My organization has a strategy:

    a. And I know what work aligns with it and what work does not.

    b. That only managers and leaders understand.

    c. But no one pays much attention to it.

    d. Strategy? What strategy?

3. Decision-making is done:

    a. At every level of my organization, and preferably by the individuals doing the work.

    b. By managers and senior leaders.

    c. By senior leaders, behind closed doors.

    d. Rarely. We can't seem to make any decisions.

4. My organization hires:

    a. Only those people who clearly belong in our culture.

    b. The best individuals we can find, with the highest credentials.

    c. Anyone who has enough experience and doesn't embarrass him- or herself in an interview.

    d. Anyone who can be trained to follow the rules and procedures.

5. In my organization, deadlines:

    a. Are based on truly urgent needs and business requirements.

    b. Are based on a project plan or set schedule.

    c. Are set by managers and leaders.

    d. Deadlines? What deadlines?

6. The perks in my organization:

    a. Are designed to restore energy and make it easier to balance/blend work with personal life.

b. Are on par with the perks of other similar organizations—just enough to compete for talent.

c. Are monitored closely, to make sure no one abuses them.

d. Perks? What perks?

The Rules

1. Rules in my organization are:

a. Invoked only during companywide poker tournaments.

b. Minimal, to protect against egregiously bad behavior.

c. Developed to ensure consistency and govern behavior.

d. Strict; enforced with zero tolerance.

2. My work schedule:

Note: Mark N/A if your schedule is based on external business requirements, such as trading or retail hours.

a. Is flexible and can flow according to my personal energy level and needs.

b. Is flexible, but only if I communicate changes to my team and manager in advance.

c. Is set and tracked by my organization; it is flexible only upon approval.

d. Is dictated by management and virtually unchangeable.

3. If I come to work late:

a. My coworkers don't really notice or care.

b. I feel the need to apologize to my coworkers and manager.

c. I will be reprimanded.

d. I won't have a job anymore.

4. If I need to take a break at work:

    a. I take it in whatever form I need, when I need it.

    b. I do so subtly, in hopes that no one notices.

    c. I ask permission or let my manager know.

    d. I wait until the designated break time.

5. If a coworker or my manager catches me on Facebook:

    a. He or she asks whether we are friends yet.

    b. I make it clear that I'm on a break.

    c. I worry that I'll be in trouble.

    d. I'll be fired for breaking through the corporate firewall that prevents access to all forms of social media.

6. If I wear jeans to the office:

Note: Mark N/A if your work attire is necessitated by your profession, such as scrubs for a doctor or nurse.

---

    a. I blend right in; it's the uniform of choice.

    b. It means it's casual Friday.

    c. It means I'm popping in on the weekend to pick up something I forgot.

    d. I would never wear jeans to the office.

Leadership

1. Leaders promoted in my organization are those who:

    a. Inspire and empower individuals to do the right work.

    b. Tend to know the right solutions and train people to implement them.

    c. Set clear rules and enforce compliance.

    d. Play the politics game the best.

2. Leaders in my organization:

    a. Trust individuals implicitly from their first day on the job.

    b. Trust individuals only after they have proved their value.

    c. Trust individuals who consistently follow the rules.

    d. Never trust individuals; they continuously monitor everyone according to company rules and policies.

3. My manager:

    a. Helps me by teaching me how to problem-solve and think strategically.

    b. Helps me by teaching me how to do things the right way.

    c. Tells me when I'm doing something wrong.

    d. Wait—do I have a manager?

4. The main role of managers in my organization is to:

    a. Develop individuals and advocate growth opportunities for them.

    b. Identify high-potential individuals and promote them up the job ladder.

    c. Supervise individuals to ensure quality work is completed on schedule.

    d. Track compliance of rules and reprimand those who break them.

5. If my manager walked in on a paper airplane contest at the office:

    a. He/she would join right in or offer to judge it.

    b. We would apologize and explain that we were taking a break.

    c. We would scramble to get back to work.

    d. We would worry about being reprimanded or fired.

6. I seek approval in my organization:

   a. Rarely; I would call it more of a conversation.

   b. From my manager, for such things as vacations and expenses.

   c. By filling out myriad forms and following processes and rules.

   d. For everything, including my break times.

Your Team and Coworkers

1. If I questioned why we were doing a project:

   a. I would be kick-starting a healthy conversation with my teammates.

   b. My manager would reiterate the importance of the project.

   c. My manager would consider me insubordinate.

   d. A deadly silence would fall in the room following my suggestion.

2. My team prioritizes work:

   a. Together, through rigorous discussion and following principles consistently.

   b. Inconsistently. We all have different priorities.

   c. Never. We try to get everything done all the time.

   d. Based on what our manager tells us to do.

3. If I quit working on a project:

   a. I could justify it by explaining the low value/impact it has for the organization.

   b. I would feel like a quitter, because I am hard on myself.

   c. My teammates and manager would view me as a quitter, not a team player.

   d. I might as well have quit my job.

4. Around my coworkers, I feel:

    a. Completely at home, even if we aren't necessarily friends outside of work.

    b. Like we get along well enough.

    c. Like I need to work hard to fit in.

    d. Like I'm from a different planet.

Your Role

1. With respect to my individual strengths:

    a. I get to apply them in my work almost daily.

    b. I get to apply them on special projects or occasionally.

    c. I hope to eventually find a role in which I can use them.

    d. I'll never be able to use them where I work.

2. If I am (or become) unhappy in my current role at work:

    a. I feel confident that I can find another role in my organization that will be better for me.

    b. I think I might be able to find a job opening on another team that would be better suited to me.

    c. I feel I have no choice but to stay in this role or leave the organization.

    d. I'd be like everyone else; no one is happy where I work.

3. I am rewarded at work:

    a. When I do a great job and produce results.

    b. When I do my job according to the best practices of our company.

    c. Based on the number of hours I spend there.

    d. By my paycheck/the job itself.

4. I know when I'm creating value for my organization because:

    a. I am given clear measures of success.

    b. My manager tells me.

    c. I'm told what to do and how to it; I have to assume it leads to value.

    d. I still have a job.

5. I know the right things to do at work because:

    a. I have a set of guiding principles to follow regarding prioritization.

    b. A set of rules and policies is in place, and I have been trained in what to do.

    c. My manager tells me.

    d. It never changes.

6. If I see something wrong in my organization:

    a. I figure out a solution and fix it.

    b. I suggest a solution to my manager or leaders.

    c. I bring the problem to the attention of my manager or leaders.

    d. I ignore it; the managers or leaders will eventually figure it out.

7. When I have worked my fortieth hour each workweek:

    a. I don't even know it; no one tracks my time.

    b. I continue working when a deadline is looming.

    c. I take a deep breath, double-down, and put in extra hours.

    d. I turn in my timecard and go home.

8. The bulk of my work:

    a. Has high-impact potential.

    b. Might or might not have an impact—it's tough to say.

    c. Is routine and prescribed.

    d. Feels trivial, meaningless, and/or overly bureaucratic.

INTERPRETING YOUR ANSWERS

Organizations are multifaceted and extraordinarily complex. It's entirely possible for the majority of an organization to be quite healthy, at the same time a department or two is massively dysfunctional. Or, conversely, an organization may have strong leadership but poor team dynamics within groups. To sort through this level of complexity, we'll look through two different lenses to help you interpret your answers to the quiz questions. Each lens provides a slightly different perspective, to help you identify areas for improvement.

Lens 1: Organizational Layers Analysis

As you no doubt surmised, the answers to all the questions are in the rough order of best (the A answers) to worst (the D answers). To begin this analysis, look at each section separately and do a quick calculation, tallying up the number of A answers, as well as B's, C's and D's. Next, make note of the distribution in Table 2.1.

Now look for trends in your answers. For example, perhaps you have mostly B's in the Your Organization's Philosophy section, but were heavy on the C's and D's in response to questions about Your Team and Coworkers. Here are some hints about what your answers in each section can tell you:

Table 2.1   Organizational Layers Analysis

Quiz Section	A	B	C	D
Your Organization's Philosophy				
The Rules				
Leadership				
Your Team and Coworkers				
Your Role				

Your Organization's Philosophy

- Mostly A's: Organizations scoring mostly A's have clear goals and the right people in place to achieve them. Further, people throughout the organization are empowered to work smartly toward those goals; and, in turn, they are treated well.

- Mostly B's: B-dominant organizations might have clear goals, but power is granted to only a select few leaders to execute on the vision. Leaders do *just enough* for their employees to retain them, but don't fully empower them to make decisions or work autonomously.

- Mostly C's and D's: Low-scoring organizations are either highly disorganized and chaotic or, at the other extreme, function in harshly authoritarian environments. In the former case, it's not clear what leaders in the organization are trying to accomplish, or who the best people are to achieve the goals. In the latter, employees are viewed as interchangeable pawns, and not trusted to act independently.

The Rules

- Mostly A's: Rules in A-dominant organizations are used sparingly. Leaders prefer to empower their employees to make decisions for themselves about what works best for their time and working environment.

- Mostly B's: Rules in B-heavy organizations are primarily used as a defense against bad behavior. For the most part, people can be flexible, but only within the constraints of the rules. There is *some* trust in the organization, but the rules remain in place as a safety net.

- Mostly C's and D's: Low-scoring organizations use rules as the primary tools to manage people. Rules abound in many forms, and provide a clear right/wrong path for employees. Inflexibility is a key theme in these companies.

Leadership

- Mostly A's: Leaders in A-strong organizations guide and develop employees, teaching them to think strategically and work autonomously. Their role is to make the most out of the organization's collective intelligence.

- Mostly B's: Leaders in B organizations "have the answers," and their job is to teach people what they are. Individuals gain autonomy only by proving over time that they know the "right way" to do things; only a select few are chosen to carry on as leaders.

- Mostly C's and D's: Leaders in low-scoring organizations are trained to control employees and hold them accountable to the rules. They may be crudely characterized as babysitters and compliance officers.

Your Team and Coworkers

- Mostly A's: Teams in A-rated organizations use productive conflict to determine the highest priorities; employees work well together and align to achieve the broader organizational mission. Diversity is not only embraced, but also seen as critical to making informed decisions.

- Mostly B's: While individuals on a team in a B-scoring organization might prioritize their work, there is little consistency among them as to what is most important. And because priorities aren't clear, it is difficult to assess the importance of projects and, therefore, justify saying no to low-impact work.

- Mostly C's and D's: Individuals in authority in low-scoring organizations dictate the work of teams, with the expectation that more is better. Because teams are given no latitude to create their own alignment on priorities, individuals might or might not get along, especially because they weren't hired for fit.

Your Role

- Mostly A's: Organizations scoring mostly A's have a vision, and teams hire individuals who really believe in it. Furthermore, because of the fluidity of teams, individuals can find roles that play to their strengths. The impact of an individual's work is clear, and is directly within his or her control; he or she is empowered to do the job in the best way to achieve the objectives.

- Mostly B's: Teams in B-level organizations hire individuals for specific jobs that have been predetermined to have importance, making it difficult to move outside of the bounds of these tightly defined roles. Everyone has a job to do, first and foremost; and even when there is an opportunity for someone to do a "passion project," it is typically managed closely to ensure that core work is not compromised.

- Mostly C's and D's: Individuals in low-scoring organizations are hired to fill rigidly assigned slots; as such, they gain no insight into the big picture, or see a relationship between their jobs and the mission of the organization. Consequently, they are almost completely disconnected from the meaning of their work. These individuals are expected to put in their time according to the rules and their training; there is little latitude outside of these parameters for them to create value or to find roles that might be more exciting or challenging.

What to Focus On   Now that you know the areas in which your organization is strong or weak, you can focus on the sections in each of the following chapters that address specific organizational, leadership, team, and/or individual layers at your company. Each chapter lays out actions that you can take to make changes in each of these layers, which represent every segment and level on the organizational chart.

Lens 2: Guiding Principles Analysis

Beyond the organizational chart, there are the guiding principles that serve as the foundation for developing freedom and inspiring excellence throughout organizations. This analysis will give you a perspective on which of the guiding principles are being fully implemented within your company, and help you identify those that are missing entirely.

For each quiz item, record the letter corresponding to your answer in the white box in each row in Table 2.2. For example, if you chose B for quiz item 1, write B in the white Impact box. Record your answer to item 2 under Right Things, and so on.

Table 2.2 Guiding Principles Analysis

Quiz Item	Impact	Energy	Strengths	Right Things	Grassroots
Your Organization's Philosophy					
1		▓	▓	▓	▓
2	▓	▓	▓		▓
3	▓	▓	▓	▓	
4	▓	▓		▓	▓
5			▓	▓	▓
6		▓	▓	▓	▓
The Rules					
1	▓	▓	▓	▓	
2	▓		▓	▓	▓
3	▓		▓	▓	▓
4	▓		▓	▓	▓
5		▓		▓	▓
6		▓	▓	▓	▓
Leadership					
1	▓	▓	▓	▓	
2	▓	▓	▓	▓	▓
3	▓	▓	▓		▓
4	▓	▓		▓	▓
5		▓	▓	▓	▓
6	▓	▓	▓	▓	
Your Team and Coworkers					
1	▓	▓	▓		▓
2	▓	▓	▓		▓
3	▓	▓	▓		▓
4	▓	▓		▓	▓

Quiz Item	Impact	Energy	Strengths	Right Things	Grassroots
Your Role					
1					
2					
3					
4					
5					
6					
7					
8					

As in the first analysis, your objective here is to look for trends in your answers for each category. For example, perhaps you have mostly B's in the Impact column, but were heavy on the C's and D's in the Energy and Grassroots categories. Here are some hints about what each category can tell you:

Impact

- Mostly A's: A score of mostly A's is an indicator that your organization has a clear vision and that individuals are empowered to find innovative ways of having an impact that is in line with the vision. Work is not judged primarily by the activities someone uses to achieve his or her goals, but by the results. Furthermore, weaving fun into the daily routine is not only accepted, but encouraged, and individuals are fully trusted to regulate their own activities and time.

- Mostly B's: While the leaders in B-heavy organizations are focused on results, they don't fully trust that individuals will engage in the right activities on their own to have the impact required. Activities are highly managed and monitored in these organizations, to ensure that individuals stay on track.

- Mostly C's and D's: Activities are the primary means of management in low-scoring organizations, and only the leadership has visibility into organizational results and how an individual might or might not have contributed to them. Activities are carefully designed to wring the highest volume of work out of individuals, who are strictly trained to adhere to them. Any activities that fall outside these parameters are strictly forbidden.

Energy

- Mostly A's: Individuals in A-rated organizations are acknowledged to have different rhythms, cycles, and preferences for when and how they work. Outside of deadlines, which are driven by business requirements or True Urgency, individuals are trusted to set their own schedules and work when they know they are fully energized and engaged.

- Mostly B's: B-level organizations use work schedules and project plans to manage a team's steady progress toward project goals, though individuals are permitted to request deviations to take care of personal needs. Generally, however, these deviations are constrained. Requesting variations from a standard work schedule too often is viewed negatively and with distrust.

- Mostly C's and D's: The management style of low-scoring organizations is to set standard work hours and plug individuals into these hours to ensure consistency. As long as employees put in their time and adhere to the schedule—usually, by means of timecards for tracking tardiness and absences—they are considered on good terms. Requests for deviations are severely limited, and too many requests may result in a poor performance rating or even termination.

Strengths

- Mostly A's: Teams in A-scoring organizations hire slowly and fire quickly. They never tolerate for long an individual who merely "fits" in a role; they insist on people who are passionate about the vision of the organization and its culture. Once someone is hired, the entire organization rallies to ensure that person can carve out a role that capitalizes on his or her strengths. To employees, the organization feels like a family, whose members share values and an enthusiastic belief in its mission.

- Mostly B's: B-level organizations spend a great deal of time carefully crafting job descriptions for open requisitions. Hiring is primarily about finding the best resume—a list of experiences and skills—for a given role. Once hired, individuals can transfer to other parts of the organization, but only if there is an opening for another tightly defined role. Finding a role that capitalizes on an individual's strengths is desirable, but not often possible, given the work that must be done.

- Mostly C's and D's: In low-rated organizations, people are hired to do very specific jobs, and there is no time to worry about whether someone feels as if his or her strengths are being used to best advantage. The emphasis is on getting the job done according to the rules; the underlying attitude is, if you don't like the job, you shouldn't have applied for it in the first place. It is a job after all; who said it should be fun?

Right Things

- Mostly A's: The key to success in A-dominant organizations is enabling individuals to choose to do only the work that will have the greatest impact and move the organization nearer to achieving its vision. A constant, vibrant debate is carried out among all of the employees to figure out what is most important, and individuals are empowered to stop low-value work and seek out more important opportunities.

- Mostly B's: Leaders and managers of B-rated organizations spend a great deal of time determining the top priorities for the organization; they are responsible for creating project plans and road maps that ensure individuals work on the "right" tasks. So, though individuals may understand the priorities, they rarely have real-time insight when those priorities shift; they are dependent on managers or leaders to communicate the changes.

- Mostly C's and D's: Employees at low-scoring organizations have no insight into organizational priorities. They are expected to do the work assigned to them by managers and supervisors. Likewise, they have no insight into whether their work has any impact, positive or negative! Individuals are given no flexibility to change course based on low- or high-value work, both because they are assigned the work and because its value is not evident to them.

Grassroots

- Mostly A's: In A-rated organizations, every individual is trusted and empowered to fix problems proactively. A typical motto is "Ask for forgiveness, not for permission," which encourages individuals to act quickly in the best interests of the organization. Transparency is key so that every employee understands the organizational goals and can make informed decisions about how to best achieve them.

- Mostly B's: Individuals are generally trusted in B-heavy organizations; nevertheless, there are processes and approval structures in place to make sure that managers and leaders maintain control over decisions made for the team. Individuals can, however, earn trust and take on additional responsibility, and they are empowered to point out problems and suggest solutions to leaders of the organization.

- Mostly C's and D's: Individuals working in low-scoring organizations are rarely trusted to make autonomous decisions. Rather, managers and supervisors are responsible for crafting robust rules and processes to guide the actions of everyone, in every potential scenario. Individuals are not empowered to go off-script; they must seek approval or escalate issues that aren't covered by existing rules or processes. Managers are further tasked with monitoring employees to ensure consistent application of the rules and processes.

What to Focus On   Each of the preceding categories corresponds to a specific chapter in this book. If there are categories for which you gave your organization a particularly low score, pay special attention to actions you can take as an individual or leader to make changes in these areas. And because these concepts are interconnected in many ways, chances are good that changes in one category will positively affect other areas as well.

Chapter 3, "The New Rules," opens a gateway from which to reflect on the rules that are guiding your organization now, to bring awareness to the pervasiveness of constraints you recognize and those you don't even notice. It's important to acknowledge the rules you follow today in order to think about new rules that will move you toward starting a Work Revolution in your own organization.

CHAPTER 3

The New Rules

I don't know why we humans hate loss so much.
It seems as though we would have evolved into
creatures that just *love* loss, can't get enough of it,
crave it, seek it out. Instead, by some design flaw,
we are stunned and devastated by things like
separation, aging, and death, as though these aren't
the very constants sure to affect every single
blessed one of us.

—Martha Beck, *Finding Your Own North Star*

We humans are notorious for resisting change and loss. We kick and scream and fight to maintain the status quo, which is why the organizations we work for might evolve but often fail to make the drastic changes needed to stay relevant in a market and, ultimately, survive. The sheer volume of coordination required to make big changes is often enough to ensure it won't happen. And when we throw in an emotional attachment to the Way Things Are (as much as we might complain about it), change is pretty much dead on arrival.

Given that change is accelerating in the business world, due to technology and globalization, our difficulties in facilitating organizational change are becoming more painfully obvious. We are failing faster because change is happening at a faster rate. Nevertheless, we have an opportunity to make some fundamental changes to our organizations. And it's critical that we do so in order to become more agile. It's also critical because of a twofold problem that is here to stay, and about which we are currently in denial: one, the always-on dilemma, which constantly fills our buckets of information to overflowing, and, two, a global workforce that follows the sun.

If we step back to observe ourselves for a moment, the scene is actually pretty hilarious:

First, we get up at a ridiculously early hour of the morning, which is exciting for only the half the population, those born with the morning-person gene. (These people are freaks, I tell you.) We proceed to the area of our closets reserved for business clothes—you know, the overpriced, boring ensembles no one would actually choose to wear. We dutifully dress ourselves according to the code outlined by the HR people at our companies, then join the hordes of fellow workers to traverse the roads at exactly the same time, jamming them up and causing a massive waste of time. (In an attempt to alleviate commuter pain, we've ingeniously created carpool lanes and other equally "innovative" solutions, such as hybrid cars and public transportation.) We arrive at work, open our e-mail inboxes, and spend the next hour or more responding to messages, thereby generating even more e-mails that spread back out to everyone else. After we've spent our most precious hours engaged in virtual, stilted conversations with a hundred different context switches, we recover over a hurried lunch, eating either terrible cafeteria food or spending $9.95 on an overpriced roast beef combo. We come back in the afternoon to attempt to do productive work, which extends far beyond our human ability to stay focused in a single day. And then we pile back into our cars to again join the masses on the overflowing roads, now going in the opposite direction, only to get home far too late to have a sensible dinner with our families.

And we're okay with this?!

We've created a world of work that, at one point, made sense—like, back when the Industrial Age felt like the Space Age. But we have far exceeded the boundaries of that era's sensibility. It is time to rethink this whole picture—to just start from scratch and rewrite the rules. The goal:

Honor the reality of our amazing, ever-present technologies and global world in a way that simultaneously respects an individual's ability to regulate energy, be productive, and contribute back to an organization so that everyone is engaged, satisfied, and successful.

As comedian Lewis Black said about our global warming issues: "It's absolutely stupid that we live without an ozone layer. We have men, we've got rockets, we've got Saran Wrap—FIX IT!!!"[1]

WHAT IS OUR REALITY?

In order to rewrite the rules, it is important to get crystal clear on our current reality. I like to think of this as a math equation. We start by listing out the known variables and the constants—the things that we know to be true and that will not change. Once we've got those, we can solve the equation to figure out the new rules that will suit us much better (pun intended).

So, what are the facts? What do we know to be true?

Fact 1: Work Never Stops

Companies are global, and our collective workdays are 24 hours long. Increasingly, we find ourselves working in companies or with clients that are literally spread across the globe. Consistent with this, technology has evolved to cope:

- *Communication is cheap*: Calling someone domestically is dirt-cheap, mostly free. Calling internationally is easy, and mostly cheap, too; furthermore, video chats and instant messaging make this almost free, save the equipment charges.

- *Travel is easy*: I can travel to the opposite side of the world in less than a day. Furthermore, I could be working from the other side of the world and my colleagues wouldn't know the difference between that and my "working from home" on any given day.

At Google, I worked closely with teammates in Mountain View, California (my location), Seattle, Washington (same time zone), New York City (plus 3 hours), Zurich, Switzerland (plus 8 hours), Bangalore, India (plus 11.5 hours—a very confusing 30-minute difference), and Sydney, Australia (plus 19 hours). Even on the Mountain View campus, which is huge, I could have been a couple of buildings away from a colleague and we would both call in to a video conference from our respective locations, to join our colleagues in Zurich or Sydney—it made no difference who was where! We all looked like two-dimensional images on the wall, and the meetings ran as if we were all in the same room, even though two of us were a stone's throw from each other and the others were thousands of miles away.

The fact that work never stops is both stifling and freeing, depending on how you look at it. It's stifling in that we feel we will never catch up, because there is always something going on. However, we can flip this on its head to realize: "Hey! If people are always working, why am I shoehorning my day into 9-to-5 hours?" We each can be doing our own work *at any time* and it would be entirely consistent with the way in which work is getting done by a global workforce.

Fact 2: Information Never Stops, and We Will Never Be Able to Consume It All

We have gotten really, really good at making information accessible; it's just as easy to generate new information to share. The problem is, the technology to help us parse and filter through all this data lags behind.

There are really only two major forms of information: *communication* and *learning*. Communication information represents all that we receive about other individuals—where they are, what they've done or are doing, and what you need to do in return. This information is mostly two-way, in that you both give and receive. Learning information includes all the data we consume to learn things of relevance to us. It's the news, new ideas, research and gossip, blogs and articles, and snippets. We have different channels for transmitting communication and learning information, though, admittedly, they often blur. Regardless, there is far too much of both types, and we are fooling ourselves if we think we can adequately consume it all.

Our mechanism for coping with this so far has been to create devices that make it much easier for us to communicate with each other and access/digest content and information *all the time*. When we walk away from work at the end of the day, most of us continue to monitor our inboxes and respond to messages until we go to sleep. Some of us even choose (or are compelled) to bring our inboxes with us on vacation.

We think, it's better to keep up with it while we are away than to go through the pain of confronting an overflowing inbox upon our return.

In essence, we are treating work as a 24-hour endeavor, though we may try to fool ourselves into thinking that we're working "only" 8 or 9 or 10 hours a day.

Let me just say this: You will never be caught up on e-mail. Never. A friend of mine once wrote me that she was having a sleepless night, admitted defeat, and got up and hopped on her computer to chip away at her inbox. At 4:00 AM, she sent me an e-mail declaring triumphantly that her inbox was down to four—FOUR!!—e-mails! My jaw dropped when I read it. E-mail nirvana! I hadn't achieved that feat in years. Of course, my inbox was so full that it was another day or two before I could get around to congratulating her (dripping with envy, I might add). Here was her response: "My inbox 'freedom' was very short-lived—lasted about one hour:)."

SOLVING THE INSOLVABLE PROBLEM OF INFORMATION OVERLOAD

Chris Crum, WebProNews.com Blog post[2]

You might say I oversubscribe to feeds. I follow too many people and organizations on Twitter and Facebook. I subscribe to too many e-mail newsletters or alerts. I'm creating too much noise for myself. But you never know where the most important nugget of info is going to come from.

It's impossible to consume it all. It really is. Even if I devoted 24 hours a day without sleep or spending time with my family or actually writing articles, I could never read every article, blog post, tweet, or status update, or watch every video and listen to every podcast and read every e-mail that I would need to truly get all of the information relevant to my interests.

(continued)

(*continued*)

The bad news, again, is that there is nothing available (that I'm aware of) that truly solves the information overload problem. Frankly, I'm not sure it's truly solvable. As more people create information, our bodies don't start requiring any less sleep, and the days don't get any longer. So we have to rely on content curation, trust building, our own picking and choosing, and optimization of our own content consumption habits.

Fact 3: People Are Different

I know, what a revelation, right? It's so obvious as to be a nonpoint.

Employees are expected to work the same hours. Do roughly the same kinds of work as the next person. Wear the same kinds of clothes. Follow the same mind-numbing policies, processes, and procedures. We have stripped out every element of variation and freedom that enable individuals to express themselves, all in service of consistency and control. It's management laziness, pure and simple.

Let me tell you a little bit about me. I am a night person, or maybe more accurately, an evening person. When I get up in the morning, it takes me a full three hours before I consider myself safe for human interaction. My work colleagues, I'm sure, will attest to this. I like having *some* function that forces me to get up, preferably around 8:00, or even 9:00; but no later, or I feel like a loser. My morning coffee is my form of daily heaven. I love to fix it (Barnie's coffee with Silk Soy creamer and honey—nothing else is quite the same), sit quietly, and either read *The Week Magazine* (my only source of news, really) or my reader on my Android tablet. Then, I like to get dressed and go be around people; but I remain in my own bubble while I respond to e-mails or do work-related reading. By noon, I feel fresh and strong, and I love to go for a run or a bike ride. When I get done with exercise, I grab my daily lunch salad, eat, and read a bit more, and then I'm ready to fire on all cylinders. I can go strong for a good six hours—preferably, in a mix of productive meetings with my teams and definitive chunks of "make-time" (which I define as uninterrupted, large-ish blocks of time), when I can focus on big problems, big projects, big work things. Then, if I had my way, I'd do a social dinner every night (versus lunch, when I'm still in my own head); then I would finish meetings after dinner, when I still have plenty of energy, but less focus. I'd end my day doing e-mail cleanup, stay up late working on my own projects or going out, and be in bed by 1:00 AM.

If you forced my sister to adopt this schedule, she'd go crazy. She's one of those morning people. Her best work time is early in the day; by afternoon, she's wiped out. Going to bed by 10:30 is completely natural to her, and she has always been that way.

You could (should!) insert your own story here (you'll have the opportunity to do this in Chapter 5, "Energy, Not Schedules"). If we all completed this exercise, we'd end up with millions of variations. And if we honored our differences, following the ebb and flow of our natural energy patterns, we'd all be much happier and healthier.

Fact 4: People Have Different Lives

Yes, again stating the obvious. Some people have families—young children and/or elderly parents. Some are young, full of energy, and craving adventure and travel. Others are nearing retirement age, but still in love with their work and not ready to give it all up. Still others are born to work; they're driven to achieve. Some view work as a complement to the rest of their lives. Some need a lot of income; others, a little.

All of these situations mean that we all have different needs and preferences regarding our work schedules, time off and vacations, travel, and a thousand other things. Given our amazing variability, it's a marvel that we find a way at all to run our lives according to such rigidly enforced schedules imposed by our jobs.

Fact 5: Different Kinds of Work Beg for Different Management Approaches

Because my work is centered around projects and products, these are the examples I rattle off most often when discussing organizations and organizational culture. But there are many different kinds of work: manufacturers, where physical goods are manipulated according to very precise workflows and machinery; retail jobs, which have natural ebbs and flows, depending on the types of merchandise and customers; customer service jobs, which require interaction with people during specific hours, set to provide help or consultation.

That said, if you compared the hours for most of these sectors across all of these different work types, you'd find the vast majority are still stuck in the 9-to-5 model. The work hours aren't based on what is best for the business necessarily; they are based on tradition—the times during which people are most accustomed to working.

In some cases, this makes sense. But in others, it's quite silly. Let's take banks, for example. They are open from—you got it—9 to 5. If you are a working person and have personal banking to do, you too are working during those banking hours, meaning you have to rush out at lunch, stand in long lines with other working people to deposit your checks and do your other banking business, thereby missing that precious downtime when you *should* be eating and, perhaps, socializing a bit. Same with dry cleaners, car repair shops, and the post office. Because they are all open during the same hours that we work, we drive ourselves crazy running our errands and getting things done.

PUTTING IT ALL TOGETHER

When we aggregate all of these realities, we are left with a very interesting picture:

1. Businesses have much more flexibility than they currently exercise to create an environment and work hours that are matched to the kinds of work their employees do.

2. Work happens 24 hours a day.

3. Information flows 24 hours a day.

4. Individuals have peaks and valleys of energy and focus, logically distributed across 24 hours, with sleep thrown in for good measure.

5. Individuals have infinite combinations of situational factors that influence their schedules and needs.

Are you seeing this? There are 24 different hours during which we can sleep, work, play, and recover; but the vast majority of companies and individuals adhere to the 9-to-5 workday, 11-to-6 sleep cycle, and 2-day weekends. How we fit in sufficient time for play and recovery is anyone's guess.

> "The best way to keep a prisoner from escaping is to make sure he never knows he's in prison."
> —*Fyodor Dostoevsky, One Day in the Life of Ivan Denisovich*

BREAKING THE OLD RULES

We are afraid to break the rules. Fear is a very dominant emotion in humans, and is at the core of our resistance to change. But when we can liberate ourselves from the rules and break a few, *just to see what happens*, the results can be extraordinary.

More and more companies today are taking the risk to break the old rules and create new workplaces. Some have done this for competitive reasons. The Bay Area, including Silicon Valley, is a great example; recruiting in this region is cut-throat, and only those organizations that provide the flexibility and the best perks get the top talent. Other organizations are responding reactively to the levels of disengagement among their employees, often spurred by an influx of gen Yers whose outside worlds clash dramatically with traditional, buttoned-up corporate cultures.

In any case, such organizations are deliberately moving away from the outdated notions of running their businesses based on activity alone, which is only roughly (and often not at all) correlated with actual business results. In other words, rather than focusing on easy-to-track and obvious behaviors—such as showing up to work and looking presentable—companies are trusting their employees to do these things and finding ways to pay closer attention to impact. The following examples of breaking the old rules honor, in turn, each of the realities of the always-on dilemma, and establish an ideal starting point for thinking about the new rules.

The 40-Hour Workweek Rule

The Rule	The Fear
You must track hours to ensure that everyone puts in 40 hours of work, the gold-standard definition of a full-time job.	If you don't have timecards/ tracking, employees will come late and leave early; they won't put in enough hours to get the job done.

The Rule Breaker: Best Buy

What the Company Did: Best Buy instituted a Results-Only Work Environment (ROWE), in which its corporate office employees are given complete control over their schedules, the number of hours they work, and their work location. Simply put, "Everyone is free to do whatever they want, whenever they want, as long as the work gets done."[3]

Results: Best Buy employees are much more engaged, and happier. The company experienced improvements across many different aspects of its culture, including:

- *Greater productivity*: Increases in productivity averaged 35 percent, perhaps directly correlated with a decrease in meetings. When time is completely at each individual's discretion, no one wants to waste it in meetings of little or no value. The system also creates a do-more-with-less culture, since no one is incentivized to do busy work that cuts into precious personal time.

- *Greater collaboration*: Team members are motivated to coordinate so that everyone can maintain flexibility with their time. They do much more crossover work—filling in for other people when they are out—and as a result, the teams have become much more agile.

- *Decreased voluntary turnover*: Best Buy saw as much as a 90 percent reduction in voluntary turnover rates; the high-performing, valuable employees want to stay.

- *Increased involuntary turnover*: Concomitant to the reduced voluntary turnover rate, Best Buy also saw an increase in turnover of the involuntary type. In other words, "You're fired." ROWE flushes out underperformers; the people hiding behind activities that didn't produce results couldn't survive in the new environment.

The Fixed-Schedule Rule

The Rule	The Fear
Employees must have set schedules so that management will know when everyone is working.	If everyone set their own schedules, coordination would be a nightmare, meetings would never happen, and customers wouldn't get the service they need.

The Rule Breaker: Credit Acceptance

What the Company Did: This is a great example from a customer service organization, not exactly your typical innovative or cutting-edge environment, particularly because the work is very straightforward and it is critical to have coverage during peak hours of customer engagement. Credit Acceptance instituted a flexible attendance policy for call center employees by creating core hours based on busy times.[4] The concept is actually quite simple: Employees work a set number of hours each month (62) during any of the peak shifts: 8:00 AM–12:00 PM or 5:00 PM–9:00 PM Mondays through Fridays, and anytime Saturday or Sunday. However, the employees can pop into these shifts without notice; they can, on a day-to-day basis, simply choose to show up for the shifts that work best for them. This is something of a variation on Best Buy's ROWE framework: "Everyone is free to show up whenever they want, *as long as the shifts get covered.*" Full-time staff is still required to work eight hours per day, five days a week, but there are no limitations on when they come in, leave, or take breaks.

Results: Call center employees at Credit Acceptance experience the autonomy enabled by setting their own schedules; at the same time, they feel good about pitching in and doing their part to offer service when customers need it the most.

The Vacation and Sick Time Rule

The Rule	The Fear
Employees get *N* vacation and sick days each year, often depending on tenure.	If you don't put strict time-off policies and tracking mechanisms in place, people will take off too much time and take advantage of the system. Employees will fake being sick to get more time off than is fair.

The Rule Breaker: Netflix

What the Company Did: Netflix had already eliminated the notion of timecards. It simply shined a light on the fact that people were working some nights and weekends, checking e-mail at all hours, and taking afternoons off here and there for sanity. Management reasoned, if we don't track hours worked in a day or a week, why are we bothering to track vacation time at all? So they revised their vacation policy and tracking to: "There is no policy or tracking."[5]

Results: The focus at Netflix is not on *time*, but instead on *results*. Sound familiar? Not surprisingly, Best Buy also has a no-vacation/tracking policy. The Netflix policy aligns with core principles that the company has chosen to embrace: freedom breeds responsibility, and flexibility is more important than efficiency, in the long term. Netflix values creativity over processes, and has given its employees the ultimate in flexibility—the right to choose when and how much time they take for themselves—rather than fussing over processes to determine exactly how much vacation time should be allocated by tenure or other arbitrary variables.

Most companies respond to growth in the number of employees by curtailing freedom and dictating processes, policies, and rules, to reduce the chaos and number of errors inherent in large organizations.

The problem with this approach is that processes drive out the top talent that thrives on creativity and personal autonomy. The short-term gains an organization generates by tightly controlling processes cannot be sustained once they start losing their high performers. In addition, overly prescribed organizations tend to struggle with change; they become unable to adapt to market shifts and remain innovative, both because their processes are too limiting and because they don't have the performers strong enough to implement those changes. It's a vicious cycle.

The Netflix no vacation policy, among others, was implemented precisely to combat this cycle. The company hires high-performance employees who are attracted to the culture of freedom and autonomy. In turn, the freedom and autonomy ensures that Netflix can continue to run with agility and an informal culture, for it has the right people in place, who have the self-discipline to navigate and avoid the chaos.

The Dress Code Rule

The Rule	The Fear
Institute a clear set of dress code rules to maintain the appearance of a respectable work environment.	Left to their own devices, employees will show up disheveled and dressed inappropriately, causing a distraction. No one will get any work done.

"[In addition to the no vacation policy] There is also no clothing policy at Netflix, but no one has come to work naked lately."
—*Patty McCord, 2004*

The Rule Breaker: Virtually any start-up in the San Francisco Bay Area

What These Companies Did: Eliminated any notion of a dress code; the words "business casual" no longer have any meaning or relevance.

Results: If you go to the campus or offices of any start-up in this region, you'll see hip, cool, happy individuals doing their work dressed in the *clothes of their choosing*. Employees are liberated from the tyranny of HR policies; they are free to be who they are, and work in the clothes that make them the most comfortable.

At the start of my career, I worked in several companies with dress codes; specifically, business casual was the rule. Consequently, I had distinct, almost roped-off sections in my closet, to separate my fun clothes from my work clothes; and, necessarily, I shopped very differently for these two sets of attire. When I started at Google, it actually took me about two years to *find* my own style. Which clothes did I really want to wear to work? What image did I want to portray? Who was I in my clothes? It was so liberating to be able to choose my clothes everyday according to how I felt, and to work for an employer that *trusted me* to choose appropriate attire. When I showed up straight from work at a dinner party or social event, people always asked, "Did you wear that to work?" They couldn't seem to process the fact that I was allowed to wear a great pair of jeans, high heels, a T-shirt, and a nice blazer (which, by the way, transitions perfectly to social events) *to work* (and not just on casual Fridays). To look and feel great at work: What a concept!

A friend of mine who is a manager in the financial industry shared a personal story from the days when men were required to wear ties on the trading floor. Of course, the trading floor was filled with high-energy young guys, none too happy to be putting on a tie everyday. Not out of rebellion but purely for convenience, this friend started putting on the same tie every day; and he tied it in a loose knot and wore it on the *outside* of his shirt collar. Technically, he was following the "tie" rule. Before long, his male colleagues decided to follow his example. When you set ridiculous rules, you get ridiculous results.

So how does a no-dress-code policy help start a Work Revolution? It comes down to personal responsibility. If we can't be trusted to pick our own clothes, we can't be trusted to allocate our time optimally for our own good and the good of the company. It sets up an Us-versus-Them mentality, which causes tension and mistrust. It's part of the Old Rules, and erects barrier after barrier to getting the right work done in the best way.

The Perks and Benefits Rule

The Rule	The Fear
Offer *just enough* perks and benefits to attract and recruit employees.	Lavish perks and benefits cost too much, and it's difficult to track their effectiveness. Plus, employees will think they are entitled to them, and come to expect, rather than appreciate, them.

The Rule Breaker: Google

What the Company Did: Offer innumerable perks (hereafter, "The Perks") and benefits. Here's just a sampling, to give you an idea:

- Unlimited access to food: Three meals a day in cafes sprinkled around the campus, complete with organic and sustainable food; microkitchens on every floor of every building, stocked with healthy snacks and drinks

- Subsidized massages, chair massages ($5 for 15 minutes anyone?), and chairs with electric massagers built in

- Nap pods and Mother's rooms

- Fitness centers; showers and locker rooms in almost every building; laundry facilities, with free detergent

- Media rooms with televisions, pool tables, and video games

- On-site service offerings, such as shuttle service to and from San Francisco on superoutfitted coach buses equipped with Wi-Fi; personal shipping through Google's shipping department; oil changes, car washes, bike repairs, and haircuts

- Minor perks, such as medicine cabinets and warm toilet seats

Results: When I started at Google, I was in awe of all that was built into the environment to make things as easy as possible for employees. The Perks are not gratuitous; they are there to remove barriers and eliminate many of the hassles inherent in running lives, to make it easier to work and get things done, as well as to recover and restore energy in sensible ways.

There was a wiki floating around Google at one time (tongue-in-cheek, I assume, though I always thought someone must have followed through on it at some point), that described tricks and tips for *living* at Google. Yes, that's right: living there full-time. And you could, no doubt about it.

Beyond simply making life a thousand times easier for the full-time employee, The Perks have an unexpected additional benefit: They create an environment of generosity. The best way to articulate this is by comparing the atmosphere at Google to another, more typical company, and the sorts of things I heard quite often in the offices there: "I'm not going to stay late to finish this! The company is so stingy with everything, why should I put in the extra effort?"

In contrast, the abundant Google perks and benefits inspire the *exact opposite* mentality. Here's an example: "I enjoyed my regular breakfast of fluffy, scrambled, free-range eggs and loads of fresh, plump blueberries and blackberries with homemade yogurt after my stress-free shuttle ride from the city to work; I just worked out in the gym, completed some important work at my ergonomically correct workstation, then took a break to go see Alton Brown chat it up with a Google audience. You want me to take on a new, super-important project, above and beyond my core responsibilities? Hell yes; bring it on."

When you are generous with your employees, your employees will return the favor, again and again and again. This is called *discretionary performance*, and it abounds at Google. People jump in all the time to do things that need to be done. "If you see a void, fill it." And they do. Googlers are empowered to "just do" the things that need to be done, and they are more than happy to pitch in when necessary.

They are also empowered to take breaks when they need them, while working hard, after completing a big launch, or finishing an important cycle. The environment, The Perks, the tools, and the freedom are about self-regulation, which is absolutely essential to the Work Revolution.

The Job Slot Rule

The Rule	The Fear
Hire candidates to fill specific, static job slots with detailed descriptions of roles, responsibilities, and requirements. If they don't fit well into their given roles, find a way to "manage them out."	Allowing employees to wander around to find their passion is nice and all (i.e., you must be nuts!), but we need to get work done around here. If we let people choose their own roles, no one would do the grunt work, and critical roles would be left unfilled.

The Rule Breaker: Semco, a company based in Brazil, is best described as a federation of business units that specialize in highly complex, premium ventures. They strive to be the high-end players in each of their business ventures, and to establish themselves as niche players in their markets. Semco's businesses run the gamut, from industrial machinery to high-tech and even environmental resources management.

What the Company Did: Semco encourages its employees to self-manage by wandering around the company, changing jobs periodically, sitting in with different teams, and exploring as much as necessary to find their place, their role, their "fit." Management believes strongly that every individual has a "reservoir of talent"; there is something for everyone, and if a particular role isn't working out, they persist in rotating them to different teams and work types until they find the right one. This is an informal practice widely encouraged across the board, but there are also several programs in place to formalize this, among them:

- Family Silverware is an internal hiring program designed to give preference to internal candidates for openings in the company. The idea is that the company would rather offer its people new opportunities, develop their talents, and perhaps help them to find something they'd like to do better.

- Lost in Space is designed for new recruits to the company. It creates the space for them to spend a full year in the company moving around to various units, exploring different interests—literally roaming as much or as little as they like. At the end of the year, they can accept a job offered by anyone they worked for in the previous year, or they can seek another opening that interests them. Why does Semco do this? Because it assumes that no one at a young age can know what they really want to do, or what they are good at.

Results: Semco has less than 1 percent turnover, and rarely fires anyone. Its employees are intensely loyal and choose to stay at the company rather than accept higher-paying roles at other places, where their freedom and autonomy would be severely curtailed.

"All of Semco's business units consistently perform above published parameters of productivity per employee," says Ricardo Semler, CEO of Semco, "because efficiency is unleashed when workers can repeatedly dive into their reservoirs of talent. Loosening up and rejecting the military model unleashes productivity. I believe this, and our numbers back it up."[6]

The Well-Defined Processes Rule

The Rule	The Fear
Develop strictly calibrated, consistent processes to ensure that everyone performs according to established standards.	Without processes and standards, quality would suffer and employees would make uninformed decisions that result in poor business results. Wild, Wild West!

The Rule Breaker: Zappos, online shoe retailer

What the Company Did: Zappos' business is heavily based on its customer service. Therefore, the company deliberately empowers its customer service representatives to handle customer issues on a case-by-case basis so they can make the best decision in every situation.[7] To that end, Zappos eliminated call center scripts and standard procedures and processes so that every employee can maintain their authenticity, and better respond to the individual needs of the customer. They are free to go above and beyond, as needed; and in doing so, they make true fans out of their customers.

Results: Despite the fact that Zappos doesn't offer the glamorous perks and benefits that companies like Google provide, it has created an extraordinary organizational culture, and its unprecedented customer service has resulted in a business model that other shoe retailers have yet to replicate.

THE NEW RULES

Okay, great: We've ditched the old rules. But what are the new rules?

Sorry folks, there are none—which is both the good news and the bad news.

A single set of rules, even if they are new, to fit every situation and organization is exactly what we have now, and exactly the wrong approach. A single set of rules is easy; black and white. It's similar to the notion of zero tolerance in schools. It eliminates any need for judgment, evaluation, critical thinking. It also quashes any sense of empowerment, individualization, and "gray-zone" thinking, which make life interesting and organizational agility possible! Zero tolerance is code for laziness. If you manage by laziness, that's exactly what you'll get in return.

There are, however, principles that can establish a flexible framework to inspire every individual, leader, and organization to make the changes that lead to a true Work Revolution. Here they are, in brief, along with the chapter number where they are discussed in detail:

Impact, Not Activities (Chapter 4)

- *Start* focusing on results—both the goals of the company and the impact of each individual—and *then* define the behaviors and activities to support this approach. Better yet, let employees discover the best behaviors and activities for them, to achieve the results and share with each other, thereby creating a strong performance culture.

- *Stop* caring about activities that are only loosely correlated (and sometimes completely uncorrelated) with actual performance, such as time clocked in and out and total hours worked.

Energy, Not Schedules (Chapter 5)

- *Start* following the energy of individuals, work, teams, trends, and opportunities, to expend the least amount of energy for the greatest effect.

- *Stop* trying to predict time, manage by time, track time, and in general, obsess about time, to create a false sense of urgency.

Strengths, Not Job Slots (Chapter 6)

- *Start* hiring only the right people for your culture, and create roles for them based on their individual strengths, experiences, passions, and desires. Empower them to find the right role and the right team. And if the cultural fit just isn't there, give individuals an easy way out.

- *Stop* hiring based on a predefined, static set of roles and responsibilities. Likewise, stop hiring the wrong people; if you can't trust them, don't hire them.

The Right Things, Not Everything (Chapter 7)

- *Start* prioritizing efforts, questioning everything, making trade-offs, and eliminating all but the important stuff.

- *Stop* trying to do it all, all at the same time. When everything is important, nothing is important.

Grassroots, Not Top-Down (Chapter 8)

- *Start* empowering individuals to contribute solutions to business problems and work toward organizational goals. Create an environment that encourages open dialog and transparency throughout the organization.

- *Stop* dictating rules, solutions, and policies that stifle independent thinking and creativity. And stop believing that leaders must know, control, and implement all of the answers.

As we continue to explore each of these principles throughout the rest of the book, I will outline actions that we can all take to start a Work Revolution, both in our personal lives and in our organizations.

CHAPTER 4

Impact, Not Activities

I learned to surf when I was 26. I took an analytical approach to mastering this sport, which meant spending a lot of time just watching other surfers. The coast of Florida along the Atlantic Ocean is a "beach break" (as opposed to the nice, neat "point breaks" in California), with seemingly endless waves approaching and closing out in the shallow waters. I remember the first time I realized there was order to what I had thought was a chaotic ritual of paddling out to what's called the *lineup*. I spotted a beginner—a wary-looking surfer handling his board awkwardly, then wading into the water, climbing on top, and beginning the long paddle out. He stroked furiously, getting knocked around by each oncoming wave, and duck-dived his board underneath to the best of his ability. He rested atop his board at various points, eyeing the distance remaining to the lineup. He then took a deep breath and continued fighting, paddling, and diving. Finally, seemingly with the last few viable paddle strokes left in his muscles, he squeaked past a cresting wave, narrowly escaping the powerful pull backwards. But he made it, exhausted, into the calmness of the lineup.

Meanwhile, I also had my eye on an experienced surfer standing in knee-high water with his board, staring out into the distance. He watched. He waited. And waited. At first, I wondered if he ever intended to actually *do* anything. But then, just as the novice surfer had barely cleared the monster wave, this second surfer deftly jumped onto his board, duck-dived beneath the weakened, broken wave, and gracefully, lightly, and easily paddled out, using smooth strokes, to arrive at the lineup only a minute after the hard-working amateur. The pro seemed to calm the waves just by looking at them, so simple did his task appear to me.

Indeed, the waves had subsided, as they do every seven waves, in what is called a *set*. According to the laws of the ocean, waves arrive to the shore in orderly groups, and between each set is a lull that can last a few minutes (sometimes many *long* minutes) before the next set arrives. The novice surfer undoubtedly worked harder. He worked longer. And in his struggle to get out to the lineup he showed determination and raw will. He was the winner! Right? But wait: Both the surfers achieved the same outcome. They both arrived past the breaking waves and positioned themselves to catch some rides. The difference was, the graceful, more experienced surfer expended very little energy, and when the next set started up, he was well prepared to paddle hard to catch a wave.

By current workplace standards, the first surfer would be considered the more valuable worker. He put in the *time* and the *effort* to achieve his goal. The second surfer, then, would be classified as lazy; looking for the easy way out. Of course, from this example, we can see how preposterous that assumption is. The second surfer was smart, smarts gained from experience. He chose not to expend his energy on activities that weren't fun and that didn't have a payout. He reduced his time in the churn and maximized his time actually riding waves.

Unfortunately, the cult of workplace management practices today focus primarily on people "looking busy," in the process often overlooking that activities for the sake of activities belongs with Alice, in Wonderland, not the global workplace.

> "Would you tell me," said Alice, a little timidly, "why you are painting those roses?" Five and Seven said nothing, but looked at Two. Two began in a low voice, "Why the fact is, you see, Miss, this here ought to have been a red rose-tree, and we put a white one in by mistake; and if the Queen was to find it out, we should all have our heads cut off, you know."
> —*Lewis Carroll, Alice's Adventures in Wonderland*

If you walk down the hall in your organization, and one after another see the flick of a wrist as each person who hears you coming quickly switching his or her screen from Facebook to "work," then you know your company is focused on the wrong matters. Don't have access to Facebook at work? Well, that's another, even bigger, issue.

ROOTS OF MANAGEMENT BY ACTIVITY

The 9-to-5 work schedule reminds me of the story of the woman who routinely cut off both ends of a cut of meat before roasting it. When asked what function that served, she replied that it was the way her mother had always done it. As it turns out, her mother cut off the ends of the meat because her roasting pan was too small to accommodate the whole thing.

Similarly today, we are blindly following management practices that have their roots in the Industrial Revolution. One of the biggest management innovations from that period was the assembly line, which reduced work for each individual down to a very specific task, which had to be done repeatedly and reliably. True, this method of organizing individual tasks transformed the work environment, and resulted in incredible gains in efficiency, productivity, and profitability. Of course, assembly lines function well only when everyone shows up on time, at the same time. There's your 9-to-5 work schedule, folks.

Frederick Taylor was one of the management innovators during the Industrial Revolution. His principles of Scientific Management served as a major force in transforming and improving the workplaces of that time.[1] He saw an opportunity to create efficiencies in the workplace by separating the *thinking* part of the job from the *producing* parts. In his framework, planners (i.e., managers) would scope out, in advance, all of the work that needed to be done in a day, then write down incredibly detailed instructions for how to do the work, including the exact amount of time each task should take.

As Taylor wrote in his book *Shop Management*:[2]

> There is no question that the cost of production is lowered by separating the work of planning and the brain work as much as possible from the manual labor. It is impossible for the man who is best suited to [manual labor] to understand the principles of this science, or even to work in accordance with these principles without the aid of a man better educated than he is.

He wanted to eliminate any thinking on the part of the producers; all they had to do was follow the directions of managers and stay on task.

He continued:

> There is no question that the average individual accomplishes
> the most when he either gives himself, or someone else
> assigns him, a definite task; the more elementary the mind
> and character of the individual the more necessary does it
> become that each task shall extend over a short period of
> time only.

Rather than an individual learning a trade comprehensively, thus
being able to perform all of the tasks associated with it, he might be
assigned one or a handful of tasks, that in conjunction with the tasks
of dozens or hundreds of other individuals, would produce the finished products. Their individual efforts were abstracted down from the
whole into tiny components, dictated to them by management.

A Century of Progress

Taylor's fundamental assumptions at the core of Scientific Management
seem comically obsolete in today's knowledge economy. Because the
shift from manual work to knowledge work happened gradually over
the century, we never stopped to consider that perhaps our roasting
pans are now big enough to accommodate that entire chunk of meat.
So what were the assumptions and realities of the early 1900s, and how
are they different now? The two biggest differences are: *level of education* and *complexity of the organizational environment*.

Educational Divide   In the early 1900s, schooling beyond the sixth
or seventh grade was rare. Because most children were destined for a
life a manual labor, high school seemed unnecessary; almost a luxury.
The high school graduation rate in 1900 was a mere 6.4 percent—
but 36 percent of those high school graduates went on to earn a
college degree.[3] Essentially, if you made it through high school, you
were firmly on the education track, and a college degree was the next
logical step.

By 1945, the high school graduation rate had risen to a respect-
able 47.4 percent, but only 11 percent of those graduates earned

college diplomas. Completing high school no longer meant that students would go on to college; it was simply the new standard for basic education.

The next 50 years precipitated a remarkable shift from high school for the masses to college for the masses (see Figure 4.1). In 2000, the college graduation rate for the general population was 33 percent; and, to put the icing on the cake, by 2009, the percentage of individuals receiving postgraduate degrees (master's, doctorates, or other professional degrees) was 10 percent—higher than the high school graduation rate in 1900!

In this context, perhaps it is understandable that Taylor called workers "simple-minded," making the broad assumption they were not capable of figuring out the most efficient methods for completing work. He insisted that only the managers could reliably do the brainwork; and it is safe to assume these were the same folks getting those high school and college degrees in that era.

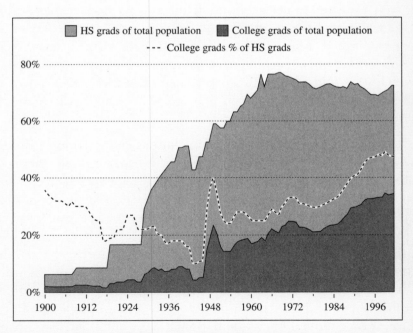

Figure 4.1   High School and College Graduation Rates as Percentage of Total U.S. Population, 1900–2000.
Source: National Center for Education Statistics, 1900–1985, 120 Years of Education, A Statistical Portrait; beginning 1986, Digest of Education Statistics, annual.
Illustration: Brian Lanier

In stark contrast, our reality today is that we have a highly educated workforce. Workers in even menial jobs have vastly higher levels of education, relatively speaking, than their counterparts in the early 1900s. Consequently, it is no longer necessary to relegate all critical thinking and judgment to management.

Organizational Complexity   The second major difference between Taylor's time and our own is the complexity of the work world. In 1900, the government classified work into 266 occupational codes across four categories (agriculture; trade and transportation; professional and personal services; and manufacturing, mechanical, and mining). The number is now close to 1,000 occupational codes, organized across 25 different categories.[4]

In Taylor's day, it was entirely possible to scope out every job within a company, and then every task within each job, that workers were expected to perform, and define how to properly perform it. In fact, this was the most efficient way of managing, as Taylor so quaintly argued. Management could anticipate virtually every scenario a worker might encounter, create rules to govern how to respond in each case, and then train workers to follow these rules, down to the smallest detail. Rule-driven management created efficiency and increased the quality of work.

Our world is many orders of magnitude more complex than it was in 1900. When I completed my PhD in experimental analysis of behavior, with a focus on organizational behavior management, and proceeded along a career path in instructional systems design, my family was dumbfounded. Not in a "we're so proud of you!" way, or even a "what was she thinking; an art history degree has no use" way. Rather, it was their way of saying, "We have no idea what the hell she does." Every time we got together, I would patiently explain the work I was doing to develop training systems for the Navy or BellSouth or another client, and they would nod politely and ask some questions. But next time around, they would ask the same question: "So, explain what it is you do again?"

In our information age, we form ideas, concepts, plans, and processes, which eventually turn into products, which often don't even exist as physical objects. Further, we work in highly complex, uncertain, chaotic, dynamic environments. We aren't shopkeepers anymore. We are "product associates," "retail consultants," and "solution architects."

The Problem with Impact

Activities are easy to track and observe. Tracking the impact (results) of our work on the bottom line, on customers, or even on productivity, takes effort. Here's how Taylor addressed this:

> There are many good managers of the old school, however, who feel that this standardization is not only unnecessary but that it is undesirable, their principal reason being that it is better to allow each workman to develop his individuality by choosing the particular implements and methods which suit him best. And there is considerable weight in this contention when the scheme of management is to allow each workman to do the work as he pleases and hold him responsible for results. Unfortunately, in ninety-nine out of a hundred such cases only the first part of this plan is carried out. The workman chooses his own methods and implements, but is not held in any strict sense accountable unless the quality of the work is so poor or the quantity turned out is so small as to almost amount to a scandal.[5]

It's not always clear how the work we do now might have impact down the line. We don't always have the tools or data to show the level of effect. And it takes time and extra steps to chase this down. So, rather than finding better ways to measure impact, Taylor took the next best step: He *managed* activities. He prescribed behaviors that led to the right results, and made sure the workers behaved consistently.

We no longer have that choice. Because today's business world moves so quickly, the moment after you define an activity to get results, the environment shifts again, and the activity just defined no longer leads to the desired results. For example, in the late 1990s, I attended an e-commerce workshop on the best way to boost a website's ranking in search results. The best method, we were taught, was to embed the desired search terms as many times as possible throughout the site. I remember thinking that the model sites we were shown looked ridiculous, full of terms like "discount flowers" and "cheap florist" plastered all over the pages of the site for a florist. That strategy worked then. But not for long. Search engine optimization is now a thriving profession, ever evolving to keep up with algorithms to figure out the best strategies to obtain top search results.

If impact is hard to track, and activities clearly lead to dead-end results, then how can we make this work? Ultimately, it requires shifting from authoritarian dictates to democratic problem solving. Table 4.1 lays out the differences between these two management approaches.

Table 4.1   Getting to Impact, Then and Now

	Then	Now
Owner/CEO	Define the products to be manufactured and sold.	Define the problem statement the employees can solve for.
Managers	Define the right way to perform tasks and track compliance.	Define guiding principles and provide support.
Individual Contributors	Employees are interchangeable. Follow rules for completing tasks.	Employees are coveted talent. Find the best way to get the job done.

THE HUMANITY OF AUTOMATION

According to Taylor's Scientific Management principles, workers were interchangeable. Because the work was highly prescribed, workers also were assigned a prescribed value—that which they could produce in a given shift—and it was essentially impossible to produce more. Worker productivity was a linear function. Under this system, it is easy to understand why workers felt powerless, and it is no surprise that they resisted automation.

In the knowledge world, in contrast, each individual contributes uniquely to an organization, and employee retention is critical for organizational success. Each individual can find creative ways to add value, exponentially increasing the value they contribute collectively to an organization. Under this system, individuals can both embrace automation and create new forms of automation themselves, given that the tools enabling them to do so are, today, ubiquitous, cheap, and democratic. In fact, creating automation has become a form of adding value!

ORGANIZATIONS AS PROBLEM STATEMENTS

For many today, meaning is the new money. It's what people are looking for at work. Clear company values, translated into the day-to-day work experience, are one of the strongest drivers of an engaged workforce, one primed for successful collaboration.
—Tammy Erickson, "Meaning Is the New Money," Harvard Business Review, March 23, 2011

The ultimate goal of every business is to make money. Businesses make decisions about how to best do this based on the capabilities of the founders and what they bring to the table. However, what may make money for a business at the start is seldom what sustains it in the long run; so the biggest challenge for companies is to evolve in ways that enable them to stay relevant.

One approach is to rely on the leaders of the organization to dictate the direction for change at every turn. The difficulty with this approach is that it requires crystal-clear, top-to-bottom communication in order to accurately and effectively transmit the directional shifts to the myriad operational segments that need to implement the changes. What this looks like in practice is a bunch of workers scrambling to implement changes they may or may not understand, even as their leaders are chasing them around to assure that everything is falling in line with the new practices—in a word, micromanaging.

Fortunately, there is another way: Point the organization in the right direction, give individuals a strategy for staying on course, and provide them the tools so they can self-determine whether they are staying the course. This alternative approach requires communicating only slight course corrections to the strategy, which translates to a much lighter burden on the leadership to oversee every little detail of the operations—in a word, autonomy.

The keys to this alternative approach are:

- A well-crafted mission statement
- Guiding principles for operations
- Measures of success

Mission Statements

In the early 1900s, companies were established to turn out very specific products. A sampling of occupations, shown in Table 4.2, from that time confirms the focus on making *things*:

Table 4.2   Occupations of the Early 1900s

Agricultural implement makers	Glassworks operatives	Organ makers
Artificial-flower makers	Harness and saddle makers	Publishers of books, maps, and newspapers
Bag makers	Iron- and steelworks and shops operatives	Quarrymen
Bakers		Rope and cordage makers
Candle, soap, and tallow makers	Lace makers	
	Leather case and pocketbook makers	Scale and rule makers
Distillers and rectifiers	Meat packers, curers, and picklers	Trunk, valise, and carpet-bag makers
Engravers		Umbrella and parasol makers
File makers, cutters, and grinders	Nail makers	
		Wire makers and workers

Source: Integrated Public Use Microdata Series USA, 1880 Occupation Codes.

A company in that era could remain profitable for decades producing the same items without ever significantly altering its product lines. For example, ice production, invented in the mid-1800s, remained a thriving business until the mid-1900s. Ice plants made ice, and there was an occupational code for "traders and dealers in ice." This concept of focusing on one specific end product, and staking an entire business or occupation on it, today would end in career suicide.

When I started my career as an instructional designer, I primarily developed training programs. Throughout the next 10 years, I slowly came to the realization that it was a huge mistake to describe my skill as "training" because that simply characterized a *tool* or a specific *solution* (I might have been called a "training maker" in 1900). A mission statement must, instead, be focused on a problem you are trying to solve. In my case, my job is to "facilitate the transfer of repeatable information and skills from those who have learned it to those who need to learn it, at scale."[6] This alternative perspective opens up a whole new set of solutions. For example, identifying experts in a company and connecting them with individuals who need access to their expertise is a valid and fruitful strategy for the transfer of repeatable information. By developing a scalable solution to connect experts to learners, I eliminate a huge swath of costly training programs by directly linking these individuals, rather than serving as the middleman. As technology evolves, we can continue finding new ways to stay relevant and get better at what we do.

In today's work environment, we solve problems. Technology changes too quickly to stake a business on one specific product or service and stubbornly stick to it. Take General Mills and Kraft, two highly recognizable manufacturers of food products. Here's how they describe their businesses:

General Mills: "Worldwide, people turn to General Mills for breakfast, lunch, dinner, and snacks."[7]

Kraft: "Anywhere, anytime, every day, our higher purpose is to make today delicious."[8]

Notice they don't talk about making food. They talk about making food convenient for people. This is an important distinction, one that lays a path for continuous innovation, change, and product development. The implications of this subtle mind shift for employees and leaders are huge.

Think about how you might craft your mission statement in the form of a problem. For example, if the ice-making companies of the last century saw their mission as "extending the freshness of food," they might have foreseen the opportunities inherent in refrigerators and freezers. But none of them did; none of those ice companies evolved with the technology. You can only get so good at making ice before you reach a dead end, which is precisely what happened to all of them.

Table 4.3 contains a few examples of both dead-end mission statements and problem-based mission statements.

Notice that the problem-based mission statements make no assumption about the medium or the product type. They are broad and inspirational, a continuous call to employees to develop ever more innovative ideas and approaches. Think about it: Would the brick-and-mortar bookstore chains have crumbled in such spectacular fashion if they had seriously adopted the problem-based mission statement in Table 4.3? Perhaps not. Maybe they would have seized new business opportunities offered by e-books, and evolved to survive the growth of technology.

Table 4.3   Sample Mission Statements

Dead-End Mission Statements	Problem-Based Mission Statements
Make T-shirts	Develop everyday wear from natural materials best suited for any type of weather.
Sell books	Connect the most novel ideas expressed in the written word to the broadest, interested audience.
Issue insurance policies	Enable individuals and businesses to manage financial risk.
Build and operate chain restaurants	Nourish and delight everyone we serve.

At the other extreme, there is also grave danger in being so nonspecific in a mission statement that no one reading it could begin to guess what the organization actually does. Here are three that fall into that category:[9]

- "Our purpose is to earn money for shareholders and increase the value of their investment. We will do that through growing the company, controlling assets, and properly structuring the balance sheet, thereby increasing EPS, cash flow, and return on invested capital."

- "The Company's primary objective is to maximize long-term stockholder value, while adhering to the laws of the jurisdictions in which it operates and at all times observing the highest ethical standards."

- "Our goal is to be the leader in every market we serve, to the benefit of our customers and our shareholders."

I didn't make these up. Each is a mission statement of an actual company, though I doubt that any of their employees reading this book would realize I was talking about their companies. In case you are wondering, the first is from a tire company, the second from a food and beverage company, and the last from an equipment manufacturer (e.g., garbage trucks).

Boiling down the operations, customers, products, and services of an organization to one core mission is incredibly hard to do; it often takes years in business to get it right. I think that is okay. If a company starts with a great idea, and a group of people who strongly believe in that idea, the mission statement can evolve as the staff settles on the ultimate problem they want to solve.

Apple, as we all know, has changed the world, arguably several times over. It started by developing personal computers that changed forever the computer industry when it introduced a graphical interface to the mass market. For many years thereafter, however, the company stalled—in fact, it almost didn't survive—and went through many leadership changes before finally realizing that Apple was about more than just computers. Just in the nick of time, Apple discovered its true gift, its core competencies. It discovered what it could do better than any other company in the world. The iPod was the first evidence of Apple's newfound mission. The iPhone came next. And then the iPad. Each of these products has clear commonalities:

- Beautiful design
- Simple and elegant user interface
- Few, but highly selective product options

At its core, Apple is about beautifully designed personal computing experiences that approach perfection.

Now, from the opposite side of the organizational spectrum, take the Rockettes, a New York institution for almost 80 years. They continue to evolve. In 2006, they hired a new director, Linda Haberman, to bring the Rockettes into alignment with modern entertainment. What did she do? As you might expect, she revamped their flagship show, the Christmas Spectacular, integrating new dance numbers and modern technology, such as 3D. However, before she changed a single kick line, she defined the essence of the group with their version of a mission statement: "Precision technique, in which individual bodies work as one to become a glittering human machine."[10] Her process for doing this was to "see how much [she] could deconstruct the Rockettes and still have them be the Rockettes." Only then did she endeavor to conceptualize how to apply that to appeal to audiences of the twenty-first century.

The problem of the right mission statement is both solvable and never completely solved. It is inspirational, yet tangible. It defines one company and one company only. It should never be stated in a way that might be applicable to any other company, even if they are in the same business. It sets an indisputable direction for the company that every single employee can see clearly, and can clearly see how they contribute to it.

Guiding Principles

Problem-based mission statements provide meaning, inspiration, and vision. But they don't necessarily answer the question of *how* a company will operate.

It is tempting to simply create rules—a set of if/then statements that provide complete clarity about the right thing to do in any given situation. Rules are conveniently black and white and, as such, assure predictable outcomes. The problem is that it is impossible to anticipate every single decision point and scenario for which a rule might need to be created.

Guiding principles are distinctly different from rules. They enable employees to approach any decision—small, large, and everything in between—with the same decision criteria that the CEO might employ. Because decision making is core to operating in a complex and dynamic world, guiding principles become the critical anchors around which everything in the organization can hang.

I'll demonstrate this through a widely relatable example: customer service. Customer service is straightforward. The title says it all: help customers. In practice, however, it's anything but straightforward. You can't just put representatives on the phones and set them free to handle calls. In a traditional call center, the customer service representatives (CSRs) are trained to handle the various scenarios it is anticipated they will encounter. They typically follow a "decision tree" for dealing with customers—for example, when they can grant returns, what the correct channels are for processing refunds and repairs. Then there are "escalation" procedures for nonroutine issues. There might even exist carefully defined exceptions that the representatives can make under very special circumstances. Of course, all of these rules are carefully drafted by managers, then painstakingly taught to the representatives, who are tracked daily for adherence. The call center operation is airtight; it's designed to cover, in a highly predictable way, every scenario that might pop up so that CSRs can resolve issues for customers with expediency.

I dealt with one such company when I dropped my mobile phone on a tile floor and destroyed the screen. According to this mobile phone manufacturer's well-documented instructions, I mailed them my phone, at which point it promptly disappeared into the abyss of its repair center. As I later learned, my phone was a "spec" model, hence this wasn't a routine repair, and the company's computer system didn't know how to handle it.

I called the customer service number (using a borrowed phone) and spoke to a representative, who dutifully submitted an escalation in an attempt to track down my phone. Then, nothing. I called again three weeks later, only to have another representative submit another escalation to check on the first escalation that had produced no resolution. Again, nothing. Two weeks later, I called again. By this time, I had no fewer than three repair tickets, which were all being tracked separately; there seemed to be no way to tie them together. Every time I called, it took me 10 minutes to explain my situation, walk through each repair ticket, and give the CSR time to understand what was going on. Finally, I asked to speak to a supervisor, and was politely but firmly told no, she couldn't do that. But she could submit an escalation.

For six months, I proceeded through this endless and unresolvable loop. At one point, about four months into it, I had a conversation with a very sweet CSR I had spoken to previously; when he realized he had talked to me four months earlier and that I *still* had no resolution, he was appalled. Finally, I had someone on the line who cared about helping me. He vowed to fix it. How? He submitted an escalation.

Eventually, I got desperate and wrote to the company through another channel, detailing the morass of futile conversations I had had to date. It was only then that I got the help I needed to find my phone and get it repaired and returned to me. It took a full six months for the repair—and I was charged full price for it.

Now, in terms of adherence to this company's rules, I can attest that the CSRs were *spot on*. They didn't break a single rule. According to their activity-driven management metrics, their service was impeccable. However, because the goal of "serving customers" was abstracted by rules, the representatives had neither the perspective nor the authority to do the right thing for me. If they had been properly focused on impact, and armed with a set of guiding principles, it would have become immediately clear that I was being failed at every turn. If each of those representatives had the autonomy to do what was necessary to solve my problem, I bet you 10 screen repairs (that's $1,000) that I would have had a more expeditious outcome.

Table 4.4 contrasts this activity-focused management style to the alternative, the impact-driven management style.

Table 4.4 Activity- versus Impact-Focused Customer Service

Activity-Focused Customer Service	Impact-Focused Customer Service
Metric: Number of phone calls per hour (the average "handle time")	Metric: Number of resolved issues per hour
Decision tree for handling specific scenarios	Decision making according to broad guiding principles
Trained to adhere to rules	Empowered to solve problems

Unlike this mobile phone manufacturer, Zappos views customer service as its primary marketing platform. Customer service is not simply an expense to be minimized; to the contrary, it *is* the business. The company's CSRs follow no scripts or rules. In fact, they are directly instructed to let their own personalities shine through, the exact opposite of standardization. They are empowered to create "wow" experiences for every customer, which might mean upgrading them to overnight shipping or even directing them to a competitor website if Zappos is out of a particular shoe style. The company doesn't measure sales on number of calls or even upsells. It focuses on making a Personal Emotional Connection (PEC) with every customer, which might translate to a single six-hour-long phone call, if that's what it takes. As Zappos' CEO Tony Hsieh puts it, in *Delivering Happiness: A Path to Profits, Passion, and Purpose,* "We're trying to build a lifelong relationship with each customer, one phone call at a time."[11] Escalations to supervisors are rare at the company, not because it has a rule to reserve escalations for only the severest of events, but because the customer service representatives are empowered to do everything a supervisor might do to solve customers' problems.

The Zappos guiding principles are stated in the form of 10 core values, which include items such as "Deliver WOW through service," "Create fun and a little weirdness," and "Do more with less." These core values are reinforced in every corner of the organization—from the leadership development pipeline to companywide communications that encourage people to blog about them. The values are coupled with an innate trust that every employee is capable of applying the principles to make sound decisions.

With Zappos in mind, here are some guiding principles for developing guiding principles:

- *Provide guideposts and rationale for decision making.* The question to ask is, "What would any individual need to understand to consistently make the same (or similar) decisions that the CEO might make?"

- *Operationalize the company's strategy and values.* Is your company looking to reach the largest audience possible, or is it interested in forging deeper relationships with a smaller target audience? Is the goal to launch quickly and iterate? Or is your brand about perfection and high quality? Guiding principles should illuminate the trade-offs that the organization is choosing to make (see Chapter 7, "The Right Things, Not Everything" for more about strategizing).

- *Show relevance to every group in the company.* Ultimately, you can't expect teams to align with the mission of the company if they can't articulate concretely how they contribute to the bottom line. Make sure every member of every team sees their connection point to the problem-based mission statement and that they understand their role in it.

You should have as many guiding principles as it takes to illuminate the path that individuals should follow on a day-to-day basis. For every rule that exists in your organization currently, consider ways of eliminating it and replacing it with a guiding principle. Then give people the freedom and autonomy to apply the principles.

Measures of Success

The final piece in the organizational impact puzzle is the feedback loop. You have direction and guideposts to show the way to get where you're going. But individuals also need to know when they are on track and what success looks like.

This is arguably the hardest piece of the puzzle to fit, and there are no pat answers about how to do it. It depends on the business; it depends on the role. It may also depend on various tasks. That said, the organization can make the commitment to invest in the technology and time it takes to provide visibility into progress and company success. Just the process of determining the right success measures may bring surprising clarity about the business; it might even help shape the mission statement and guiding principles. Measurement provides meaning. If individuals understand how the work they are doing is contributing to the company's success, they will be much more motivated to contribute more, smarter, and better.

I don't know how Zappos measures its success, but I would guess that its CSRs would want to know how many of their PECs account for future business.

The good news is that technology advances are making measurement more feasible and cheap. For example, web analytics tools are transforming the marketing world. The old adage went something like: "Half of my advertising dollars are working; I'm just not sure which half." Now it's possible to determine how specific ads lead to very specific purchases, and whether the investment in the ads was worth it in the first place. As technologies continue to evolve—web, mobile, computers, artificial intelligence—each of us will continue to gain much deeper insight into our impact on the company's bottom line.

LEADERS ASKING QUESTIONS

The problem-based mission statement and set of guiding principles comprise the new set of tools for leaders and managers. It's not about telling people what to do. It's about giving voice to the direction of the organization and teaching individuals how to think about getting there. It is now the job of a manager to teach individuals how to think strategically.

Ask, Don't Tell

I've had to work hard to become an effective manager. I'm not one of those gifted leaders who inherently knows how to inspire people, and gets energy from coaching and working with them. I typically dread one-on-one meetings with my direct reports because it means getting out of my own head-space (a place I really like to be), listening intently, and making the time meaningful for both of us. For an introvert like me, this is exhausting!

At the same time, I find management ultimately satisfying. I think of it as an opportunity to multiply my effectiveness through other individuals. Specifically, I see the role as:

- Using my experience to help individuals sharpen their skills. These days, though, I find that I rarely have to do this. In many cases, my direct reports *are far better than I am* at performing specific tasks. They have, for example, better Excel skills, better relationship-building skills, better course design skills, better project management skills. Which means that I spend most of my time …

- Asking questions about the bigger picture and strategy. For example: "Yes, you could certainly develop solution X for this team, and I have no doubt that it would be top-notch. But would that be the best use of your time? What is the desired outcome? How can we scale that for the rest of the organization? Is this more important than project Y?"

I call this the Ask, Don't Tell policy of management. My goal is to ask all the right questions to help individuals do the problem solving, in a way that aligns with the guiding principles of the organization. After we have worked together to figure out *what* to do, then I can always take myself out of the picture and let them figure out *how* to do it.

Share the Impact

The second major role of managers is to make the connection between the work that individuals and teams are doing, and the impact it is having (or will have) on the organization. While it is difficult to determine the exact degree of impact each individual's work will have, that doesn't mean it's not worth trying to do. This should be one of the highest management priorities within an organization: Find ways of illuminating and measuring the impact of every individual.

As a manager, this is the most precious form of motivational juice on the market. Show individuals the impact they are having. Make the connection between the work they have contributed and the resulting increases in, say, customer happiness, employee productivity, or company revenues. Invest in systems and technologies that capture metrics and data that show impact. Finally, reward individuals based on their relative impact. I'm not saying that 100 percent of someone's salary should be precisely calibrated against his or her contributions; but you can choose to award bigger bonuses and salary increases to those individuals who find ways of creating impact. I recommend reading *The Sin of Wages*[12] by William Abernathy for more on rewarding performance based on impact.

INDIVIDUALS AS INSTIGATORS

If you could walk into every single company on the planet and spend some time observing the individuals who work at them, over time you'd uncover groups of individuals who, for various reasons, have greater impact than the rest of the employees. Regardless how enlightened or conservative an organization may be, there are always ways for certain individuals to figure out how to increase the impact they're having on the organization. This section is about just that—how can you, as one individual in a much larger organization, focus on impact?

You might ask, why bother? If you aren't rewarded for your innovations, and managers don't care, what would be the point? First, you'd feel far more engaged with your work—if you have to work, you might as well make the most of it and take pride in what you do. Second, by the very act of focusing on the work you do that will have the greatest impact, you'd influence everyone around you to do the same, essentially kick-starting a more widespread change process. I'm talking about grassroots efforts, which can add up more quickly than you might imagine.

Be prepared: Focusing your work on the impact it has requires becoming a bit of an instigator. You'll have to relearn how to ask everyone around you a very important and sometimes annoying question: Why?

Why?

Children are very good at asking the question why, usually preceded by "but":

Mom: "It's time to go to bed."
Child: "But why?"
Mom: "Because I said so."

Perhaps, as parents, we might be patient for the first thousand times our children ask why. But then the question begins to exhaust us, in part because we are reluctant to admit the truth. Consider this scenario:

Mom: "I need you to go to bed so I can have an adult conversation. And, frankly, the odds of winning Candyland are driving me mad. I need a glass of wine."

The unfortunate side effect is that, by the time we are adults, we are conditioned never to ask why. Asking why in high school was seen as an act of insubordination, mainly because the algebra teacher was tired of pretending that knowledge of the subject would be of any remote use in the real world. Asking why in the workplace feels contrarian, so we just don't ask it anymore.

We must revive the practice of asking why in the workplace. This may be the *single most important action we can take in starting a Work Revolution*, regardless of our role or position or company. Ask why. Then ask again. Ask why five times if that's what it takes to uncover a problem statement. You don't need to work for a company that lavishes on The Perks to ask why. Everyone is free to do so; anyone, anywhere, can ask why. If the answer happens to be, "Nobody really knows; we've just always done it that way," then you better figure out whether the roasting pan is still too short to fit the meat.

If anyone gets offended or annoyed by your asking why, it can only mean two things:

- He or she has no idea how to answer you.

- He or she has a reason, but it's too nefarious to admit.

There are two specific situations in which asking why is particularly productive: challenging rules and uncovering problem statements. In both cases, asking why breaks down the "we've always done it that way" barrier.

Challenge the Rules In case you haven't already noticed, I'm not a big believer in dress codes. In fact, I rail against them every chance I get. Are there situations and legitimate business reasons for people dressing a certain way? Absolutely. When I present at a conference, I put on a dress or a skirt. When I was in a role to meet with potential clients, I dressed smartly. But I didn't need my manager or the HR director to tell me how to dress in these situations. I already understood that these interactions demanded an extra layer of polish. Guiding principles would have worked just fine for me in those cases.

In my first job, my company had a large military base as a client. It was important to project competence and reliability, highly desired characteristics in a potential vendor. Knowing this as a guiding principle, each time I met with them I chose to wear business suits. However, back at my office, it should not have mattered at all whether I wore jeans or casual business attire to write storyboards and review lessons.

I'm not suggesting that you start by challenging your company's dress code (typically, a highly impenetrable institution). What I am saying is that you can start small. Here's a sample script:

Manager: "For every meeting we must use our new Meeting Agenda cover page."

You: "Why?"

Manager: "Every participant should know the topics of the meeting in advance."

You: "Why?"

Manager: "I go to too many 'update' meetings."

You: "Why don't we come up with alternatives for sharing updates so that we don't feel it necessary to hold meetings to do that?"

| Manager: | "Right, well, okay. That's reasonable. And maybe we can use the next meeting to go over principles of good meeting management?" |
| You: | "Yes." |

Phew!

Uncover Problem Statements   Suppose one after the other your manager comes to you and asks you to do a task, a colleague from another team asks you to collaborate on a project, and an employee asks to purchase a $500 software package. If you choose to comply blindly with each request, you are missing an opportunity to deeply engage with both your work and your colleagues. In each of these cases, the requestor has already closed in on a particular solution. It is your role to take a step back, revisit the problem each is trying to solve, and work together with all of them to determine the best possible solution.

Let's break down each of these scenarios.

Scenario one: Your manager asks you to create a spreadsheet listing every manager in the company (see Table 4.5).

Table 4.5   The Random Manual Labor Request

Option A	Option B
Manually create the spreadsheet by copying and pasting each manager's name from the HR database.	Ask what problem your manager is trying to solve, and discover that she wants to distribute an e-mail to all of the managers in the company and needs the distribution list.
	You know that an e-mail group list is dynamically generated from HR data. You give her the group e-mail and point her to the handy new template script you just created to automate the entire process of generating personalized e-mails.
Total time: 5 hours	Total time: 5 minutes
Level of engagement: zero	Level of engagement: 100 percent, followed by a feeling of satisfaction that you helped solve a problem in a much better way.

Scenario two: Your colleague is running a training program, whose participants have provided feedback about how to restructure it to improve the class. She has asked you to partner with her on making the design changes (see Table 4.6).

Table 4.6   The Collaboration Request

Option A	Option B
Take on the redesign project, even though you already have a full plate of projects. Complete the redesign based on participant comments, a task you find particularly onerous.	Ask what problem your colleague is trying to solve, and discover she wants to boost the course survey satisfaction scores. You analyze the suggested changes and determine that the redesign wouldn't materially change the objectives and justify the time investment. You engage in a healthy debate with your colleague and realize in the process that the class would be better managed by a partner team, who, it turns out, is eager to take it over.
Total time: 40 hours Level of engagement: 15 percent—barely enough to make it through	Total time: 2 hours Level of engagement: 100 percent, and saving 20 percent of time for you and your colleague in the next quarter.

Scenario three: An employee has asked to purchase a $500 software package for creating surveys (see Table 4.7).

As you can see in these scenarios, unless you understand the full context of the core problem statement, you can never fully engage in your work. It often takes a few round of questions to get there, but the results and impact will be far greater.

Permission to Call "Bullshit"

An underlying theme for individuals-as-instigators is the implicit and explicit permission to call "bullshit" when things just don't make sense. Naked emperors shouldn't be allowed in the workplace.

In this regard, note that it is far easier, and better, to give others permission to call out *your* bullshit than it is to do it for others.

Table 4.7 The Approval Request

Option A	Option B
Approve the $500 software package and hope the employee doesn't come back later with questions about how to use it.	Ask what problem he is trying to solve, and discover he wants to launch an employee engagement survey. You're aware that the knowledge management group recently installed an open-source survey tool that would get the job done; but you also know that another team is working on a new, innovative approach for measuring employee engagement through other means. You take part in a rich debate with both teams and the requester about employee engagement and surveys, the results of which are new insights that guide the direction of everyone involved.
Total time: 5 minutes	Total time: 1 hour
Level of engagement: zero	Level of engagement: 100 percent, with a far better outcome that aligns with the guiding principles of the company.

Invite people to pick apart your solutions. Illuminate the problems you are trying to solve well before anyone has to ask. Admit you may be approaching solutions from a biased and partially uninformed perspective. When colleagues observe you doing this, chances are high they will follow suit (though you should still ask why for everything that is unclear in this regard).

The farther along people in your organization move toward starting the Work Revolution, the easier it will be to call "bullshit" on things. Take Best Buy: Recall from Chapter 3 that in its quest to create a results-only work environment (ROWE), the company ditched the 40-hour workweek rule. The company even created a new term: "Sludge," defined as "any negative comment we make that serves to reinforce old ideas about how work gets done."[13] Best Buy facilitates Sludge sessions with teams, who document comprehensive lists of all the Sludge in their work environment. Then they take major steps to eradicate all forms of Sludge. It takes a concerted effort, one that can, and should, begin with each individual.

WHAT DOES WORK LOOK LIKE?

Sarah Bloomfield, Senior Learning and Development
Specialist, Google

Close your eyes for a moment and imagine someone working. What is she doing? Wearing? Where is she, and who is she with?

You probably pictured someone at a desk, either staring at a computer monitor with rapt attention, or talking on the phone, leaning back in her chair. Was the person wearing a suit? Khakis and a button-down shirt? Maybe you pictured a team in a conference room, or meeting with a client.

Maybe you thought of someone working from home (WFH). But in many organizations, WFH seems to stand for "not really working." Did you envision someone in ripped jeans and tennis shoes? Of course not. You can't work dressed like that.

But these are the old ways of thinking, the ones we need to abandon. Why? Because they don't necessarily impact performance. In fact, requiring ways to dress, or forcing people to relegate themselves to windowless cubes, might do more harm than good.

Here's an example: When do you do your best thinking? If you have a nasty, hairy problem to solve or a nut you can't seem to crack, what works for you? Two things help me achieve an ideal problem-solving flow: going for a walk and playing the piano. Why? Where walking is concerned, the rhythm of my steps and the fresh air on my face revitalize me, and I feel my thoughts converge. For other types of challenges, especially those related to people, I head for the piano. It's an activity that I've long enjoyed, and it

(continued)

(*continued*)

engages many parts of my brain simultaneously. It distracts me just enough that I am able to walk back to my desk and finish up a proposal or document.

If you walked into the office and saw me seated at a piano keyboard, what would you think? Would you think me lazy? Would you ask me if this were a scheduled break? Would you assume that I'm a low performer?

How can you accurately describe what thinking looks like? And is it only supposed happen in one way or in one place? I'm a knowledge worker; at best, I produce words I can print on paper. Like most knowledge workers, it takes me longer to think than to type. And add this consideration: The people I most need to think with are not likely to be in the room with me. In the age of national or global businesses, we are often great distances from our teammates. In the last five years, I've shared the same geographic location with my manager for a year, at most. So 80 percent of the time I've had a manager who sits more than 700 miles away. Does he or she care if I'm wearing a skirt? Or when I go to lunch? And what of my teammates in far-flung places—in Europe and in Asia? Do they care if I think at my desk or while on a jaunt around the business park?

Exactly.

Because the nature of work has changed, we must not focus so much on the *how* of working. Yes, there are certain elements that might not change as readily as we might like—say, not being able to work from home for security reasons, or being limited to lengths of breaks because of regulations. Yet if we really examine our working practices, there are many that could be easily modified.

How can you change this today?

1. Figure out how you do _____ best. It might not be thinking, though that's an easy example. If you edit book proposals, when are you at your sharpest? If you design software,

what setup works best for you? Think not only about times of day or places, but of other environmental factors that would help you. On the flip side, define what hampers your work. For example, I know that if I wear yoga pants and a baggy sweatshirt when I work from home that I'll be far less productive than if I dress as if I were headed to the office.

2. Get clear on your deliverables. What is the end product you must produce, and when is it due?

3. Take a small step. Would you rather meet with your boss in a coffee shop than a conference room? Ask. Would you be more productive if you could wear jeans on days when you don't have client meetings? Ask.

4. Persist in the face of resistance. If you hear no, have another option ready. If you can't change what you wear, immediately suggest instead that you'd like to shift your lunch hour. Explain to your manager or leader that you understand what is expected of you, and that you will deliver. Does your manager still say no? That's a sign.

5. When your manager agrees, give a sincere thank-you.

6. Deliver at the same or even higher quality. Thank your manager for giving you the chance to prove that doing something that was comfortable for you gave him or her the desired result.

7. Ask for something else. Deliver. Repeat.

It might not seem that wearing Pumas is a giant victory for working the way you want; or that a weekly one-on-one takes place on a walk. But continue to perform without a hitch and, little by little, you'll get to work the way you like.

One last hint: Remember to remain open-minded toward your colleagues. What might keep you energized might drain others of energy—and, believe it or not, some people might prefer to think at their desks, distraction-free. Be clear about deliverables, focus on results; try not to focus on all the details.

MORE ON IMPACT TO COME

Focusing on impact, not activities, is the overarching principle in the Work Revolution. Every other principle in this book further illuminates the ultimate goal of creating impact:

- In the next chapter, "Energy, Not Schedules" I address the obsolescence of standard work hours and time cards, and explain how to follow the natural rivers of energy to do more with less.

- The notion of treating individuals as problem solvers and indispensable talent is core to the ideas in Chapter 6, "Strengths, Not Job Slots."

- Asking *why* is key to the prioritization process, and is the subject of Chapter 7, "The Right Things, Not Everything."

- Making the shift from authoritarian management to democratic problem solving is detailed in Chapter 8, "Grassroots, Not Top-Down."

As you delve into each of these chapters, you'll see that they crisscross, relating over and over to the fundamental theme of empowering individuals to solve problems for the organizations they work in.

SUMMARY

The Work Revolution requires making a shift from static business models and rules to dynamic problem solving and guiding principles. The role of the leader becomes that of a support person, while individuals take action to find answers to the why question. This shift is summarized in Table 4.8.

Table 4.8   Summary of Impact, Not Activities, for Organizations, Leaders, and Individuals

Organizations	Discover the core competencies of the organization, and express them in a problem-based mission statement. Develop a robust set of guiding principles that inform decision making at every level of the organization. Define measures of success, and invest in systems and technologies that show the connection between efforts and results. Ditch all the policies and rules that are disconnected from results and focused on activities.
Leaders	Teach individuals to think strategically about their work. Ask a lot of questions to figure out what to do, then set people free to figure out how to implement the solutions. Give frequent feedback on the impact of people's work.
Individuals	Ask why. Then ask why again. Or ask, "What problem are we trying to solve?" Give one another permission to call "bullshit," to question the importance and reason behind everything.

CHAPTER 5

Energy, Not Schedules

Project plans. Work hours. Deadlines. Due dates. Milestones. What do these concepts have in common? For starters, they all purport to contribute to productivity, by drawing arbitrary lines in the sand and defining who will do what, by when. In a very crude way, they impose organization and drive teams toward goals. But their only common denominator is *time*.

We are so obsessed with time in the workplace, often to the exclusion of many other important factors, that we've become almost immune to the issues that actually matter. Time is finite. We each get a very limited quantity of it; thus, rather than letting it rule our lives, we should honor it as the very limited resource it is by doing everything in our power to conserve it or spend it wisely. This is a fine line, so I'll use an obvious example to help make it clear.

How long does it take you to get to work from your home? When I ask people this question, most often, I get two different answers. The first: "Well, during rush hour it takes *X*." The second: "During off-peak times, it only takes *Y*." The second answer is irrelevant, unless you are one of the rare individuals who has the luxury of working during off-peak hours, or has the flexibility to set your own hours. Organizations requiring their workforces to arrive at the same time and leave at the same time (for nonbusiness reasons) essentially waste everyone's time, thereby reducing the overall energy individuals have to expend on the stuff that matters.

Ultimately, there are several fundamental problems with using time as the gatekeeper to the workplace. For starters, humans are laughably bad at predicting the amount of time it will take to get something done, due to a litany of cognitive biases, such as the *planning fallacy* (the tendency of people to underestimate how long it will take to complete a task) or *anchoring phenomenon* (the tendency to focus too much on a single piece of information in making decisions), both well documented in psychological research. If you ask a group of individuals, even on the same team, to estimate how long it will take to write a piece of code for a new software feature, put together a PowerPoint presentation, or compose a report, their estimates will be both wildly divergent and, usually, inaccurate. Why? We fail to factor in the start-up costs of getting our bearings for the assigned task (e.g., research, previous work completed, input gathering), the cost of fielding interruptions once we've ramped up (e.g., checking e-mail, perhaps hundreds of times a day), the cost of switching from one task to another (e.g., answering an e-mail, troubleshooting a problem for a colleague), and the cost of myriad unknowns that will pop up as obstacles to completing the task (e.g., lack of the right tools or materials). We are much more adept at comparing the *relative effort* of two different tasks, say software development experts who have devoted a lot of time trying to solve estimation problems.[1] If you ask members of a team whether task A or B will require more effort, independently they tend to be in agreement based on their past experiences and perspective, assuming they have familiarity with both tasks.

Another fundamental problem caused by time is that it creates False Urgency. When you are working alone on a project, it's perfectly acceptable to set some time-based goals to get things done. We do, after all, respond well to goals in the behavioral sense. However, it's not uncommon to run into situations in which one person's deadline conflicts with another person's. On the surface, it's impossible to know which of the two is more important. If someone asks for help with a task and follows up the request with, "It's due by the end of day," we tend to comply without questioning the truth of the deadline, for fear of seeming rude, difficult, or even insubordinate (especially if it's your manager or another executive). We don't want to be the ones causing a colleague to miss a deadline! Deadlines are critical, indisputable. The problem is, they obscure the True Urgency driving the work, resulting in rampantly poor prioritization within an organization.

Finally, our focus on time serves as a crutch. When our salaries are based on time, our work on deadlines, and our days on number of hours we work, we—all of us—are taking the easy way out. It's the lazy person's method of management, the lowest common denominator that everyone can point to and easily track and report—"I worked 72 hours this week!" Sadly, this causes organizational blindness to the issues that really matter: the mission of the organization, individual performance and contributions, customer needs, and the current operating environment.

When we free people from assigned schedules and defined hours of work, and make them the stewards of their own time, amazing things can happen. Individuals feel a huge sense of relief and autonomy. Their focus on their projects will be on the potential positive impact they might have. Everyone starts making smart decisions about how to use their time, both to sustain their energy and for the benefit of the company. Releasing ourselves from the tyranny of time opens up a whole new world, one in which "rivers" of energy suddenly become visible as they flow around us.

RIVERS OF ENERGY

Rivers are complex bodies of water. They are defined both by the landscape around and beneath them; in turn, they alter that landscape over time. They have currents and ebbs and flows; they also have bends, falls, rocks, and other obstacles. Some rivers are deep enough to be navigated by ships, whereas others can be traveled only by kayak or canoe. Their variation is endless, and their beauty breathtaking.

Changing the course of a river is exceedingly difficult, sometimes literally requiring moving mountains; nevertheless, we can learn to navigate a river and take full advantage of the energy it generates. We can create more efficient boats that are perfectly suited to the properties of every kind of river. We can learn to ride a river's whitewater and become better swimmers. We can invent tools to read the contours of river bottoms to better inform navigation. We can build dams to harness the power of a river to generate electricity. In short, though there are many things about a river that are outside of our control or hard to change, when we learn to harness the energy of the river in ways that are within our control, the impact of our efforts multiplies.

We can think about running our organizations in the same way. Some organizations, such as technology companies, may choose to ride the wild, rocky rivers where the waters are swift and the payoff is large. Other organizations, such as traditional manufacturers, may choose to travel the wide, smooth waters—taking the slow but steady route. The leaders in an organization make choices about how to navigate the river—from the right boats to the right people in the best positions— and how to coordinate the activities of the people on the boats. These choices are made to take the fullest advantage of the energy of a river, while avoiding the obstacles along the way.

When you begin to look for rivers of energy within your organization, you will find unexpected and creative ways to do more with less time. If the goal is produce the greatest impact for your organization, following the energy of individuals, your team, and the environment will enable you to multiply your effectiveness and that of your organization.

In the rest of this chapter I address two major sources of energy: the energy of individuals and the energy of value. In the first, the focus is on following rivers of personal energy. The second, the energy of value, refers to aligning your teams and organizations to tap into natural sources of motivation, for greater efficiency and impact.

THE POWER OF RIVERS

It's no coincidence that the Nile, Tigris, Euphrates, Yellow, and Yangtze rivers gave rise to the cities at the heart of early modern civilization. Towns grew up around these rivers because of their inherent advantages: irrigation for crops, clean water for drinking, and easy transportation to other cities. The rivers served as a multiplier for progress, and the axes of power rose and strengthened along these rivers to produce the Egyptian kingdoms, Mesopotamia (Greek for "land between the rivers"), and the Xia, Shang, and Zhou Dynasties of early China.

THE ENERGY OF INDIVIDUALS

For some time now, we have been ingeniously tapping into the power of the Internet and computers to take productivity to a whole new level. But, ironically, in this age of knowledge workers, we have reached a plateau in terms of capitalizing on the energy of individuals. The default mode of leadership is still the one-size-fits-all treatment of employees, constrained within inflexible work hours. Of course, when work hours are based on business needs that are truly urgent, such as global 24/7 call center coverage, it's entirely reasonable to assign schedules and expect individuals to adhere to them. However, there are many organizations and teams for which this is not the case, and the potential for change in these environments is enormous.

Following Your Energy River

Rivers are great analogies for thinking about maximizing impact through personal energy.

Who are you "in the wild"? No, I'm not asking what you do when you cut loose. I'm asking how you structure your days and activities when you have zero professional or personal pressures on your time. A great reference point for answering this is college. Which classes did you pick: the early-morning ones, the late-afternoon ones, or the evening classes? Did you cluster your classes back-to-back or spread them out evenly within a day or week? When did you study: morning, afternoon, or night? And where: with friends or alone; at a coffee shop, the library, or your dorm/apartment?

How about your workdays now? When do you have the best focus/concentration? When is your most creative time of day? When would you pay $1,000 for a nap? The answers to these questions should give you pretty solid clues about the rhythms of your personal energy. And when you learn to follow the peaks and troughs of your energy for work and rest, you can multiply your productivity and maximize your potential impact.

Remember (as if we need a reminder!), our time is finite. There are only so many hours in a day that we can work. And if we are forcing ourselves to work during our "junk" hours, we are wasting precious time, reducing our productivity, and fighting against the currents of our energy river. In Chapter 3, "The New Rules," I stated the obvious fact that people are different. When I am forced to follow a fixed work schedule, from 8:00 AM to 6:00 PM, with a one-hour lunch break, here's how it plays out for me (see Table 5.1).

Table 5.1   How I Function in a Fixed Work Schedule

Time	Activity	Emotions/Feelings
6:00 AM	Wake up, eat breakfast, get ready for work	Angry
7:30 AM (ish)	Leave for work.	Hazy; it's hard to think straight enough to make sure I'm not forgetting my pants.
8:00 AM	Arrive at work, respond to e-mails.	Fuzzy; productivity around 10 percent of peak; Is this a. . .what day is this?
9:00 AM	Work	At 20 percent productivity; generally have a hard time forming coherent sentences in meetings.
10:00 AM	Work	At 30 percent productivity; starting to feel human—just a little.
11:00 AM	Work	Starved! More awake, though; at about 40 percent productivity, and finally slipping into a groove.
12:00 PM	Lunch	Annoyed that I have to stop work and my momentum; worse, I have to forage for food and fight the lines of massive lunch crowds.
1:00 PM	Work	Distracted. Need to get back into a groove; at 30 percent productivity.
2:00 PM	Work	Finally feeling strong, with surge of productivity—50 percent.
3:00 PM	Work	Gathering steam—60 percent!
4:00 PM	Work	Ugh; my usual afternoon slump. Back down to 30 percent productivity.
5:00 PM	Work	Over the slump; feeling alive, refreshed, and firing on all cylinders! Creative brain is spinning. At 100 percent—finally!
6:00 PM	Time to leave	Seriously?! I was just getting started.

Total hours worked: 9

Average level of productivity: 41 percent of peak

Total productivity (hours worked × percent productive): 3.7 hours

In contrast, when I apply my idealized evening-person schedule and follow the flow of my energy river, I respond as shown in Table 5.2.

Table 5.2 How I Function in a Natural-Energy Schedule

Time	Activity	Emotions/Feelings
6:00 AM	Still sleeping	Bliss
7:30 AM (ish)	Wake up, make coffee.	Resist getting up, but slept well; long enough.
8:00 AM	Read articles related to work, respond to morning e-mails.	Head is hazy, but the coffee is sinking in. I can take in a lot of info, but can't really put much out yet; productivity (because of nature of tasks) 50 percent.
9:00 AM	Get ready for work, eat breakfast, leave.	Pause from working, to let myself wake up a bit more.
10:30 AM	Arrive at work, dive into some big tasks.	Productivity at 100 percent; I've had three full hours to wake up, barely enough time for a nonmorning person—but, hey, I'm a go-getter!
12:00 PM	Exercise	Perfect time of day for physical activity—I'm awake, energetic, and not hungry for lunch yet.
1:00 PM	Have a working lunch.	Eat while I catch up on more e-mails and do any other reading I need to do; at 50 percent productivity.
2:00 PM	Work	Feeling strong; energized from food and exercise, and firing on all cylinders; at 100 percent productivity.
3:00 PM	Work	Still going strong; maintaining 100 percent productivity.
4:00 PM	Work	Ugh; my usual afternoon slump. Productivity down to 30 percent. Go for a quick walk.

(continued)

Table 5.2   How I Function in a Natural-Energy Schedule (*continued*)

Time	Activity	Emotions/Feelings
5:00 PM	Work	Over the slump and feeling alive, refreshed; firing on all cylinders! Feeling creative, my brain is spinning; at 100 percent, again.
6:00 PM	Work	Feeling very productive; making huge progress; still at 100 percent productivity.
7:00 PM	Work	Starting to wind down, do wrap-up tasks, and plan for tomorrow; organize my work; at 50 percent productivity.
7:30 PM	Leave the office	Hungry for dinner

Total hours worked: 8.5

Average productivity: 80 percent of peak

Total productivity (hours worked × percent productive): 6.8 hours

As you can see, my average productivity rating almost *doubles* when I'm working in the flow of my natural energy river. When I'm not, as shown in Table 5.1, I worked a solid nine hours but at only a fraction of the productivity I'm capable of, meaning that many of those hours were a complete waste of my time and energy. Compare that to when I worked on the schedule that is best for me: I got twice the productivity from each hour I worked, plus I gained additional energy from a sense of accomplishment. I interacted better with people, I was able to form complete sentences, and I got in my daily exercise.

My point is, it's important to figure out for yourself when you're at your best. Once you've determined when you work most effectively, versus when you aren't quite capable of human interaction, negotiate a schedule that aligns with your natural flow of energy. If, for example, you are a morning person and love getting to work early, volunteer to collaborate virtually with a team located in a time zone that is hours ahead of yours. If you aren't a morning person, do everything in your power to work with teams *behind* your time zone. I once had the opportunity to work out of New York for a month while my primary team members were all on Pacific time. Every day, I gushed about how lucky

I was that I *never* had to attend meetings before noon! This was heaven to me; and I was always happy to stay late for evening meetings, given that my energy peaked at that time.

I believe we should all advertise our "morning handicap"—sort of like a golf handicap. Mine would be +3, meaning that I'm not fully awake and alive until three hours after 9:00 AM. If you are a morning person, yours might be −2, meaning you are one of those annoying (okay, not annoying; I'm just jealous) early birds that chirp their way cheerily to the office at 7:00 AM, fully awake and firing on all cylinders. I've known software engineers with a +5 handicap; they would arrive to the office at 2:00 PM and work until 11:00 PM or midnight every single day. It worked for them!

FIVE TIPS FOR MANAGING YOUR ENERGY, NOT YOUR TIME

Jenny Blake, author of *Life After College: The Complete Guide to Getting What You Want*

"Life is a marathon, not a sprint."

"I'm in this for the long haul."

"I can see the finish line—not letting up now."

"I'll sleep when I'm old," or "I'll rest after I finish this next big phase."

"I'm so passionate about what I'm doing that I don't even *need* a break!"

If you're anything like me, you've uttered one or more of these motivational phrases to yourself as you pursued a big project or business idea. We often try to do it all—build our business, eat healthy foods, stay fit, be social, take care of our home and loved ones, and be cheerful on top of it all.

It can be exhausting.

And contrary to all the popular mantras, treating life and business like a marathon might not actually be in our best interest.

(continued)

(continued)

MY ILL-TIMED BOOK BREAKDOWN

I experienced this firsthand after having a complete and utter break-down three weeks before my book, *Life After College: The Complete Guide to Getting What You Want*, was set to come out.

I had been working on the project for over two and half years, and in the final months I ramped it up to an obsessive around-the-clock endeavor (in addition to my full-time job at Google). I felt like I was on mile 23 of a marathon—I could see the finish line and it was not the time to rest or let up.

Because I wasn't willing to take a break, life knocked me on my ass (that's the technical term) and forced me to rest. Despite the fact that my book was going to be released in three weeks, and I had an impossibly long to-do list of important tasks to complete, I was a miserable, crying, nonfunctioning mess. Even though I was incredibly passionate about my project, not building in any rest stops had been a recipe for disaster.

THE ALTERNATIVE: MANAGE YOUR ENERGY, NOT YOUR TIME

Tony Schwartz, author of *The Power of Full Engagement*[2] recommends that we manage our energy not our time. Rather than treating our life and businesses as a marathon, Schwartz advises we treat them as sprints and recovery (recovery being key here!).

We all know we are going to have big sprints—that's what makes pursuing a project or business so exciting. But it's imperative that we build in equal parts recovery.

Five Tips to Make Room for Recovery

1. Schedule it. No matter whether or not you think you need a break, schedule fun or relaxation activities in advance and stick to them.

2. Double the break you think you need. I know how this goes: "Sure, I'll take a break—I'll give myself a whole hour off!" Not good enough. Whatever the break you think you need, double it.

You are most likely underestimating the toll that all of your hard work is taking on your body and mind—even if you're having fun.

3. Enlist family and friends. If you schedule a weekend getaway with family or friends, you'll have no excuse but to unplug. Family and friends can be great accountability buddies for taking the breaks you need.

4. Make a list of the benefits of R&R, and brainstorm your favorite rejuvenation activities. I know that even after reluctantly taking a break, I will come back refreshed, more cheerful, and more creative—which puts me in an even better position to do my best work once I'm back at it. Making a list of the benefits will help motivate and remind you to actually take the breaks you've set up. At a loss for what to do? Make a list of any/all activities that bring you joy or relaxation. For me that's reading, yoga, a glass of wine (with chocolate) and watching a few shows on Hulu.

5. Break down your biggest goals into achievable, measurable chunks, and reward yourself often! For every day that you make a massive to-do list, add a reward item at the end that brings you joy. Maybe it's reading a book or a gossip magazine, or going out to dinner with a friend. For many of us, we only take breaks or celebrate when we hit the *big* goals—but those can take months to achieve. Instead, break them down into smaller parts and reward yourself for all of the smaller milestones you hit along the way.

Forbes, May 30, 2011. www.forbes.com/sites/yec/2011/05/30/5-tips-for-managing -your-energy-not-your-time.

Navigating a Team of Rivers

While it might be a fun exercise to design your dream work schedule, it's another matter entirely to make this work for an entire team. But it's actually not all that complicated if you focus on one thing only: True Urgency. True Urgency represents all the deadlines, priorities, and schedules that are driven by *real* needs of customers or other important external factors that dictate the nature of your work.

As a leader, you can create a flexible work environment by loosening all the parameters around working times that aren't bound by True Urgency. Some teams, such as trading groups or retail stores, will always be bound by a set schedule (e.g., trading hours, store hours determined by peak customer traffic). But for many teams in the knowledge space, there may be no hard-and-fast schedules. When this is the case, you have the luxury of freeing your teams to work when they are best able to function and coordinate with each other. True Urgency can and should be central to the entire team's schedule and priorities. As long as the team members understand what is truly urgent about their work, you can negotiate with them to ensure everyone is contributing fairly.

For example, recall from Chapter 3 the example of Credit Acceptance, the company that broke the fixed-schedule rule. It supports a range of days and hours during which the company offers live customer service, some of which represent peak call times. Surely, in this environment everyone can't have their own schedules, right? Wrong. In 2008, Credit Acceptance implemented a creative plan under which everyone was required to cover a set number of four-hour shifts during peak times. Beyond this, they could come in for any combination of four-hour shifts to fulfill their remaining work hours. Moreover, they *didn't need to inform the team ahead of time* which shifts they planned to work; they could just show up when it suited them, according to their rivers of energy. As a team, the company met its True Urgency needs during peak call times, but then provided individuals autonomy, freeing them to manage the rest of their hours according to their personal needs and preferences.

To accomplish what Credit Acceptance did, it is important to use common language with your teammates to clearly convey the distinction between workgroup coordination activities and True Urgency, so that they can make sound decisions about when they will work and how they will coordinate with one another. Absolute deadlines cannot, of course, be negotiated, but coordination activities such as team meetings (helpful for keeping things on track, maintaining peer accountability), joint working sessions, and any other real-time interactions can easily accommodate the working preferences of team members for the purpose of capitalizing on their individual energy cycles. As a leader, you are the key to setting the tone with your team, to break them of the habit of work driven by False Urgency and work schedules.

TIP

Create a shared calendar on which all team members can list their working hours and reference those of others. This calendar can be used for scheduling meetings and otherwise coordinating the staff. When teams need to work closely together, they can use this calendar to help make it happen.

The Workplace as Individual Energy Charger

I recently toured the offices of IDEO in Palo Alto, California. IDEO is an incredibly successful company, known for design innovation. Its consultants advise a wide range of companies about how to think about design, to help them home in on the ideal products to solve interesting and challenging customer problems.

Like Google, IDEO's offices bear little resemblance to those of a typical company. I saw a large group of employees (dressed, of course, according to their own taste rather than to a prescribed code) disbanding from a large get-together in the café. Tom Kelly, the general manager, showed us the materials experimentation station—a huge drawer fully stocked with every kind of cool substance and material—designed to enable individuals to tinker and think creatively about their potential applications. I also saw a hollowed-out van used as a conference room, and toys and bikes everywhere. And it didn't look to me as if people were actually *working*. But that's the best part: They clearly were. It's just that work at IDEO looks very different from the traditional image of people glued to their computers, typing away in isolation.

The most important step an organization can take to support individual energy renewal is to change the definition and expectation of what work looks and feels like. If we expect people to log eight hours a day churning out e-mails and reports and presentations and sales calls and…, we are setting them up for burnout. Simply, it is not possible for anyone to sustain that level of concentration over that period of time.

In my own case, I've implemented a routine that pays dividends for my state of mind and productivity every workday. It's based on a behavioral research concept called the *post-reinforcement pause*, which refers to a very predictable response in any organism.[3] Let's say you train a pigeon to peck repeatedly at a round disk, and after every 50 pecks, food is delivered as a reinforcer of the pecking behavior. Or, alternatively, food is delivered on the first peck after a two-minute interval. These are called *fixed schedules of reinforcement*: either the number of responses or the interval of time is constant between the delivery of the reinforcers. What researchers have found is that, once the food reinforcer has been delivered, the pigeon takes a break. Every single time, over and over: Peck, peck, peck—food! Take a break. Even when it is in the best interest of the pigeon to resume pecking as soon as possible on the fixed response schedule, the pigeon still takes a break!

I have now taken up the practice of granting myself post-reinforcement pauses. When I finish writing an e-mail that required a great deal of thought, I take a break. When I complete a tedious set of tasks that entailed referencing 10 different documents to reconcile details, I take a break. When I finish coding a dataset, I take a break. Depending on the size of the task, I may take a short break—simply get up, walk down the hall to get some coffee, and stretch a bit. If it's just before lunch and I've put in a hard morning, I go outside for a run (particularly rewarding upon completion of *any* big task and on a beautiful day). I might walk outside, go to the bathroom, or make a personal phone call. If you tracked my movements on any given day and posted a time-lapse video on YouTube, you might draw the conclusion that I couldn't possibly be getting any work done given all of the breaks I take! In fact, the number of breaks I take is *precisely* why I am able to get so much done. After each break, I engage in a mini-renewal session, after which I'm ready to jump back in, fully energized for the next task.

It all comes back to the notion of energy versus schedules. Scheduling work breaks and forcing people to take them according to the schedule is counterproductive. It leaves no room for employees to make decisions about when they actually need a break; it also artificially limits the number of breaks. Allowing employees to follow their own energy cycles, and take breaks as they need them, ensures a fully charged workforce that can truly make the most out of every workday.

This is the real reason that Google installs Foosball and pool tables, nap pods, massage chairs, gyms, bikes, pianos, video games, and micro kitchens throughout its campuses. Google uses every imaginable way to enable its employees to recharge throughout the day. The campus might look like a playground, but it's actually an intricately designed recharging station, with something for every employee in the company.

THE ENERGY OF VALUE

Value has energy, and it creates energy. The stock market is driven by the pursuit of value: People invest in a company when they believe it has value, and they sell when the value goes down. When we start businesses, we believe that the products or services we are offering have value to customers. If I value something, I am motivated to pursue it.

The greater the value, the greater the energy. I believe value is like money. Money is a universal incentive (in behavior analysis terms, a *generalized reinforcer*) because it can be exchanged for an infinite number of physical or virtual goods. Value is like money for energy; regardless of the task, and whether it aligns with my core strengths, if it has value, I will generate some kind of energy by engaging in it. Interestingly, when we are engaged in activities that have inherently low value, our personal energy flags; thus, it acts as a barometer of sorts for potential value. Google has a frequently touted motto: "Focus on the user and all else will follow."[4] I propose a minor modification: "Focus on the *value* and all else will follow."

The Role of Individuals in Finding Value

In the summer of 2011, I made the big move from California to New York to start my new job—coincidentally, right when I was starting to write this book. Between the time I finished my old job and was to start my new one, I had three weeks—yes, three weeks!—with no formal work obligations. Given my tight book deadline, I set the audacious goal for that period of writing three chapters—one per week—to get a great head start on the process. Here's how it went:

Week One: I had planned a trip to Scotland, where I had a speaking engagement. Five days of travel and only four hours of speaking, so plenty of time to write! Except that I was in a new country, and there was so much to see... And I found I had no energy after finishing up my job transitions (a huge post-rein-forcement pause). In the end, I managed to write 1,000 words on the airplane ride home; better than nothing.

Week Two: Selling stuff, packing stuff, coordinating stuff, in sum-mer heat and no AC; saying goodbye to people, and paying an emotional toll. Result: No writing at all; not a word.

Week Three: First week in New York: no routines, few friends, tons of free time. Day one: Couldn't help but explore the city! Day two: Long bike ride around the city and over to New Jersey; came home exhausted. Day three: Now, I really needed to write! No more excuses. I stared at the computer, but my apartment was uncomfortable, with no good work setup; my back was killing me and my brain was frozen. I worked and reworked the same sec-tion, making no progress whatsoever. Day four: New tactic; try the library. Too loud; who knew? Try a coffee shop; too hot, open air. Back at the apartment: exhausted, took short nap. Two-thirds of my day now gone.

By this point, I was really beating myself up. I mean, this was day four of week three and I was absolutely and completely stumped. Everything seemed to be conspiring against my mak-ing any progress at all. Finally, mercifully, I let myself crack open a new chapter to write (no, not a beer; though, that would certainly have been my next strategy). As I started the process of planning the new chapter, then writing the introduction—boom! It all made sense! The chapter I had been struggling through was all wrong. It didn't fully fit into the structure I had originally outlined, but I finally gained the clarity to see where it did fit, and what it should say. I made the notations to that chapter, flipped back to the new one, and proceeded to pound out 1,500 words in about one hour, despite the summer heat, my weariness, the poor working space—all of it. It all just flowed so easily.

Clearly, my brain had been throwing up every roadblock it could think up, in the form of low energy and a billion distractions. I had been focusing on every factor except the most important one: that the chapter I was attempting to write was low value! I was trying to fit a square peg in a round hole. It was only after I unraveled the mystery that all of the bottlenecks and obstacles disintegrated before my eyes; consequently, my energy blossomed.

Low-Value Signals   No doubt you can recount moments like these. You have work that you just can't seem to motivate yourself to complete. Every time you approach it, your brain triggers hunger or sleepiness or *anything* to avoid doing the task. My theory is that this is our brain's way of sniffing out work that is of low value to us. The problem is that we've layered so many societal expectations around getting work done that we are blinded to the underlying root issues.

I've managed a few dozen individuals over the years, with a wide array of backgrounds, skillsets, experiences, and passions. I found that every single one of them had a bullshit detector worthy of Sherlock Holmes. Yet very few of them ever realized it. Here's how our interactions would unfold:

- They feel low energy in approaching a task or specific responsibility.

- Try as they might, they can't muster the energy to complete the task, and they miss a deadline or two in the process.

- Sheepishly, they come to me hoping I can motivate or pep-talk them through the stalemate.

- As we discuss it, we realize that the task, itself, is bullshit. It might once have had meaning, value, or potential impact (or it might not have). In any case, it no longer has the potential to make a significant impact, due to a multiplicity of factors. The conclusion? They should drop it.

- They walk away from the conversation feeling light as a feather, renewed, and full of energy.

It's clear to me that our gut reaction to bullshit tasks is usually right-on; but our work culture is such that giving up and leaving something unfinished is regarded as a sign of laziness, a half-assed effort, or even cheating. We can't let go of these things because doing so reeks of quitting, of failure.

And yet we should. We usually know at our core when something is not worth doing. But we are conditioned to push past this knowing, leading ourselves to believe that our resistance is more a reflection of some personal dysfunction, a character flaw, or a deficit in willpower. If we can't articulate *why* we believe something is low value, we tend to believe it is ourselves who should change, not the task. What we fail to acknowledge is the power of our brain to pick up on thousands of subtle cues—so subtle as to be beneath our consciousness. If we learn to pay attention to our energy level, we can fast-track the process of discovering the greatest sources of value in our work.

The Energy of Decision Making   Our energy levels help us to identify low-value activities. The same brain processes that piece together multiple cues around potential value are the same ones that can play a large part in decision making. Gut feeling, intuition, sensing—all of these terms relate more or less to the same thing. They tell us to push aside the distractions and the thinking/logic that are leading us astray. *Of course*, analytical thinking is absolutely critical in the business environment. However, we tend to overvalue analytical thinking to the detriment of our intuition. They both have a place; they both are critical. We spend a lot of time in school sharpening our abilities in analytical thinking, but spend virtually no time at all honing our intuitive skills. The result? We often overlook opportunities to learn something valuable from our gut instincts, and in fact, miss many insights our analytical thinking skills obscure.

John K. is a managing partner at a trading firm who has been trading commodities for about 10 years, so long he claims to have completely lost his ability to be a thoroughly analytical thinker. I believe him; for when I interviewed him, he had a hard time extracting the core principles to explain how he does his job—he's that entrenched (and successful) at what he does. His job is to make quick decisions based on information coming into him, hard and fast—thousands of decisions every day—using his gut instinct as a guide. His job is to be right more than 50 percent of the time. (An aside: This sort of metric boggles my mind; if I did my work right 50 percent of the time, I'd be fired for poor quality. But in the financial industry, beating the odds, even by a sliver, is good enough; quite lucrative, in fact.)

John states that the number one mistake his guys make (yes, there are all guys in his office on the trading desk) is to base decisions on what they can *explain*, not what they actually think is right. He tries to teach them to listen to their gut—the quiet, often dissenting voice that tells us to make seemingly irrational decisions (at least, according to the experts)—to make decisions they can't fully explain or defend. But, undoubtedly, those decisions are informed by thousands of pieces of information accumulated over time. And they are often the right ones. But how to teach this effectively to a bunch of young guys hung up on proving themselves? *That* is a different question.

There are two compelling reasons for relying on our intuition. First, it can be a huge timesaver. Our intuition-based conclusions are often just as accurate as our thinking-based conclusions, but they take a tiny fraction of the time to reach (which, in our trading example, is critically important). In the realm of social psychology, this is called *thin-slice judgments*. The research on this shows that the conclusions we draw in the first few seconds of an interaction with someone correlate extremely closely to judgments based on extended interactions.[5] For example, two researchers were extensively trained in conducting interviews, evaluating candidates, and making judgments based on extensive and time-consuming analyses of the interviews. Separately, a large number of objective observers were shown a very short video clip of these same candidates walking in, shaking hands, and sitting down for their interviews. Based solely on this clip, the objective observers' judgments of the candidates fell remarkably in line with those of the extensive interview evaluations on 9 of 11 categories. In other words, 15 seconds of uninformed observation yielded virtually the same results as those derived from approximately an hour's worth of interview time and analysis by trained interviewers. Clearly, harnessing your intuition, and knowing when to use it to your advantage, can serve as a huge timesaver.

Second, we often can derive better outcomes by relying on our intuition. I interviewed some folks in the intelligence community (who, for obvious reasons, can't be named). These amazing people deal with all kinds of nefarious characters in the course of their intelligence-gathering duties. They have to be able to determine whether the individuals they work with are reliable, have good intentions (toward us), and are truthfully stating their motivations (even if their motivation is money or other less than fully honorable incentives). The job of these men and women is to interview possible sources of intelligence, gather information about them, and in short, do all of the due diligence that is possible to determine whether or not they can be trusted. But in the end, before making the final decision about whether to work with each of them, they ask a very simple question: "What is your 'Blink'?"—Malcolm Gladwell's term for thinking without thinking.

What they are getting at is that usually you have a gut instinct about a person. You might not be able to articulate *why* you feel the way you do, but there's no denying it. Your brain detects signals that you might not have words to explain. But they're there, they're powerful, and, probably more often than we realize, right on target.

One intelligence officer—I'll call him Aaron—relayed a story about working with an Al-Qaeda source in the Middle East. The source claimed to be an Al-Qaeda Amir (*amir* means *prince* in Arabic, the term used to denote a leader of an Al-Qaeda operation). In the intelligence community, this was a huge boon—to get a high-level leader on board to provide intelligence is the equivalent of discovering a gold mine. It was a high-profile operation, and a lot was riding on the possible intelligence coming from this man. When Aaron first joined the team that recruited the Amir, he ventured out on a routine meeting with another officer. The two picked up the Amir, to transport him to the meeting spot; during that very first ride, Aaron recalled that he felt a strong uneasiness. Over the next few meetings, his negative energy about the Amir continued to mount, though he couldn't articulate *why* he felt this way. Still, it compelled him to dig deeper into the case.

After sifting through the mountains of documented interviews with the Amir, Aaron stumbled across the Amir's accounting of a "training trip" he had taken to Iran. Because of Aaron's deep expertise on Middle Eastern issues, this tripped an alarm in his mind. Training in Iran?! This was a major revelation; completely new information. If true, it would open an entirely new line of intelligence—groundbreaking, in fact. Aaron went back to the Amir to conduct another round of interviews, specifically regarding the Iran training trip. Not surprisingly, it took him little time to uncover the inconsistencies and flaws in the Amir's story. And shortly after these discrepancies started to emerge, the Amir's entire story collapsed. It turned out he was not an Amir at all; he faked the role as a way to make money. As embarrassing as it was for the intelligence team that initially recruited him, finding that out probably saved lives.

The point is, Aaron trusted his initial gut instinct, then followed this energy and applied his analytical skills to test his hypothesis that the Amir was a fraud. In retrospect, he was able to look back and pinpoint suspicious behavior. For example, when he and his colleague picked up the purported Amir for meetings, he would sweat profusely, and seemed nervous as a cat. In Aaron's experiences with other terrorists, he noted the complete opposite posture—they were swaggering, unapologetic, and cocky. Still, it wasn't a stretch for the other officers to interpret the fake Amir's nervousness as a sign he was paranoid of being caught by his own organization; but, ultimately, they too were suspicious of his behavior. But since they couldn't articulate the logic behind why they felt suspicious, they didn't have the courage to stand up and question the fake Amir's authenticity based on a "feeling."

As the complexity of our information-heavy world continues to increase, we must improve our ability to decipher the signals our energy sends us. And while it will always remain important to use our analytical skills to decipher puzzles, we also need to learn to use our gut energy to develop hypotheses, which we can then test, rather than try to sort through an infinite number of possibilities in our worlds.

Discovering Organizational Channels of Value

While individuals can each play a role in surfacing and eliminating low-value activities in our jobs, we can look at the organizational level of our companies to find channels of value through which our efforts can blossom and grow. In other words, our work should align with channels of value, and when it doesn't, initiatives and projects will fall flat.

A good example from my personal experience of a failed organizational initiative was the launch at Google of the Personal Development Plan (PDP as it came to be called). The PDP was a tool designed to facilitate the conversation between managers and their direct reports about their careers. It featured all the typical questions: What do you enjoy doing the most? Where do you see yourself in five years? It was an online form that was stored in the performance management system, which was convenient if you happened to get a new manager or wanted to return to it again in the future.

PDP wasn't a terrible failure, really. I'm sure the people who actually used the form got some value out of it. But by and large, it never caught on, and it tainted the whole notion of career development at the company for a while afterwards. I heard versions of this conversation many times:

"We should do something about career development. People say they want career paths."
"Oh, we tried that before. We rolled out PDPs, and no one did them."

Why did the initiative fail? To understand what was behind it, we need to take a step back to look a bit more closely at the ABCs of behavior.

The ABCs of Behavior   We can look at any given behavior—our own or that of others—and make some very good guesses about why that behavior occurred, thanks to the work of B.F. Skinner[6] and behavior analysts who followed him. When I refer to a *behavior*, I mean some action that is directly and indisputably observable. "Getting angry" is not a behavior; yelling loudly, throwing plates, and stomping are. Anything that prompts a behavior to occur is called an *antecedent*, and anything that happens as a result of the behavior is a *consequence*, as diagrammed here:

Antecedent ⇨ Behavior ⇨ Consequence

An antecedent can be an e-mail, a sign, or an alarm—anything that serves as a prompt for some behavior. Traffic lights are quintessential antecedents, prompting the well-known behavior to stop on red. It's in the consequences of behavior, however, where the real power lies. Consequences can be positive or negative. They can happen immediately after the behavior occurs or sometime in the future. Some consequences are certain to follow a behavior; others are completely uncertain. And, often, there are many consequences for a given behavior. But here's the most important point: The probability of a behavior happening again is completely dependent on its consequences, and whether they were positive (thus, reinforcing the behavior) or negative (reducing the probability of the behavior happening in the future). Traffic lights would be ineffective as antecedents if they weren't so highly linked to consequences. If you run a red light, chances are very strong that you'll get a negative reaction: You'll get honked at, be pulled over by a cop and be handed a ticket (or get one in the mail), or, worst of all, cause an accident or a near-miss.

None of this is very hard to grasp. In fact, it's quite intuitive. So it is amazing how rarely people think about this with respect to their own behavior, and especially the behavior of their children, spouses, pets, and coworkers!

Consider a common example: A mother and her young daughter are at the store. The toddler spots cookies she wants (antecedent). She points and asks for the cookies (behavior). The mother says, "No sweetie, not today" (consequence and antecedent). The little girl starts to cry (behavior). The mtother consoles her (consequence), but still says no (antecedent). The girl throws a tantrum, drawing the attention of everyone in the store (behavior). The mother gives in and buys her the cookies (consequence). The child stops crying. What do you think is going to happen next time?

When we think about this in the organizational context, it's not much more complicated or surprising. I run an exercise using the *ABC model*[7] to demonstrate this with software engineers in manager training classes. We spend about five minutes listing out each of the antecedents and consequences for the behavior of writing documentation for their projects, which is an important behavior. Documentation ensures that other software engineers can understand the code and how they might use it. Table 5.3 contains a snapshot of a typical analysis.

There are a healthy number of antecedents there—many of which seem to be powerful. And there are some positive consequences at play, too. So why don't the engineers consistently write documentation? We can use the PIC/NIC Analysis® to take a closer look at those

Table 5.3   The ABC Model

Antecedents	Behavior	Consequences
Verbal reminder from team lead	Writing documentation on a project	Adds more time to complete the project
Written checklist of project responsibilities		Lost time writing new lines of code or adding a feature
Twelve engineers e-mailing questions about the project		Hassle of tracking down the details from the team for documentation
One engineer complaining about lack of information		Fewer questions about the project
Two other projects inappropriately using one of the application programming interfaces (APIs)		Thank-you's from engineers reading the documentation
		Questions from engineers reading the documentation
		Proper use of APIs
		Thank-you from team lead
		Annoyance of checking documentation periodically for freshness

consequences with respect to whether they are positive or negative, immediate or future, and certain or uncertain (see Table 5.4).

Consequences that happen immediately and with certainty are those most likely to influence the probability of the behavior. So when we look at the consequences in Table 5.4, we see that the only ones that are immediate and/or certain are negative (the "NICs")! Regardless of how many positive consequences there are, they are all in the future and largely uncertain. When we look through the lens of the ABC PIC/NIC Analysis, what emerges is a much more understandable picture of why behaviors are (or are not) occurring.

Table 5.4   ABC PIC/NIC Analysis

Consequences	Positive or Negative?	Immediate or Future?	Certain or Uncertain?
Adds more time to complete the project	**Negative**	**Immediate**	**Certain**
Lost time writing new lines of code or adding new features	**Negative**	**Immediate**	**Certain**
Hassle of tracking down the details from the team for documentation	**Negative**	**Immediate**	**Certain**
Fewer questions about the project	Positive	Future	Uncertain
Thank-you's from engineers reading documentation	Positive	Future	Uncertain
Questions from engineers reading documentation	Positive	Future	Uncertain
Proper use of APIs	Positive	Future	Uncertain
Thank-you from team lead	Positive	Future	Uncertain
Annoyance of checking documentation periodically for freshness	Negative	Future	Certain

© of Aubrey Daniels International, 2012, used with permission.

Going back to the failure of the PDPs at Google, it is pretty clear why they never took off:

- They took a lot of time to complete. (negative)
- They required commitment from both the manager and direct report. (negative, difficult)
- They necessitated scheduling one or more meetings to discuss. (definitely negative)

- They were kind of hard to do—who really knows what they want to do in five years? (negative)

- There was no requirement to complete them. (negative)

- Everyone, both managers and direct reports, had too many other things to do that were more pressing. (True Urgency, negative)

- They were buried in a remote location in the performance management system (negative), so there were very infrequent antecedents to complete them.

Finally, as far as the positive consequences of the PDPs were concerned, no one actually used them for the purposes of matching individuals to internal positions. They might have proved useful at a later time, but for what and how, no one was really sure. So, clearly, all of the immediate and certain consequences for completing the PDPs were negative, and the positive consequences were so vague and future-based they virtually had no influence at all!

Leveraging Channels of Behavior   Channels of behavior—which we can also glimpse through an ABC PIC/NIC Analysis—can be used as powerful energy sources. Whether we are developing products for users, delivering services to customers, or launching internal initiatives in our organizations, it is important to stay focused on how and where behavior naturally occurs, as this points to valuable opportunities. Like energy, behavior, too, is like a river. In fact, William Schoenfeld and John Farmer coined the term "behavior stream" in 1970 to describe the way behavior and the stimuli in our environment continuously flow.[8] When you align with behavior streams, you are leveraging the antecedents and consequences that are already in play, essentially saving you a load of work and improving your chances of success.

Take, for example, the San Francisco Bay Area business Cater2.me. The founder started with two primary observations: First, the local gourmet food truck business was booming. People flocked to food trucks because their chefs were passionate about their food (there are *a lot* of foodies in the Bay Area). Second, many of the start-up tech companies in the area provided free lunches for their employees, as a perk (similar to

Google and Facebook, though the start-ups were not big enough to hire their own chefs). Cater2.me was founded on the potential of connecting these two behavior channels—the employees who might normally seek out the gourmet food trucks on lunch breaks and the chefs who couldn't quite figure out how to market to the start-ups in a scalable way.

Cater2.me states its mission as "connecting inspired kitchens with the masses."[9] Essentially, it finds the best local chefs and provides an easy system for companies to order their food, bridging the gap between the two parties.

Behavior channels can come in many forms. Whatever your target audience, start by taking note of their natural patterns and habits. For example, let's say we decide to tackle the career development problem in an organization, the right way. We know two things to be true:

- A successful leadership program is already in place; senior leaders clamor at the chance to attend it, and actively jump through many hurdles to do so.

- The employees in the organization have shown a strong desire to interact with senior leaders, to gain a better perspective about what they value.

A successful career development initiative would take advantage of these existing behavior channels. First, a prerequisite for leaders planning to attend the leadership program might be to identify successors—individuals on their teams they could mentor, to eventually take their places after they, themselves, took on greater responsibilities. Second, after attending the leadership program, the senior leaders might be asked to commit to offering 10 hours of advice sessions to employees in the organization, who could sign up to discuss their careers with these leaders—the expectation being that time with men and women at this level would be in high demand, and employees would jump at the chance to discuss their careers with them, thereby multiplying career development by tenfold over the current participation rate in the leadership program. Further, the identified successors could participate in their own leadership development program, thus expanding the cycle of career development.

Organizational behavior channels can be found everywhere—in the company culture, its systems, principles, and biases, all of which organizations naturally develop over time. Channels also include any work that is in progress and fully resourced in an organization, such as programs that are already running and have garnered popular success. When you tap into these energy streams, you can boost the impact of and ease with which work is done, to reap multiplicative returns on your team's effort.

Here are some questions to ask to help uncover potential behavior channels:

- Where do employees spend most of their time while working and on breaks? Where do they enter and exit? Where do they make and drink their coffee?

- Which company Internet (and intranet) pages attract the most visitors? Why are people visiting them, and what are they getting from them?

- Where are pockets of volunteerism in your organization? What are people doing because they are passionate about it?

- What are the most commonly used channels of communication within teams? Across teams? Within the organization?

- What are the big deadlines that drive True Urgency in large parts of your organization?

- What is the timing of the cycles in your organization that regulate important milestones, such as bonuses, raises, performance reviews, and other required administrative tasks?

The answers to these questions can point you to natural channels of behavior that might serve as good launch points for the work you are doing. You can also ask these same sorts of questions about your customers to find strong external channels of behavior.

ELIMINATING BAD ENERGY

While tapping into behavior channels can multiply efforts to generate greater impact in your organization, it is the elimination of the "energy suckers" that may, in fact, be the most important effort you can make to maximize energy, companywide. Energy suckers can be anything that slows work and people down, erects obstacles, or generates toxic energy and feelings. They can be individuals, or even group dynamics. They can be leaders or managers who don't appreciate the fragility of human nature and the emotions of their employees. Energy suckers also can come in the form of bureaucracy, politics, and passive-aggression.

The telltale signs that you have brushed shoulders with bad energy are the listlessness, discouragement, pessimism, and sour emotions it causes. I'll highlight next what I see as the top three most insidious energy suckers in companies, those that destroy more positive personal energy than a marathon in 100-degree heat.

Energy Sucker 1: Bureaucracy

The most common, and perhaps most widely recognized, energy sucker is bureaucracy. It is like a kudzu vine in an organization: Once it starts growing, it rapidly multiplies, until it covers, and smothers, every corner of the organizational chart. Bureaucracy includes rules that have been written to prevent some unwanted behavior (e.g., hoarding red staplers, engaging in copy room sex, or leaving moldy food in refrigerators). It takes just one bad employee doing something really stupid or egregiously wrong to prompt an HR person to write a rule to prevent said bad behavior from occurring in the rest of the organization, as if it were catching, like some kind of raging virus.

Rather than dealing directly with the misguided employee(s), bureaucrats seem to get greater satisfaction by explicitly stating, for example, that employees should not load a cart with videotapes to the point of overflow, and shove it recklessly down an aisle past old ladies because you are too lazy to walk it to the other side of the store to restock the shelves. That is the only scenario I could conjure up to explain the following policy in a (soon-to-be-obsolete) video store, as told to me by a former employee:

> If you had four movies or less, you could carry them. If you had five movies or more, you had to get this big cart and wheel the five or more movies around on them. The carts weren't allowed down the smaller aisles, so if you had more than five movies, you could park the cart at the end of the aisle then carry no more than four movies at a time down the aisle.

Right.

In 2009, President Obama developed an initiative to eliminate bureaucracy where it settles in deepest: the government. The SAVE Award solicits ideas from federal employees to make the government more effective and efficient, and each year, the top ideas are integrated into the president's budget.[10] One of the 2009 winning solutions highlights the unneeded complexity of processes that can develop over time:

> When Forest Service personnel collect money from the public (e.g., selling a pass or collecting campground fees), we take that money, count it, drive to a bank to convert the cash into a money order, and then turn the paperwork, checks, and money order over to a unit collection officer. The unit collection officer then recounts the receipts, makes two copies of the money orders and checks, creates a bill for collection, waits 24 hours for the bill to print, fills out a remittance report, runs two calculator tapes of receipts (one for her and one for the bank) and mails the package (via certified mail) to a bank in San Francisco, CA. . .Why can't we just deposit our collections into a local bank?

It requires vigilance and an organizational culture that abhors stupid rules and processes to keep bureaucracy at bay. Flushing out bureaucracy at regular intervals has the added effect of saving small little pockets of energy each and every day for every single employee, which translates to cumulative energy gains of enormous proportions.

Energy Sucker 2: Passive Aggression

This energy sucker is, at least, rooted in the very noble effort not to hurt other people's feelings. But it still is insidious. When people avoid having tough conversations, it destroys time and energy, both for the individuals who are holding back on the critical feedback, as well as the uninformed individuals who have no idea they've done something wrong. The most successful organizations are those that create a culture that encourages open dialog, even when the subject matter is difficult. I call this being *kindly honest*, which is distinctly different from being brutally honest.

Why is this so important? Because when individuals are encouraged to be strong and honest communicators, they waste less energy stewing over problems, going down the wrong path, or spinning their wheels through veiled disagreements. No one likes to have the tough conversations, but when an organization supports genuine and direct openness, no problem is too difficult to solve.

Energy Sucker 3: The Worst of All—Bad Managers

Bad managers (aka: fire-breathing dragons) come in many different forms:

- The hopelessly incompetent, who flail around in their jobs, create havoc, and cause confusion for all the poor souls who report to them.

- The ruthless, who pressure their employees using fear-driven tactics, to maximize short-term gains by wringing every ounce of productivity out of them, and without a care for the dead bodies lying in their wake.

- The ignorant and/or oblivious, with an EQ (emotional intelligence[11]) negatively correlated to their IQs; they are completely unaware that human beings actually *have* emotions.

I am lucky that I had a bad manager. I realize that might seem like a strange statement to make, but I'm grateful because the experience gave me a point of comparison, enabling me to relate to others who, sadly, still have bad managers. Besides, I had only one.

The fact of the matter is, the effects of a bad manager can permeate every crevice of your being. If you are a passionate person, and care about doing a good job, there is nothing worse than working for a manager who doesn't acknowledge your work, doesn't believe you are doing a good job, or, even worse, sabotages your work environment in every way possible. After all, these are people who have power over you!

Primarily in this book I present principles and suggestions, as opposed to rules and requirements. That said, what you are about to read is the one thing that you absolutely, without exception *must* do (assuming you are in a position to do so): *Remove bad managers from their roles*. I assure you, the damage they will do if you leave them in place is far worse than the temporary setbacks for a project or a team. By leaving bad managers in place, you will lose precious, valuable, committed, and high-talent employees who would rather abandon an organization than put up with the hell of a bad manager. Better to reassign these managers as individual contributors. Or let them resign gracefully. If you have no other choice, fire them. Just please don't "promote" them out of their current role to another leadership position.

SUMMARY

Focusing on energy, rather than schedules, in the workplace requires looking for ways to conserve energy, generate energy, sustain energy, and follow energy. Energy isn't stagnant; it's either increasing or decreasing, always. Pay attention to all of the sources of energy that invigorate you, your team, and your organization, and eliminate or avoid the things that zap energy and create drag. Table 5.5 contains a summary of suggestions for doing this.

Table 5.5   Summary of Energy, Not Schedules, for Organizations, Leaders, and Individuals

Individuals	Get clear on your river of energy: when you work best and when you shouldn't work at all.
	Advertise your morning or night handicap, and negotiate a work schedule that flows with your river of energy.
	Schedule recovery time after cycles of hard work—within each day and for longer-term projects.
	Pay attention to your gut signals regarding low-value work.
Leaders	Highlight True Urgency projects and deadlines.
	Empower workgroups to coordinate the best schedules for individual team members.
Organizations	Create workspaces that enable individuals to recharge.
	Align work with natural channels of behavior.
	Eliminate bureaucracy and bad managers.
Everyone	Redefine what work looks like.
	Be kindly honest, not passive-aggressive.
	Focus on value, and all else will follow.

CHAPTER 6

Strengths, Not Job Slots

"What do you want to be when you grow up?"

I hated this question as a child. I felt ignorant of my occupational options, of which I only really understood doctor, lawyer, teacher, and astronaut. It's like an Eskimo asking someone from Florida what type of snow she likes the best. First, it doesn't snow in Florida; second, there's more than one kind?!

The notion of career counseling in high school is laughable, in my opinion. In my personal experience, it consisted of taking a test that narrowed down a list of occupations for which I *might* be suited. I stared at the final list blankly. I had no idea what most of the jobs were, and had even less of an idea how to learn more about them. I remember my career counselor gushing about the job of an actuary, part of her honorable attempt to entice me with lesser-known occupations: "If you like math, you'll love this job!" Hmmm…what kind of math? And why would I like this? I had visions of doing math homework all day, every day; and though I *liked* math, I simply couldn't muster any enthusiasm for the prospect of working at an insurance company, crunching numbers.

Hiring individuals in the workplace, no matter the profession or business, has tended to follow the same line of reasoning, and is just as fraught with meaninglessness as career counseling. It goes something like this:

1. Write a laundry list of job tasks and responsibilities to define a job slot, for which you are given headcount to fill.

2. List a bunch of educational requirements and years of experience you think correlate to the job level.

3. Compare a stack of resumes to determine those that are the closest fit in terms of experience to the job qualifications. Eliminate the resumes with bad grammar and spelling errors.

4. Interview candidates to verify their experience and make sure they are a good fit.

5. Submit the best candidate for approval by a broader committee or group of higher-ups, who have absolutely no context on the needs of the team.

On the surface, this process works reasonably well. It is generally easy to find people who have relevant experience and can contribute quickly on a team. But the job-slot hiring model has some serious problems, and many companies are starting to acknowledge this by changing their approach to it. When we bring someone on for a static set of job tasks, we are blinding ourselves to their full capabilities and potential. They might have loads to contribute above and beyond the rigidly defined job slot, but the mentality is, we need them to do only what we hired them for. Straying too far outside of these bounds spells trouble for employees, in the form of raised eyebrows and questions from managers about whether they are focusing enough time on the core job assignment.

In the case of many organizations that are beyond the start-up phase, for anyone to move outside of the bounds of a job slot the "right way" requires jumping through hoops, called "internal transfers." Companies meticulously dole out precious headcount to their various departments, and if someone finds that his or her strengths align better with another part of the organization, he or she is essentially stuck, and must wait it out until more headcount opens up, a replacement is hired, and approval comes from the manager, the other group's manager, HR, the CEO, and probably 10 other departments along the way. And even should the person manage to get through those hoops, he or she will then probably have to suffer through a series of interviews with the new team, every bit as scrutinizing as those given to external candidates. I can't think of anything more bureaucratic and contradictory to the notion of agility. Furthermore, a staffing process like this casts individuals as little more than chess pieces, stripping them of their humanity and individuality.

There is a better way. Rather than using job tasks as the starting point, start with the people. How would you characterize your organizational tribe? What kinds of individuals succeed and are loyal to your organization? How might you round it out if you hired more diverse employees, who think differently, and bring different experiences and strengths to the job? Only in the very last moment (and probably not until you've brought them on board) should you even consider the job tasks at hand; if you hire the right people, the rest will follow.

To repeat: The starting point of a new staffing model is the individual. The responsibility lies within each of us as individuals; we must learn to be clear about what we do well, what we love to do, and what kinds of organizations we believe we will thrive in. We must let go of the archetype of job drudgery, and open ourselves to the idea that we can actually do what we love. When we are willing to voice our personal strengths, we send a clear invitation to our organizations to use us in the best possible way, for both of us.

STRENGTHS, TALENTS, PASSIONS

Doing easily what others find difficult is talent.
—Henri-Fréderic Amiel, *The Private Journal of Henri Fréderic Amiel*, 1935

There are many terms and definitions for strengths. Here are four to consider:

- Tom Rath, with the Gallup Organization, defines talent as "a natural way of thinking, feeling, or behaving" that, combined with practice and skills, forms strengths or the "the ability to consistently provide near-perfect performance."[1]

- Christopher Peterson and Martin Seligman define character strengths as virtuous traitlike habitual patterns that are relatively stable over time.[2]

- Marcus Buckingham takes a more practical approach in *StandOut: The Groundbreaking New Strengths Assessment from the Leader of the Strengths Revolution*, defining strengths as what you do in your most powerful moments and how you can make an immediate impact at work.[3]

- Mihalyi Csikszentmihaly, in *Flow: The Psychology of Optimal Experience*, explains that *flow* is complementary to strengths: It's how you feel when you are fully engaged, through application of your strengths.[4] Flow is the ideal place, where you are pushing yourself, but in alignment with your abilities.

I won't add my own definition of strengths here; I prefer to defer to these, which I think are great. But functionally speaking, you'll know you've hit on a personal strength when the work you are doing excites you, pushes you to extend yourself, and makes the time fly. Your strengths might be present in some contexts and not others; they may be quite specific to environments and/or the people around you. Your strengths might have nothing to do, whatsoever, with the subject matter. Then again, they might.

NAMING YOUR STRENGTHS

It's not hard to argue that it would be wonderful to work in a job that played to your strengths. What's difficult is to define your strengths. For some reason, we find it very easy to think about subjects—math, science, history; we also have no problem segmenting ourselves according to industries—finance, technology, healthcare, education. But we have a heck of a hard time describing what it is we do well. We simply don't have a well-developed vocabulary for this; plus, it doesn't exactly roll off the tongue.

"So what do you do?"
"I think strategically, find important connections between different parts of the organization and define the core mission of teams."
"Oh."

Also, it doesn't fit very well on a business card.

Some people seem to have been blessed with self-knowledge from the moment they could form words. I've heard stories of individuals who "just knew" they were destined to run their own company, or become a software engineer or a paleontologist. For example, Betty Skelton (1926–2011), one of very few women pilots in her day, set light-plane altitude records and performed daredevil stunts. She said that, as a child, she just knew she was destined to fly. At the age of 8, she was requesting brochures from airplane manufacturers; and at age 12 she had completed her first solo flight. She spent her career pushing the gender boundaries in both air and auto sports. In 1999 she was asked, "What makes you tick?" Her answer? "My heart makes me tick, and it's my heart that makes me do these things. I don't think I have any better answer than that, except that everyone is built a little differently, and my heart and my will and my desires are mixed up with challenge."[5]

The rest of us (myself included) still aren't quite sure what we want to do when we "grow up." To figure it out, ask not: "What do I want to *be*?" Instead, ask: "What kinds of things do I want to *do*?" This is a freer way of thinking about our careers, because it doesn't require us to come up with one answer. When Betty Skelton ran out of challenges in the air, she moved on to cars, setting several records in that sport, too. You might come up with 20 different answers, and each of them might be applicable to many different kinds of industries and jobs.

My sister and I have very different jobs. I work in corporations to facilitate learning and employee development. She works in the Middle East as an analyst on counterterrorism issues. In spite of these obvious differences, we have come to realize that, in practical terms, our jobs are almost exactly the same. I watch for signals in an organization to determine the problems we need to solve. She pays attention to signals in an entire country or region to determine where there are problems. I distill concepts down to digestible learning pieces and direct them to the right "students." She distills international intelligence down to the most critical information and directs it to the right policymakers. We both spend an inordinate amount of time parsing overwhelming amounts of details into their core essence. Not coincidentally, we have very similar strengths. The dissimilar paths we've taken should encourage you that it's not about finding that one perfect job. It's about uncovering your core strengths and finding environments in which they are particularly valuable. There might be *many* applications for your strengths.

There are many ways of figuring out your strengths. One simple practice is to catch yourself in the act of having fun at work. I recommend keeping a notepad with you at all times at work for, say, a month, and record every time you find yourself either:

- Humming along, feeling content, excited, or challenged by a task.

- Angry, anxious, annoyed, bored; or procrastinating in a big way.

Pay attention to your physical energy, too; notice what it is you do that seems to give you energy, and, conversely, what robs you of energy. In both cases, it's important to figure out what it is about the task or situation you particularly love or hate. For example, I love taking qualitative information and determining how and where to extract themes from interviews or open-ended survey questions. I have come to realize I love doing this because it plays on my strength of capturing core messages; moreover, I find the process of coding this information interesting, whereas many find it tedious. The more of these moments in your day you can record, the better your chances of picking up on patterns to give you clear ideas about what you do well. Ultimately, the best job for you is one that minimizes those energy-devouring experiences and maximizes the number of energy-rich projects.

THE THREE P'S

In *We: How to Increase Performance and Profits through Full Engagement*,[6] Rudy Karsan and Kevin Kruse suggest three P's for finding true engagement in work: passion, purpose, and pay.

- Passion is about following your ultimate dream.

- Purpose is about figuring out who you want to help, or which areas you want to serve.

- Pay represents what you can do to earn a living.

  The intersection of these is what they call the "career-life bull's-eye," the sweet spot for work.

I also recommend taking one, or several, of the easily accessible strengths assessments (see Table 6.1). Strengths Finder 2.0[7] and StandOut[8] are both fun, and free with the purchase of the accompanying books. After completing such an assessment, you might walk away with profound insights; at the very least, you might pick up some vocabulary to help you better describe your strengths. In any case, I recommend tapping in to whatever tools you can find to help you better define and name your personal strengths.

I don't think I fully understood my strengths until my mid-30s. Early in my career, I would routinely get frustrated with people when they worked mindlessly on projects without understanding the big picture. At one time, I was known as "Dr. Tables" because of my penchant for organizing information into tables to identify the parallels and connections between items. The lightbulb finally came on when I took the StrengthsFinder 2.0 assessment, and "Strategic" showed up as my top talent theme. Finally I understood why I got frustrated when other people around me lacked strategic insight; it was because strategic thinking came so naturally to me. This talent was like the air I breathed; it was simply part of my makeup, and so *me* that I didn't even notice it. Once I realized that it was special, and uncommon, I became much more intent on applying this skill whenever possible at work. Strategic thinking was my *gift*, and something of great value to the organization. That realization was a turning point in my career.

Table 6.1   Strengths Assessment Tools

Assessment	Defined Strengths	Sample Strengths
Clifton StrengthsFinder (Gallup)	34	Futuristic, Intellection, Communication, "Woo" (short for "winning others over")
Values in Action Inventory of Strengths[9] (Peterson and Seligman)	24	Creativity, Persistence, Social Intelligence, Humility
StandOut (Buckingham)	9	Advisor, Creator, Pioneer, Teacher

Here are a number of other personal examples to show how strengths assessments and self-reflection can help you create your own personal portrait of strengths and nontalents:

- I hate networking—"working a room" to meet people and chat it up. Not coincidentally, "Woo" (winning others over) ranked almost dead-last for me, according to StrengthsFinder.

- On the other hand, I love public speaking, particularly when I am presenting a new perspective and want to challenge people to think about issues in a new way. It is therefore not surprising that "Stimulator" and "Influencer" were my top two strengths according to StandOut.

- I also love connecting with individuals who have something in common with me, and engaging in long conversations about our mutual interests. This is called "Relator" in StrengthsFinder, and shows up in my top 10.

- I love data and numbers as they relate to organizations and people. "Analytical," another of my top 10 strengths, might explain this.

- I hate personal finance, and I have no idea how this relates to my strengths.

- I love coming up with creative solutions and ideas to solve specific problems (aka: "Ideation," among my top five strengths).

- I am terrible at visual design and generating blank-canvas ideas. I need context.

- There are very few topics I don't find interesting; I could work in virtually any industry, except for banking, since, like personal finance, it bores me to tears. Learning ranks high for me in every assessment I have taken, explaining my job flexibility.

STRENGTHS OF A TEAM

Individuals are widely varied as to whether specific tasks create or destroy their personal energy. We all have different strengths and experiences, meaning that one person's hell can be another person's playground. For example, as I've already mentioned, if you put me in the middle of a networking happy hour where I don't know a soul, you'll see me wither up under loads of anxiety. Put my friend, Brant, in this same situation, and he lights up, chatting up people, getting to know them, being exhilarated by their stories. I'm an introvert, whereas Brant is a classic extrovert, so it's easy to understand that we would have different responses to the same situation.

The biggest obstacle to achieving strengths-based leadership is shifting the team away from a guilt-based work environment. We feel bad about handing off work we dislike to someone else. We also feel guilty when we enjoy our work. We are conditioned to believe that work equals suffering; so when we love what we do, we seem to think we are cheating the system. But it is critical to remember that we all love and hate different things. And as teams adopt a strengths-based approach, the guilt associated with work will start to fall away, and we will start to realize that we can all feel engaged in what we do.

As a leader, there are concrete things that you can do to bring out the strengths of the individuals on your team, including allocating work according to those strengths and shaping your team to fill any strength gaps.

Allocating Work

Fortunately for any organization, the sheer number of individuals in it almost guarantees a wide diversity of strengths. If there is a task you hate, chances are very good that someone, somewhere, in the organization actually loves it.

I put this theory to the test when I was charged with leading a three-person team at Google (myself and two others). Our mission was to facilitate team effectiveness in the engineering organization; we called ourselves the "Team team." There were a lot of teams, so we had to do a lot of work to make sure our approach could be applied to all of them, around the globe.

One of the first things I did when I took on the role was to sit down and list every single responsibility that related to achieving our goals. This ranged from conducting interviews with teams, facilitating team-building sessions, creating content for our programs, designing custom events, training engineers as peer facilitators, and building an internal website to support everything. I developed a questionnaire on Google Forms, comprising the 30-some-odd tasks I came up with; and for each one, I asked every team member to rate them based on these two questions:

- How skilled are you at completing this task?
- How much do you enjoy this task?

For the skill question, the answer scale ranged from "I can perform this task easily, with near-perfect results" to "I am terrible at this task; put me on it at your own risk." For the enjoyment question, the answers ranged from "I was born to do this!" to "I'd rather gnaw off my arm than do this, it so utterly destroys my energy." I feared the results would be that everyone loved and hated the same things, and we'd be stuck doling out grunge tasks all around. This was not an unreasonable fear; after all, the three of us were all trained instructional designers. Fortunately, and to my great delight, this was not the case. As it turned out, Josh was our content creation guru. He loved developing new team-building content, which none of the rest of us were particularly interested in doing. Sarah was, hands down, our facilitator guru. She was gifted in recruiting and developing engineers as facilitators; for my part, I could think of no worse task for myself. I, of course, loved the strategy components. And all three of us loved and were particularly good at facilitating team-building sessions, as that's what attracted us to the work in the first place; luckily, there was plenty to go around.

This example illustrates the distinction between the old notion of *job slots*, as rigid sets of requirements for a very specific set of tasks, and *strength-based roles*, which are defined more by the individuals involved, according to a loose set of responsibilities spread across a team. Allocating work based on the skills of individuals, supported by the energy they each get from performing the tasks they're assigned, frees them to have important conversations about what needs to be done and why. It also broadens their thinking, to help them discover new strengths and capabilities they don't know they have.

The process of work allocation is much different on a strengths-based team. Rather than breaking down work into small tasks and assigning each of those tasks to individuals, it is better to first take stock of your goals and your team's various skillsets:

- *First, define the vision for the team*: What are you trying to achieve? Rather than focusing on defining the tasks that need to be done, take extra time to clarify the team's vision and goals; make them crystal clear.

- *Next, take stock of your team's strengths*. Not everyone has an easy time articulating their strengths, so the leader should invest time to help individuals figure this out. To that end, invest in strengths assessment books for everyone on your team, and sponsor a team lunch at which everyone shares their results. Ask individuals to identify their favorite projects and explain why they enjoy them. In short, do whatever it takes to facilitate self-awareness.

- *Finally, empower the team to negotiate what needs to be done based on who is best aligned to do each task*. Be clear about the results that are important to target, then let the team figure out the best way to hit them.

Filling the Gaps

Once you understand the strengths of your team and the work that needs to be done, any critical gaps will become clear. What strengths are missing that are key to achieving your objectives?

Going back to the example of the "Team team," we discovered that our strengths were quite complementary. Together, we almost completely covered the spectrum of strengths required to reach our goals. Almost. None of us could stomach the thought of managing the project plan, writing project updates, or completing the website.

For those tasks, we recruited another team member, Stephanie, who became our project manager extraordinaire. She turned out to be masterful at filling in all of those gaping holes. She saw needs that had never occurred to the rest of us, and she chased down ways to meet them. She even wrangled us into a weeklong group session, to pull together the website. And because we were a fully distributed team, we did it via video conference. In short, we were able to organize our very small team into strengths-based roles to generate excitement, increase productivity, and ensure engagement for all of us. And we launched our project on time, in full.

If your team has a significant strengths gap, there are three ways to think about filling them:

- Embrace automation.

- Find creative ways to use existing team members.

- Recruit new members to join your team, as needed.

Embrace Automation   Narrative Science, a company launched in 2010, develops algorithms to translate piles of numbers into readable, engaging news stories—from sports stories to financial reports. Its raw material is data. Here's an example:

> Michigan held off Iowa for a 7–5 win on Saturday. The Hawkeyes (16–21) were unable to overcome a four-run sixth-inning deficit. The Hawkeyes clawed back in the eighth inning, putting up one run."[10]

Such a story doesn't sound like it came from computers, which is why its power is so astonishing. At first glance, you might think this kind of technology would threaten the jobs of sports writers. In my opinion, they should *embrace* it. Who wants to write yet another recap of a baseball game? That's not exciting. Technology like this does something important: It removes the grunt work from our daily lives and leaves behind far more exciting tasks that are perfectly suited for humans. Journalists can focus on the really important stories, those that require digging into details, in search of connections only a human mind could make.

On our "Team team," Stephanie saw an opportunity to automate our tracking process—who we were working with, what the status was, and who was responsible for next steps. She partnered with an engineer whose specialty was creating scripts to automate Google Docs tasks, and within a few hours, he had a working prototype. By the time we fully launched our project, our automated tracking system had been fully tested and was ready to go; and no one was stuck maintaining the complicated spreadsheet, which previously entailed nagging people several times a quarter to make updates.

Creating a strengths-based team on which individuals get to apply their strengths for the majority of their workday requires finding ways to ditch grunt work. Automation is key to this meeting this challenge. Automation enables the human-appropriate work to rise to the top. Let computers do the crap work.

Creative Fillers As much as I hate networking, there are times I just need to suck it up and do it. And I admit, I've made some fortunate connections with people I've met through networking happy hours. Even so, I know that no matter how much I work at it, I will *never* like networking. So, I do the next best thing: I fake it. I put on a big smile and act as if I am the most confident person in the world, someone who thinks nothing of sipping a drink while sitting completely and utterly alone in a corner. I pretend I can slip gracefully into an interesting conversation with total strangers, who might, in fact, be boring me to tears.

My point is, I have learned to supplement my ironclad fake-it routine with something much more sensible, which is to tap into my actual strengths to "make it work,"—Tim Gunn style, author, with Kate Moloney, of *Tim Gunn: A Guide to Quality, Taste, & Style*:[11]

- I am a learner, and I love to hear about people's jobs, about what they do.

- I also love ideas, so by crossing from my world into the world of others, I find new ideas and ways to think about how to solve problems.

When I explicitly tap into my learner/ideation strengths, not only can I survive the happy hours, but I can make them productive and useful. Of course, as soon as I leave, I head straight home and collapse in complete exhaustion.

I'm convinced it's also possible to find creative ways to fill the gaps on teams with existing individuals, by encouraging them to stretch and do things that aren't directly in their zone of comfort and expertise. And if a task is important enough—that is, will have major impact on the project—individuals on the team will step up and get it done; they will make it happen. It's important to note, however, that creative fillers are short-term solutions. Teams may be willing to be flexible, but not for long, so the rewards need to be explicit (e.g., spot bonuses, team lunches after reaching a tough milestone). This strategy can, ultimately, lead to team burnout, so use it sparingly.

Recruit New Members   As stated previously, recruiting additional individuals to join your team is the ideal method of filling gaps. Your gap might be obvious, such as the project management gap on the "Team team." In this case, we knew we needed someone like Stephanie, whose strengths were organization and coordination. She filled the gap on our team perfectly.

But what if it's not evident that you have a gap? Perhaps the issue might be better characterized as an imbalance. While the breadth of strengths on a team is bound to be wide, it can still fall prey to imbalances. This might happen when, say, the manager hires too many people due to a similarity bias (a phenomenon confirmed through research studies in which hiring managers show a preference for candidates similar to themselves). It can also happen when a specific type of person dominates a particular profession, such as the hypergregarious sort who tend to gravitate toward sales. It might also happen by chance. In my work with teams throughout my career, I saw two examples that stood out for me.

The first team comprised a group of managers—about a dozen of them—who wanted to solidify their mission and make strategy decisions about their future. They were the nicest group of managers I had ever met, which foreshadowed the issues they were dealing with. As it turns out, almost every one of them was "blue," in True Colors parlance.[12] True Colors is a simple assessment that segments people based on their personalities and working style, and blue represents harmony, inclusion, and peace. We quickly came to realize that the "blues" had difficulty making decisions. They shied away from conflict, which meant that they couldn't engage in productive debate to move decisions forward. And because the team was overloaded with "blue" leaders, the balancing solution involved putting in charge a leader who was the exact opposite—a "green" impartial, analytical problem solver.

In the second case, I was running a team-building session with a fairly large group of people—about 20. The very first exercise I ran with them entailed figuring out the best way to get the entire team through an obstacle course at a fast time. I didn't give them a time limit for strategizing—and, oh boy, did they strategize! They spent close to 20 minutes generating ideas, tossing them back and forth, and then discarding them; they never came to a consensus about the best one, not until I forced them to do so. Later in the day, for a leadership exercise, I segmented the team based on strengths. It was no surprise at all when virtually all of them ended up characterized as strategic thinkers, according to Tom Rath's and Barry Conchie's definition in *Strengths-Based Leadership: Great Leaders, Teams, and Why People Follow*.[13] Only two were strong in execution. This was a team full of strategists, with no one to execute their ideas!

If you find that your team stumbles over the same type of issue again and again—decision making, execution, building relationships, or something else—check whether your collective strengths are too heavy in one particular area. If this turns out to be the case, then it should be clear what other types of people you need to hire—anyone not like yourselves! You might, also, consider transferring some team members to other projects, where they might need an influx of said strengths. However you decide to proceed, begin by getting clear on the strengths you need to meet your goals, and then seek team members who can fit this bill.

BUILDING AN ORGANIZATION ON STRENGTHS

The process of creating a strengths-based organization means answering two critical questions:

- What kinds of individuals belong in our organization?
- How can we best use the strengths of each individual?

Conversely, for an individual considering a job in an organization, the questions are:

- Do I belong in this organization?
- How can I best use my strengths within this organization?

The first question addresses the organizational culture and the individuals most likely to thrive within it. The second is about facilitating the process of matching those individuals to the right teams and roles, allowing them to find their true "homes" within the organization. I devote the remainder of this chapter to focusing on these two goals.

Organizational Culture: Who Belongs Here?

The economic crisis of 2008 hit everyone hard, particularly finance companies. The Focus Consulting Group was curious to learn what distinguished the companies that survived the hard times, those that *thrived* during them, and those forced to close their doors. To answer that question, the firm conducted an assessment of 65 different asset management companies that fell into one of these three categories. The assessment covered culture, leadership, and other factors related to success. The results showed notable distinctions in the organizational culture between these three groups of companies; but what stood out to me was the response to the question: "Do we have the right team members to accomplish our goals?"[14] This is the item on which the failed companies scored the lowest, ranking them in the lowest 2 percent in their industry on this dimension. Is it any surprise at all that they failed? Clearly, if you don't have the right people on board, you are almost guaranteed to fail.

Jim Collins, in his book *Good to Great: Why Some Companies Make the Leap—and Others Don't,* found that the high-performing companies his team studied subscribed to the principle of "first *who*, then *what*."[15] In other words, get the right people on board—those who want to be "on the bus" together. Only after you have the right people should you begin to think about what they will be doing. Collins outlines two major advantages of putting the *who* before the *what*:

- *Adaptation*: If you hire people to fill specific job slots, and then the company needs to change direction, you've got problems. You have too much structure and too many silos, which erect barriers to change. Have the right people? They'll be committed to making the shifts and steering the bus in the best direction, *together*.

- *Motivation*: When people are connected to each other and to a common vision, their motivation will be intrinsic. You won't have to manufacture excitement to increase productivity, or tightly manage them through rules.

But who are the right people? It depends on the organizational culture.

As I've said before, each of us struggles to describe our individual strengths, partly because there is no universal vocabulary for this purpose. Similarly, it's difficult to succinctly describe the culture of our organizations. I see an organization's culture as a concept similar to that of an individual's personality. If you stepped back and characterized your organization as a person, how would you describe him or her: Introverted or extroverted? Traditional and conservative, or creative and cutting-edge? Analytical or intuitive? Whatever the answers, it is important to find people who can relate to and support your organization's personality. If you hire an individual who is a creative renegade for a traditional, conservative company that doesn't value open debate, he or she will probably crash and burn in spectacular fashion.

Company culture describes the way individuals collectively go about working toward achieving the organizational mission (refer back to Chapter 4, "Impact, Not Activities" for more about mission statements). Culture should be at the core of the strategy where you define how you serve customers and bring products to market. For example, you can see the cultural variations among the different airlines, which on the face of it offer the same service. The major carriers portray a culture of hierarchy, evident in their frequent-flyer programs complete with tiers and differential treatment for various customer levels. Southwest's culture, in contrast, is portrayed as casual and fun, with a laid-back environment, which matches the airline's strategy of catering to leisure customers. As another example, Virgin America has introduced a culture of sophistication and design, featuring sleek airplane interiors and built-in video capabilities, which include food and beverage orders—not to mention power outlets at every seat. It's no surprise that Virgin's main hub is in San Francisco, servicing Silicon Valley workers and the social media start-ups in the city. And when you fly on each of these airlines it's no surprise that their crews have personalities that match their cultural characteristics. Southwest's crews can be heard cracking jokes; whereas you won't find a more serious group of flight attendants than those on the bigger carriers.

The Organizational Culture Assessment Instrument (OCAI) defines four basic types of organizational cultures:[16]

- Clan culture, characterized by a familial environment, with loyalty as a core value

- Adhocracy culture, where innovation and risk-taking are key

- Market culture, with a supreme focus on driving results through tight accountability

- Hierarchical culture, heavy on procedures, formality, and structure

There are many other variations of cultural categories, but this list gives you an idea of the themes and concepts that are helpful in describing how individuals in your organization behave collectively.

The mission of an organization, overlaid with the culture, provides a clear picture of what it might be like to work at a company. It suggests the types of individuals who will fit best in the environment, as well as the types that might clash. This is an important point: It is critical to understand what "flavors" of personalities you want interacting throughout the organization.

Seth Godin's concept of *tribes* is a great one for finding the right people. He defines a tribe as "a group of people connected to one another, connected to a leader, and connected to an idea."[17] Further, Godin references faith as a defining characteristic of a tribe: Do members of the tribe share a *belief* in what they are doing every day?

FITTING IN VERSUS BELONGING: THE COSTS AND BENEFITS OF CONFORMITY

Joe McCarthy, author *Gumption* blog

Brené Brown has been researching the costs and benefits of vulnerability for the past 10 years. Among the insights she shares in her recent book, *The Gifts of Imperfection: Let Go of Who You Think You're Supposed to Be and Embrace Who You Are*,[18] she makes an important and insightful distinction between fitting in and belonging, and how that distinction relates to personal and professional growth.

Brown shares two lists of recurring themes that emerged from the thousands of stories she's collected from people over her years of research into shame and resilience. The first list characterizes people who enjoy a strong sense of love and connection; the second list characterizes people who don't.

Do: worthiness, rest, play, trust, faith, intuition, hope, authenticity, love, belonging, joy, gratitude and creativity.
Don't: perfection, numbing, certainty, exhaustion, self-sufficiency, being cool, fitting in, judgment and scarcity.

The inclusion of belonging in the first list and the inclusion of fitting in on the second list immediately jumped out at me, as I had previously thought of these two terms as synonymous. A little further on, Brown notes that she was [also] surprised at the distinction, and offers definitions for the two terms:

Fitting in is about assessing a situation and becoming who you need to be to be accepted. Belonging, on the other hand, doesn't require us to change who we are; it requires us to be who we are.

She goes on to define belonging in more detail:

Belonging is the innate human desire to be part of something larger than us. Because this yearning

(continued)

(*continued*)

is so primal, we often try to acquire it by fitting in and by seeking approval, which are not only hollow substitutes for belonging, but often barriers to it.

The issue of fitting in versus belonging is also an implicit theme in John Hagel, John Seely Brown, and Lang Davison's book, *The Power of Pull: Institutions as Platforms for Individual Growth*:[19]

> Rather than molding individuals to fit the needs of the institution, institutions will be shaped to provide platforms to help individuals achieve their full potential by connecting with others and better addressing challenging performance needs…. Rather than individuals serving the needs of institutions, our institutions will be crafted to serve the needs of individuals.

Large organizations have traditionally tended to promote conformity and to treat employees as standardized parts of a predictable machine, who suppress their intrinsic creative instincts in return for extrinsic rewards. Although the tactics employed by managers in most large organizations to encourage conformity are not generally drastic, they reflect a common underlying premise: we know what is best [for you].

However, if one believes that innovation is more likely to occur at the edges than the core of an organization, and be practiced by people who are taking risks rather than conforming to written or unwritten rules, then the cost of conformity is to sacrifice innovation, and the benefits of innovation will accrue to those organizations that are willing to embrace nonconformity… or perhaps even anti-conformity.

Few large organizations are willing or able to embrace—or even accept—nonconformity, much less anti-conformity. This is why many large organizations attempt to import innovation via acquisitions… and why so few innovators stay on with their acquiring benefactors beyond the point at which their stock options vest… and why so few imported innovations turn out to be sustainable.

I suspect this corporate emphasis on conformity is also why so few employees of large organizations are willing to be courageous, vulnerable, and authentic in their work[places] … and why so many employees feel so disengaged. A recent Gallup survey[20] revealed only 31 percent of U.S. workers feel engaged in their work; 51 percent are not engaged, and 18 percent are said to be actively disengaged, undermining their colleagues and sabotaging or exhausting resources that might otherwise fuel innovation.

The Welsh poet David Whyte, author of *The Heart Aroused: Poetry and the Preservation of the Soul in Corporate America*, offers some wisdom once shared with him by a Benedictine monk at a moment when the budding poet was experiencing disengagement and burnout in his work: the antidote to exhaustion is wholeheartedness.[21] These words of wisdom gave Whyte the gumption to conduct the courageous conversations that enabled him to successfully renegotiate and redefine his work in a way that aligned more naturally with who he was… and who he was becoming.

Reflecting back on Brown's "Do" and "Don't" lists, I believe that the "Don't" list aligns more closely with most employees' experience in the workplace… which may explain why wholeheartedness is more the exception than the rule in most workplaces.

Gumption, January 16, 2011. http://gumption.typepad.com/blog/ 2011/01/ fitting-in-vs-belonging-the-costs-and-benefits-of-conformity.html.

We're Just Not That into You

We need to keep innovating our hiring practices to find people who belong in our organizational cultures. The question is, how can we fairly assess candidates for "belonging"?

Semco, one of the pioneering organizations in the Work Revolution, has but one prerequisite for full-time employees: "A material connection with the very heart of the business that makes us unique."[22] The company hires based on a highly intuitive, gut-reaction process; no list of requirements in sight. Instead, the hiring teams draft a list of qualities they are looking for in a candidate. The interview, likewise, is a collective process. A group of candidates is brought in to interact with a number of Semco employees—perhaps 40 at a time—with the goal of seeing how the candidates handle the dynamics of personal interaction. It is just as important for the candidates to determine whether they belong in the company as it is for the team to determine whether the candidates would be a good match for the company. The processes that follow the collective interview are all geared toward ensuring the candidate is exactly right, and these processes are nothing short of rigorous. Clearly, at Semco, the hiring bar is set high. Once the company brings employees on board, it fights like hell to help them find their place in the organization; after all, it expects to keep them for a very long time.

Jen Bilik, the CEO of Knock Knock, the stationary and gift company famous for the WTF stamp, talks about hiring in terms "casting." The company instituted a work-style assessment that focuses on the traits of job candidates, for the purpose of looking closely at individuals in terms of how they will get along with other coworkers. As Bilik puts it: "We hire slow and fire fast…. You hire a resume, but you work with a person."[23] Knock Knock is also crystal clear about the company culture in interviews to ensure candidates understand that, just because Knock Knock has an informal culture, it does not mean people can screw around and not be productive.

The global talent management company Development Dimensions International (DDI) sees a healthy trend toward companies assessing formal and informal culture fit as an essential element in best-in-class selection processes for external hiring, internal promotions, and even special assignments.[24] These organizations recognize that hiring folks or assigning them roles in which they quickly feel they *belong* is more fruitful than trying to change longstanding personality traits (such as a desire for independence, style of dress, or preference for great diversity versus task repetition). Better cultural fit leads to higher employee engagement. High engagement, according to DDI's 2004 study, is linked to tangible business outcomes, including revenue growth, profitability, and customer and employee satisfaction.[25]

Unfortunately, while companies acknowledge the need to focus on cultural fit, there is precious little advice about how to achieve it. The way I see it, the best working analogy for finding the right people for your organization (or determining whether you wish to join an organization) is the dating process. Successful, strong relationships start with two individuals who know who they really are and what is at the core of their essential selves (i.e., strengths, culture). Then they form some notion of what they are looking for in a mate. The dating process is about determining whether the "stats" and interests of individuals, on paper or in an electronic dating profile, translate to a real-life connection. Finally, the relationship comes together when the couple negotiates the time they spend together, personal space, roles, and communication. I'll use this dating analogy to describe a hiring process that focuses on cultural alignment.

We evaluate potential mates along many dimensions. Charlotte Kasl, in her book *If the Buddha Dated*, lists eight different dimensions along which we bond with others: physical/material, intellect, interests, values/lifestyles, psychological/emotional, creativity/passion, spirituality, and essence.[26] Here's how I translate these to the organizational environment:

1. *Physical/material*: In dating terms, this would be a person's basic "stats"—height, weight, hair color, age—as well as income level. In terms of a job candidate, the equivalent is the resume—years worked, degrees earned, previous organizations served. For an organization, this comprises the basic About Us profile—revenues, product lines, years in existence, and executive officers.

2. *Intellect*: How important is continuous learning in your organization? Do individuals value street smarts over academic

credentials? Do employees find academic endeavors fun and challenging? Or do employees place the greatest value on unconventional education? In any case, this is a big indicator of values, which also set the vibe in a company. An individual with an Ivy League education is not likely to find fulfillment among a group of supersmart geniuses who all dropped out of college to join a start-up and change the world.

3. *Interests*: This is a big one for dating: What are your hobbies? How do you spend your time? Which movies and TV shows do you like? In job terms, what are your areas of interest or your areas of expertise? This also extends to the organizational tribe: What are common hobbies across your population? What are general and specific interests that might create bonds between individuals and groups?

4. *Values/lifestyle*: If your organization requires crazy all-nighters, due to frequent tight, True Urgency, deadlines, you should seek employees who thrive in the excitement and under pressure. If your organization values, instead, slow and steady, and consistency, then you want individuals who are looking for stability in their jobs, perhaps because their top priority is a new family.

5. *Psychological/emotional*: This addresses authenticity, honesty, and openness. Do the people in your organization feel free to speak openly and debate honestly; can they be respectful during conflicts? If personalities are so divergent in your company that they cause, or deny, conflict, then you've got the wrong mix of people.

6. *Creativity/passion*: How is creativity expressed in your organization? How core is innovation to your business? What are people passionate about who work there? Are they "yes, and. . ." types (as in, "Yes! That's a great idea. And we can also do this.")? Or do they like to pick apart ideas at the outset to find all of the reasons they might not work?

7. *Spirituality*: Obviously, this is a critical factor in personal relationships, but it also links with the notion of faith in what you are working toward professionally. Do the people

in your organization believe in the company mission? Do they share a belief in the importance of their work?

8. *Essence*: This boils down to whether individuals share a natural interpersonal connection with others in the organization. Do they hang out with each other outside of work? Do they enjoy each other's company?

Organizations can use this list to gain clarity about the various aspects of culture. It takes courage to admit what your organization is about and who really belongs in it. For example, it might be tempting to hire a gifted graphic designer who can bring an amazing design sense and polish to your marketing organization. But if his tattoos, earrings, and penchant for lively debate will be seen as inappropriate by others in your conservative job environment, have respect for your respective differences and do everyone a favor, including the candidate, and take a pass on him. Otherwise, it will only cause pain down the road for both the employee, who just wants to be himself, and the organization, trying in vain to rein him in.

As a job candidate, it's important to assess each of these items when you interview with a company. Treat it as a checklist for gathering data along each of the dimensions, to determine whether you think you belong in the company. And don't forget to listen to your gut instincts: Did your interactions fuel a fire of excitement in your belly, or did your "Blink" tell you to be wary?

THE CLASH OF CURRENT AND ASPIRATIONAL CULTURES

Barry Stern, PhD, Vice President,
Development Dimensions International

What is your current organizational culture, and how does it match up with your aspirational culture?

(continued)

(*continued*)

I have come to believe that too many of us are looking in a fun-house mirror when it comes to owning up to the nature of our existing cultures. All too often, senior leaders limit their effectiveness by living in a world far removed from day-to-day cultural realities. Despite engagement surveys spelling out dissatisfaction, they ignore the culture issues and the sentiment of the rank and file; it's simply more fun to focus on the future. As a result, they fail to deal with the tough "blocking and tackling" of cultural change. This distorted picture leads to huge cultural and talent missteps.

Just recently, a Fortune 500 executive voiced his frustration to me. In his opinion, the company had gotten it "half right"—and he shared aloud his dark thought that, perhaps half right was actually worse than "all wrong." Executives within the company articulated the ideal success profile of key positions to align the knowledge, experience, and personalities to their aspirational culture. Well intentioned indeed, they failed to consider how, once the open requisitions were filled with such revered and divergent talent, they would nurture, protect, and leverage these new assets in their current culture. After all, they were in fact hiring cultural misfits.

But hire them, they did. These top-notch folks, who liked to work in fluid, nonhierarchical team-based environments, would work long hours, but might not get to the office promptly at 8:00 AM. They valued agile project management processes, but responded poorly to a manager peering over their shoulder. They were like aliens to the organization, dropped awkwardly into a highly conventional, hierarchical culture. Disturbance and dysfunction prevailed, and two years later, not one of them remained. The common explanation was the company was special, and these folks "just didn't get it." In reality, the organism rejected the foreign body.

Our challenge is to knock the distortion curves off of our mirrors and ask ourselves coldly, "What are we today, and how huge is the gap between that and where we want to be tomorrow?" And then we need to recognize that the journey, always exciting, can sometimes be very painful. Are some of the outliers in your current organization the seeds of your cultural growth? How are you nurturing their growth? What are they truly held accountable for? Do they even know who they are, and are they given opportunities to be with each other? Are their leaders being held accountable for their cross-pollination throughout the organization? These are but a few of the tough questions that I encourage us all to pause and consider.

Home within a Home

> When I draw up my playbook, I always go
> from the players to the plays.
> —Bud Grant, Hall of Fame Minnesota Vikings coach

Marcus Buckingham defines a strengths-based organization as "a workplace in which employees spend more than 75 percent of each day on the job using their strongest skills and engaged in their favorite tasks, basically doing exactly what they want to do."[27] But wait! Isn't the point to make money? How is it possible to satisfy both individual employee happiness and the goal to meet profit margins? There is actually mounting evidence to suggest that focusing on individual strengths leads to greater efficiency and higher performance levels at organizations. Employee engagement contributes to all the right numbers: better quality, higher productivity, lower turnover, greater customer satisfaction, and greater profits. Consider:

- The cost of replacing employees who leave an organization can range from 25 to 200 percent of their annual salary, according to the American Management Association.[28]

- The Deloitte Shift Index shows (two years running) that passionate employees are more than two times as likely to actively seek knowledge and make connections with other individuals in the organization, which the firm characterizes as "inter-firm knowledge flows."[29]

- According to a study on asset management firms during the financial crisis, the firms that thrived ranked 20 percent higher than the industry standard for developing engaged employees.[30]

- The *Forbes* "Best Companies to Work for in America," list, which represents the organizations with the most satisfied employees, earned annual returns of 14 percent, double that of the markets.[31]

- Chip Conley, CEO of the Joie de Vivre hotel chain, made major changes to his organization after the dot-com bust and 9/11, both of which negatively impacted his business. He created an environment of meaning, recognition, and self-actualization, in true Maslow fashion, to enable employees to reach their full potential. Over the course of the next eight years, annual revenues tripled.[32]

The key to building an organization of engaged employees is figuring out how to best match individuals to the right opportunities, based on strengths and moment-to-moment needs. This is aspirational; I believe there is much room for innovation in this area before it can be carried out on a large scale. At the same time, I believe the answer lies in one major theme: fluidity.

Create Fluidity

When I joined Google in 2006, I felt like I had found my tribe. I loved the sales training team I was on, and I enjoyed the work. The team needed help in translating their instructor-led product training to online learning, something I knew I could do practically in my sleep. Though it was a good entry point to the company, I knew I wouldn't be able to grow in this role over time. So, after a year and a half contributing to this team, an opportunity came along to join Google's central human resources organization, called PeopleOps (for People Operations), and I took it. I spent a year there, doing some good work, enjoying the individuals I worked with, and learning a lot about myself. But I couldn't get excited about creating solutions for a generalized audience without crisply defined problems; I knew I was better suited for a role directly embedded with an internal customer

STRENGTHS, NOT JOB SLOTS

with very specific problems. So after two and a half years, I transferred to my third role at Google; this time in the engineering organization. I joined a team charged with delivering learning and development solutions to software engineers. It was here I began to thrive. I felt I had found my home at Google, where I had room to grow; I also felt I was tapping into my full range of strengths, on a near-daily basis.

Three roles in less than three years may sound like a lot, but I knew I needed to find the one that fit me like a glove, and I persisted until I found it.

Fluidity requires:

- Lowering the barriers that prevent people from moving around in the organization.

- Incentivizing leaders and teams to share resources.

Many organizations are already getting better about sharing resources across the business. For example, rotational programs generate movement to expose individuals to different teams, which starts the momentum for fluidity. Cross-team collaboration initiatives also encourage individuals to mix across team lines, to gain a wider perspective of the organization. Cross-pollination of individuals across the organization encourages interaction with other teams, which might be doing other work better suited to their strengths. To these ends, think about:

- Hosting an innovation tournament[33] to solve a specific company challenge. Pair up teams with other teams they rarely interact with.

- Holding an off-site strategy session with two or more teams to work on streamlining operations between groups.

- Facilitating case study sessions so individuals from various teams can share challenges they have worked through.

- Developing rotational assignments—even one week in length—to allow individuals to complete mini-projects on different teams.

Anything that increases the frequency and depth of cross-team interaction ultimately contributes to greater fluidity within your organization.

Another strategy for achieving fluidity is to create a common organization-wide language for describing new opportunities on teams in terms of strengths. This common language can point to strength areas that are specific and relevant to your organization. For example, I conducted a series of career development interviews with Google engineers to understand what they were looking for in growth opportunities. The conventional wisdom held that all of the engineers wanted to be in a start-up environment, working on new ideas that might become the "next big thing" for Google. To my surprise, that is not at all what I found. There were, of course, some engineers who were looking for just that. However, I also talked to engineers who wanted very different things:

- One engineer actually hated start-up projects; he cringed at developing prototypes that he knew would be thrown away. He preferred working on a project once the prototype was complete, and figuring out how to make it work on a larger scale.

- Another engineer didn't care about working on products at all. He wanted to build the tools and infrastructure that would span 50 or more different engineering teams. He loved creating projects that had wide-reaching impact.

- Yet another engineer considered himself to be a "launcher." That is, he loved being on a team that was struggling to get over the finish line. He would come in, work through obstacles, and push the team to get the product out the door.

For Google projects, it makes sense to label transfer opportunities according to the phase of the product. Is it in start-up prototype? Or are people needed who can figure out how to scale a product for millions of concurrent users? For every organization, these opportunity "tags" can be anything that distinguishes the maturity of projects, idea generation versus problem solving versus execution, level of interaction with teammates and customers, or any other facets of roles that might inform individuals about potential fit.

Fluidity is, essentially, the grease on the company's wheels, enabling individuals to find the roles that align with their strengths. After they are hired into an organization, and are confident they belong, the goal is to open channels that facilitate the flow to match strengths throughout the organization.

Summary

Starting a Work Revolution means finding every opportunity to do work that is perfectly suited to our strengths. When this happens, time flies; we actually *gain* energy from working. If we could create a world in which everyone was doing their life's work, there would be energy explosions every day, on every corner of the planet.

Table 6.2 offers a recap of all you can do to shift away from job slots to strengths.

Table 6.2   Summary of Strengths, Not Job Slots, for Organizations, Leaders, and Individuals

Individuals	Define your strengths—observation at work and assessments are great tools.
	Share your strengths with your manager and leads.
	Ditch the guilt around ditching work that doesn't work for you.
Leaders	Define the vision for the team; what you are trying to achieve.
	Assess the strengths on your team.
	Allocate work based on strengths alignment.
	Fill team roles by focusing on diversity of strengths.
	Embrace automation.
Organizations	Define your organizational mission and culture—what you do, and how.
	Hire the way you date—find people who belong.
	Create liquidity between roles and teams so that individuals can find their true organizational home.

CHAPTER 7

The Right Things,
Not Everything

A great company is more likely to die of indigestion from
too much opportunity than starvation from too little.

—Packard's Law

If everything is important, then nothing is.

—Patrick Lencioni

Surfing, for me, is one of the most soothing experiences on the planet. I love nothing more than to sit past the breaking waves, feeling the sun on my skin and the undulating water underneath my board; it's my definition of utter peacefulness, with the sounds of dry land just out of earshot. It's also such a cool sense of community, with all the other surfers perched on their boards, staring into the horizon, arms crossed on their chests, legs swaying just below the water's surface.

Until the waves come. Then the peacefulness erupts into jockeying and chaos, every surfer anticipating where the waves will crest, where the peaks will pass through. The "winner" is the surfer who takes off closest to the peak of the wave furthest outside; according to surf etiquette (yes, there is such a thing), that person officially has the right-of-way; he or she wins the wave. Therefore, it is critical to paddle furiously to get into the wave, because it can just as easily pass right on through and leave you behind.

Beginner surfers chase after every ripple. Every little swell in the water that even remotely resembles a wave will prompt them to take off, trying their hardest to match the speed of the wave and drop into it. Not surprisingly, they catch very few of these elusive waves; worse, they take themselves out of position in the lineup. Then, when the big, breaking waves pass through, they are too tired to paddle for them, or they are in the wrong place entirely.

The really good surfers, in contrast, know exactly where to be. They willingly "give away" the smaller waves to those around them, watching the amateurs try to take off on unreliable, low-power waves. Then, when everyone around them has exhausted their arms and fallen out of position, a set wave invariably emerges on the horizon. It is beautiful, perfectly shaped, like a photo straight out of *The Surfer's Journal*. It carries enormous power, enough to pluck up the knowledgeable surfer who is in the right position, delivering to him or her the most divine ride on the planet. The novice surfers let out a loud growl of envy as the winner winds his or her way up and down the wave, almost taunting them as they duck out of the way and try not to be pummeled by the breaking wave.

I would estimate that 75 percent of the learning process in surfing involves wave selection and positioning. It's about spotting the good waves and putting yourself in the right position to snag them. If you take off on every wave, you end up with nothing but tired arms and a few paltry closeout waves that throw you over and deposit you on the floor of the ocean, where you must fight and paddle to make your way back out to the lineup.

But when you are disciplined to wait for the right wave, you are rewarded with the Wave of the Day. No one else is in position to take it but you; and you do, listening to the hoots and hollers of the rest of the surfers (the "props") as you pass by. And if that is the only ride you catch during that surf session, it is enough to reverberate in your soul for days.

In each and every one of our jobs, at every business, there are so many things we *could* be doing. Ideas are abundant. Information flows quickly. Opportunities are rampant. Our workforce is smart enough to put these elements together to churn out some pretty amazing products. The problem, in fact, is that we have *too* many opportunities and not enough time to take them all. Something has to give.

This reminds me of my New York apartment storage dilemma. I grew up in Florida, where real estate was cheap and houses were big. Our family home was a typical Florida ranch style, with walk-in closets, an attic, a two-car garage, and tons of storage space; it never registered in my mind as being particularly noteworthy. So when I moved to New York this past year, I was shocked to learn that closets were actually considered a *feature*, meaning you had to tell your broker explicitly that you wanted closets in your apartment. To me, this was akin to someone saying, "Oh, you need oxygen to breathe? You should have mentioned that." Today, though I'm the proud tenant of a Manhattan apartment, *with closets*, I view household organization in a whole new way: To my New Yorker's eye, every open patch of wall has the potential to hold shelves; every drawer and cabinet must be optimized for objects of corresponding size and shape. The Container Store is like Disneyland to me. And because my living space is finite (by which I mean, barely big enough to hold my household effects), if I buy something—anything!—I have to consider what will have to be displaced to make room for it.

In the world of information and opportunities, time is like New York City closet space. In the past, we could do everything—read the newspaper in the morning, go to work and complete our assignments, come home to watch the evening news, possibly while flipping through the mail, prepare a family dinner, and sit down to eat it; and there would still be time to watch primetime television for a couple of hours.

Today, we try to fit all of this in and more: e-mail, Facebook, blog subscriptions, online news and gossip, regular work, side projects, start-up projects, volunteer projects, Meetup groups. Still, at the end of each day, we go to bed feeling guilty because we didn't respond to *every* e-mail in our inbox. Our metaphorical closets are overflowing. We can either organize the hell out of them, or we can ditch the clutter and get *very clear* about what is important to keep in our lives. This is about choosing to spend our time on the *right things, not everything*.

Admittedly, this principle isn't one of those provocative, flashy concepts you might expect to read about in a book about revolutions. But sometimes the most powerful concepts are the simple ones, those sitting right under our noses, and which maybe we aren't very good at implementing. And the more complex and global our jobs become, the more this principle becomes critical. Organizations that "do the right things" to the exclusion of everything will beat their competition, while creating a sustainable work environment. Individuals who do so will emerge as well-balanced, smart contributors; and their leaders will become hot commodities.

Choosing to do the right things is not easy. There are two significant barriers to saying yes to the right things and no to everything:

- We are not certain what the right things are. If we pick the wrong things, we lose. But if we try to do everything, we're sure to get *something* right.

- We don't like saying no. Saying no means disappointing customers who don't get that feature they asked for; letting down teammates who want to collaborate with you; or appearing obstinate to your boss.

Fortunately, there are ways of getting past both of these barriers, starting with the most important but least-recognized leadership skill.

AND THE NUMBER ONE LEADERSHIP SKILL IS...

Leadership is a vague and hotly debated concept; I often hesitate to admit I do leadership development as part of my job; but it *is* my job, and therefore I've given it lot of thought. There are a lot of leadership programs out there—some very good; others, not so much. Most leadership programs, typically, start with a definition (as if we'd never heard the term). For example:

> "Leadership is organizing a group of people to achieve a common goal."[1]

> "Leadership is the process of social influence in which one person can enlist the aid and support of others in the accomplishment of a common task."[2]

Note that the focus in these definitions is on, respectively, *organizing people* and *enlisting support*. But in each of these something is left unaddressed, leading me to ask:

- Which common goal?
- Which common task?

Zeroing in on that *one* goal and that *one* task is, in my opinion, the most difficult part of being a leader. To develop stronger leaders in an organization, I could roll out programs covering a wide range of leadership behaviors and concepts: inspiring people and communicating effectively; project management and accountability; coaching individuals, rewarding performance, setting strategy, and even developing other leaders. In doing so, I would exhaust all of my training resources. Alternatively, I could focus on the single most important leadership skill, the one that no one seems to notice but that is core to virtually every leadership task in business: *prioritization*.

That's right: I believe that the future of leadership development lies in prioritization. Think about it:

- Struggling with decision making? This typically involves a disagreement over choosing the best options.

- Arguing about strategy? Individuals can't agree on a single approach.

- Having difficulty negotiating with a team to deliver on an important product component? This is usually an indication there is disagreement between teams over what is more important.

- Failing to manage burnout on your team? This means, probably, they have far too much on their plates.

Each of these issues would be resolved through better prioritization.

The key to finding, and doing, the *right things, not everything*, is prioritization.

STRATEGY *Is* PRIORITIZATION

I'm a big fan of strategy. I claim it as one of my strengths, though I am guilty of misusing the term. Granted, it has a broad meaning, but at its core, strategy is about prioritization.

I'll use an easy example: cupcakes. When cupcakes became the biggest dessert phenomenon of the early 2000s, I wondered what could possibly be so special about a cupcake to garner all of that attention. As it turns out, there are a lot of ways to differentiate a cupcake:

- *Focus on convenience*: I admit to having a fondness for the cupcakes of the '80s—Little Debbie's, Hostess, Tastykake. The companies that produce them focus on packaging and broad distribution to grocery and convenience stores; their cupcakes remain "fresh," despite having a long shelf life. High quality, however, is not the aim of these companies.

- *Focus on premium ingredients*: Most cupcake shops in New York feature baked goods that are delicious because they are made with the best ingredients. Affordability is *not* a factor here, and neither is shelf life. These treats sell out before the end of the day, every day—and they don't last long in the buyers' hands, either.

- *Focus on creative ingredients*: Cupcakes are the new Dairy Queen Blizzards. How about a cookie dough cupcake with the dough in the middle and cookie crumbles on top of the creamy icing? A peanut-butter-and-jelly cupcake? Or even a maple bacon cupcake?

- *Focus on healthy ingredients*: Gluten-free, vegan, sugar-free (substituting agave syrup) cupcakes? You bet. They won't win any county fairs for best in show, but you can indulge in these and not feel (as) guilty.

You, too, can make cupcakes, like every other baking entrepreneur out there. But first you have to figure out what your strategy will be to differentiate your cupcakes from all of theirs. This is the crux of strategies, as shown in Table 7.1.

Table 7.1   The Role of Strategy in an Organization

Mission Statement	Why a Company Exists
Guiding Principles/Values	How individuals behave in a company
Strategy	**The competitive game plan**

I'm not suggesting that this is a new way of thinking, or particular to the Work Revolution. I am suggesting that we double-down on strategy as a core foundation in creating vibrant organizations. If you've got a solid strategy, you have nailed one of the most important, and difficult, components of the Work Revolution.

An organization's strategy makes clear what the business will optimize for, and just as importantly, what trade-offs it will make. For example, Google has chosen to optimize for simplicity in its user interface, designing products that are so intuitive they don't require training or explanation. Not surprisingly, the company has *not* optimized for customer service. Google has billions of users; it knew early on that serving them all would be a losing battle. It's not that there's no customer service—there is! I worked with many of the incredibly hard-working individuals in customer service. But they can't possibly provide rich, personal customer service to every user who has an issue with Docs or Reader. That's why Google has chosen instead to be creative in how it scales customer service processes and operations.

Back in 2008, David Collis and Michael Rukstad wrote an article for the *Harvard Business Review* titled "Can You Say What Your Strategy Is?" (This, by the way, is a must-read for any entrepreneur and leader.) In it they laid out an exceptional model for strategy statements, which includes:[3]

- A time-based objective

- The scope (customer or offering, geographic location, vertical)

- Advantage (how you will differentiate from your competitors)

For example, Edward Jones, a brokerage firm, hashed through every word of its strategy statement to get it exactly right:

To grow to 17,000 financial advisers by 2012 by offering trusted and convenient face-to-face financial advice to conservative individual investors who delegate their financial decisions, through a national network of one-financial-advisor offices.

In it you can see the time-based objective, the defined customer, and the advantage—the trusted, convenient, one-financial-advisor offices—that provide very personal attention to the conservative investor. This strategy statement directly pointed to the best decisions to align the company for success:

- Offices located in rural/suburban strip malls, for convenience; not high-rise office buildings

- Large training programs, to hire and train advisors from outside the industry (there weren't that many around!)

- Investment primarily in mutual funds and blue chips, not options and commodities, to align with the conservative investor

Strategy is vital to an organization's ability to focus on the right things. It provides a built-in "decision-engine," around which projects and parts of the company are determined to be either worthy of extra investment or needing less attention. When you are clear about the trade-offs you are willing to make, prioritization naturally follows. It becomes the first level in deciding what work teams should do and what to take off the table. As Collis and Rakstad put it, "A well-understood statement of strategy aligns behavior within the business. It allows everyone in the organization to make individual choices that reinforce one another, rendering those 10,000 employees exponentially more effective." Basically, the strategy statement gets people doing the right things.

ELIMINATE THE BOTTOM, PUSH TO THE TOP

The principles behind the *right things, not everything* are nearly identical for individuals and leaders; both individuals and teams make decisions about what they will do in a day, a week, a quarter, or a year. As an individual, I stare at my to-do list every day, trying to figure out the most important tasks that need to get done. As a leader, I stare at the list of projects and initiatives that align with my organization's strategy, trying to figure out what to tackle next. It's the same process, just on a different scale.

After leading a fairly large group of people who were working on disparate projects, I finally gave up on the idealistic notion that there is an absolute ranking of importance for every goal. First, we rarely have the opportunity to consider all of our options at the same time. Opportunities trickle in over time, and we have to make case-by-case decisions about whether we will accept any one of them; we can never know what other opportunities might pop up tomorrow, or next year. For example, I love speaking at conferences, and get a lot of offers to do so. However, these opportunities are offered at unexpected times, so saying yes to one might preclude my saying yes to another that might be offered in the future. Second, we rarely know with certainty what the impact of any project will be. We have to make a lot of guesses and estimations. Prioritization is, at best, a messy bet, and it changes over time.

As a result, the prioritization approach I have adopted is a much more layered approach, a multistep testing process of ranking and elimination. Each test breaks down decision making into relatively easy steps that guide you to do the right things.

Test 1: Mission Worthiness

First, make a list of your current set of projects or opportunities. It is critical to maintain your list of projects and opportunities in the form of *goal*s that state what you are trying to accomplish. If you lose sight of why you are doing something, you can't properly prioritize it. For example, "train managers" is not a goal; it is a means to an end, and that end is not clear here. A better goal statement might be: "Increase the quality and frequency of manager feedback to employees."

Next, gather the critical ingredients:

- One well-formed mission statement
- List of guiding principles
- Organizational strategy

Put these ingredients together, and pass each opportunity or potential project through them, as you might if they were combined in a strainer. This first test is a yes/no decision as to whether the goal broadly fits within your mission and strategy statements, and whether it would line up with your organizational culture. If it's a no for any critical ingredient, it's a no, period.

For example, I have food allergies. It is very easy for me to say no to corn, oranges, rye, oats, and sweet potatoes, as eating them makes me itchier than a dog with fleas. Beyond that, my guiding principles are healthy eating, convenient breakfast and lunch options, and occasional dinners at exceptionally nice restaurants. The healthy-eating principle also has led me to ban certain foods from my diet entirely, because I know that if I eat them I will lose complete control over my willpower: chocolate croissants, Chipotle burritos, fried cheese, and anything with Nutella on it. In order to allow the fine-dining experience (c'mon, it's New York!), I eat healthy salads almost every day of the week, for lunch. My feeling is, it is just not worth spending the calories on any other mediocre takeout food.

Once you move past the high-level yes/no decision, you'll still be staring an unwieldy list. So, now what?

Test 2: Eliminate the Bottom

For some reason, it is much easier to eliminate the stuff at the bottom than it is from the top. I think this is because there are fewer items at the bottom, and they are easy targets that help us avoid making the tough decisions. For example, when people ask me what my favorite foods are, I hem and haw and put a thousand caveats around my answer. It depends on my mood, where I am, who I'm with, how good the restaurant is, and on and on. However, ask me what I dislike, and I can easily rattle off the list: chicken, green olives, bleu cheese, and all brown liquors except dark rum. Not much ambiguity around that.

So fine, start at the bottom. What are the obvious goals that have low potential impact? Look at the full list and do the mental exercise of picking out the bottom items using whatever criteria are relevant. When you've eliminated the painfully obvious bottom items, go back and do one more round. This might be a bit more difficult, and you might start getting into debates at this point, either in your own mind or with teammates. But it should still be fairly easy to do.

Test 3: Push to the Top

The third test isn't about stack-ranking goals at the top; this is still too hard to do. All the caveats that I place around my favorite food choices actually do matter, very much. Instead, it's about *pushing* goals to the top by viewing them through a varied set of prioritization lenses. Rather than asking what my favorite food is, the question becomes what I want to eat *tonight*.

Prioritization lenses can vary widely from organization to organization and from one individual to another. But there are a few standard lenses that can get you started.

Effort/Impact   Evaluate each of your opportunities by estimating the *value* of reaching the goal (what will it yield?) and the *cost* of doing it (in terms of effort, time, or actual investment dollars). Value divided by cost will give you an estimate of relative value among the opportunities. Which of your opportunities are easy to do and have high potential impact (value/cost = a high number)? These are dubbed "low-hanging fruit" in corporate-speak. Push them to the top of the list. Any goals that cost more than their value are simply not worth doing; eliminate them.

Urgency/Importance   Just because something is urgent does not make it important. As explained in Chapter 5, "Energy, Not Schedules," you must stay vigilant to recognize False Urgency work. One way to do this is to add the importance dimension (you can also use the value/cost calculation). Of all the urgent projects or tasks, which of them are truly important? The truly urgent and highly important projects will rise to the top rather naturally. Urgency is something we all understand; but we are probably doing a lot of work in the low-importance bucket, also known as *reactive work*. You might need to start saying no to some of the True-Urgency, low-importance work. But say yes unequivocally to the truly urgent and highly important stuff.

As an example, sometimes, being the first to launch in a market carries a huge advantage. Scan the opportunities and see whether there are projects or initiatives that present this first-to-market advantage. If so, push these to the top. Another way to think about this is in terms of opportunity cost. If you don't do something now, are you giving up the opportunity to do it in the future?

[Fill in the Blank]   What additional prioritization lenses are important to you and/or your organization? These additional lenses might reveal the more *intangible* aspects of value, those that aren't easily captured in numbers. For example, your team may choose to prioritize the topmost customer request each quarter—not because it has the greatest potential return in terms of profits, but because it creates goodwill with customers.

In the team domain, make sure members understand each and every prioritization lens and the principles behind them. These should become part of the team's shared language, particularly the ones specific to your team. For individuals, post a list of your prioritization lenses at the top of your to-do list. It should be the first thing you see each time you add and prioritize potential work.

Putting It All Together

Once you've applied all the relevant tests, you should be left with a list of goals at the top and in the middle, followed by those you have eliminated. For the trashed goals, document the reasons you made a *no* decision:

- Did the cost outweigh the value?
- Did it fail the mission-worthiness test?
- Did it fail on another prioritization dimension?

By documenting eliminated goals, you are compiling a valuable historical document, a reminder of the logic behind prioritization decisions. It is just as important to know what the team is *not* doing as it is to know what they are. The estimates of value or cost might also change at some point in the future, bringing some goals back to life.

Now it's time to focus on the goals at the top. Can you tackle all of them, right now? If yes, congratulations—you've done a splendid job of prioritization. If no, you've got one final test to apply: hiring. If you know your team is short on the resources they need to complete the top priorities now, assess the number of people it would take to get the job done. If you have enough legitimate items at the top to justify either hiring new team members or recruiting an assistant to help you out, you know you are on the right track. However, if you look at the list and determine that the potential impact would *not* justify a new hire, go back to each of the prioritization tests and reassess.

I'm not suggesting you actually go out and hire someone at this point; doing the mental exercise of reconciling the list is what's important. There are additional strategies you can implement at the team and individual levels to help you decide how to handle an overflowing list of the right things.

TEAM PRIORITIZATION

I hate project management. It's not just the Gantt charts that send shudders up my spine; it's the inflexibility of the whole process. Once you've figured out goals for a team, detailed all the supporting tasks, and plugged in ownership and dates and dependencies for each task, it is an onerous process to make changes. I'm not sure whether it's the inflexibility of the tools or the collective mind-set. In any case, traditional project management tends to stifle interaction with the organizational environment. If anything new or different pops up during the project, there are significant logistical barriers to integrating specified changes into the plan. Changes tend to cause a ripple effect on the whole endeavor, requiring new dates, owners, reprioritization, contingencies, and communication. Worse, when tasks are laid out at the beginning, they often get separated from the original goals. And when the goals become obsolete, for any reason, individuals rarely know this and continue blindly along, completing meaningless tasks on "the plan."

A brilliant former colleague of mine, Chris Lopez, is an expert in lean/agile practices[4] in software engineering; he has worked with many different teams to help them streamline their development processes and increase their ability to get stuff launched (such as products, features, or services). When he explained to me an entirely different method of project management, I was bowled over by how obvious and simple it was. Its focus is always on the right things. Here's the basic idea:

- Let's say you have five different initiatives at the top of your list (the "right things"), each of which will take your team one week to complete.

- Each initiative will produce a weekly payoff of 100 units of value for your organization (active users, dollars earned, man hours saved, stock shares—the exact unit doesn't really matter).

If you create a typical project plan, chances are good that each team member will own one initiative and make steady progress on it until completion. This makes sense at the surface level: Every initiative is highly important, so you should do them all now! Table 7.2 shows what this looks like:

Table 7.2   Tracking Individual Project Ownership and Value

Week	Progress	Value Earned This Week
1	Five initiatives started and in progress	0
2	Five initiatives in progress	0
3	Five initiatives in progress	0
4	Five initiatives in progress	0
5	Five initiatives completed	0
6	Five initiatives implemented	500
	Total value gained over six weeks	500

Let's say, however, that you choose to tackle one initiative at a time, with the entire team collectively focusing on each one until completion (assuming that it is possible to break down the initiatives so that multiple people can contribute). Table 7.3 shows what that looks like.

The point to note here is that once an initiative is completed, it contributes value to the company *immediately*, as well as over the remaining weeks while the other initiatives are in progress. That means, when you move on to the second initiative, the first is already contributing; then the second kicks in, and so on. By choosing to

Table 7.3   Tracking Collective Initiatives and Value

Week	Progress	Value Earned This Week
1	Initiative 1 started and completed	0
2	Initiative 2 started and completed; 1 implemented	100 (Initiative 1 in play)
3	Initiative 3 started and completed; 2 implemented	200 (Both initiative 1 and 2 paying off)
4	Initiative 4 started and completed; 3 implemented	300 (Initiatives 1, 2, and 3 all working for you now)
5	Initiative 5 started and completed; 4 implemented	400
6	5 implemented	500 (All initiatives now yielding value)
	Total value gained over six weeks	**1,500** (Represents the cumulative value of each initiative paying off each week it is in play.)

chunk tasks in this way, you are adding value more quickly to your organization. The other cool thing is that the team experiences a sense of completion much more frequently, which is both reinforcing and exciting. An additional side effect is that the team bonds together around shared tasks, and learns to allocate components according to the best person for the job (i.e., strengths). Coordination is key; when the team is focused on a joint challenge, they become motivated to make it happen.

In practice, of course, projects and initiatives are not this neat and clean. We often don't have a clear view of their potential impact, and our estimations of the effort necessary to complete them might be off. However, what's important in this approach is to ask one question at the beginning of each week: What is the most important goal we should be working on *right now*? The team learns to adapt to changes in the environment, such as new opportunities or urgent/important projects. The "if it's important enough, we should all be doing it" mindset gives clarity around the right things. So while the initiatives at the top of the list might shift and change over time, your team is always in a position to do the most important thing, quickly.

Individuals

As an individual, you might be working on teams, by yourself, or both. Managing your list of the right things requires a slightly different focus, one tailored to you as an individual. Beyond the prioritization lenses detailed previously, there are two more tactics that will help you to get clear on the right things.

As in Chapter 6, "Strengths, Not Job Slots," the first tactic here is to understand what kind of work aligns with your strengths. Ultimately, if you have a list of equally important and potentially high-impact tasks, prioritize the ones that capitalize on your strengths.

An easy way to do this is using what Martha Beck, in her book *Steering by Starlight: How to Fulfill Your Destiny, No Matter What*, calls the "shackles test."[5] Shackles are an excellent visual analogy to depict what it feels like to be working on a task that is deeply ill-suited to you: You lose energy; you feel trapped. You become bored, tired, disengaged. You'd rather go clean your toilet than do the assigned task. For example, creating project plans is a very shackles-on endeavor for me. On the other hand, developing a strategy for increasing manager effectiveness in an organization is quintessentially shackles *off* for me—the complete opposite! My mind soars; I get excited; I can't wait to dive in. It's my work-candy.

It may be hard initially to distinguish between shackles on or shackles off for all but the most obvious examples. But once I started doing this exercise regularly, I found I could fine-tune my shackles meter quite accurately. I actually find myself applying the shackles test 10 or even 20 times a day for everything, from what I want for lunch to whether I will accept an offer to speak at a conference. The more you use it, the better you get at assessing whether something is in line with *you*.

The two essential questions to ask are:

- What can I contribute best to?

- What do I abhor doing?

When you muster the confidence to start answering this honestly for yourself, it will be much easier to do this with your team. Remember, what one person abhors, the next person might love. So if you hang onto a task out of guilt, you might, in fact, be keeping it from the very person who would celebrate the opportunity to do it.

The second tactic is somewhat unintuitive: Learn to be a quitter—by which I mean, learn to quit what just isn't working.

This principle is critical for the right-things principle to work. Jim Collins and Morten Hansen, in their book *Great by Choice: Uncertainty, Chaos, and Luck—Why Some Thrive Despite Them All*, dissected companies that thrived in uncertainty and chaos to understand what made them great and how they coped in such environments. One of the hypotheses they tested was whether the successful—or 10X, as they called them—companies were better at predicting what would succeed for their businesses.[6] In fact, they found this was not a factor. What the 10X companies *did do* was fail fast. They put stuff out there, assessed whether it was working, and abandoned it the moment the evidence mounted against it (I'll come back to this topic in Chapter 8, "Grassroots, Not Top-Down"). This is the corollary to the right-things principle; we can't always know what the right things are, and we are sure to do some things that turn out to be wrong things.

There are two primary reasons we have a difficult time quitting. First, we have a sunk-cost bias. Once we have invested in something, we hesitate to abandon it. Our biggest fear is wasted time, money, and/or effort. For example, when you go to a theater to see a movie, you spend time and effort to get there; you park, pay for a ticket, and find a good seat. But, if you hate the movie, you should leave. Staying does nothing but waste more of your time. Fundamental business classes teach this concept; once time/money has been invested, you should not make decisions about whether to continue based on that factor. It is a "sunk cost."

The second reason we hesitate to quit is largely cultural. Americans are raised to be go-getters; they are taught never to quit. Quitting is seen as a sign of weakness. (In Asian cultures, the focus is more on discipline and perseverance.) Not quitting is a healthy and important lesson for children; but once we become adults, we need to unlearn it, for many reasons. Once we know we *can persevere*, we need to learn to make clear choices about what is truly worth sticking to. There are so many goals we can chase after; we have to advance to the next level of "don't be a quitter" by following this rule only when the opportunity is right for us.

As an individual, it is up to you to flag projects that aren't going in the right direction. Pay attention to your energy signals, and ask about their impact. If you don't speak up, no one will know, and you'll waste precious time on work that is definitely not worth doing. And as a contributing and valuable employee, you owe it to yourself to give the very best of *you* to your work; you as well as your organization will benefit.

TOSS PRODUCTIVITY OUT

Leo Babauta

For at least a couple of years, *Zen Habits* was one of the top productivity blogs, dispensing productivity crack for a nominal fee (your reading time).

I'd like to think I helped people move closer to their dreams, but today I have different advice: Toss productivity advice out the window.

Most of it is well-meaning, but the advice is wrong for a simple reason: It's meant to squeeze the most productivity out of every day, instead of making your days better.

Imagine that instead of cranking out a lot of widgets, you made space for what's important. Imagine that you worked slower instead of faster, and enjoyed your work. Imagine a world where people matter more than profits.

If any of that appeals to you, let's look at some traditional productivity advice, and see why we should just toss it out.

1. *Get organized.* Sounds good, but getting organized is just rearranging the chairs on the deck of the Titanic. It does nothing to stop the ship from sinking. Instead, simplify. If you have a desk with five things in it, you don't need to organize. If you have a closet with only a handful of

clothes, it doesn't need a closet organizer. If your day has only one or two appointments, there's no need for a detailed schedule organizer. Simplifying means making important choices about what's important, rather than ignoring that question and just trying to cram everything into your day (and space) in a logical way.

2. *Keep an idea list.* The idea is that whenever you have an idea, you should write it down. Then you'll never lose an idea, and you'll always have a list of ideas that you can come back to. Sounds great, right? Except in practice, the idea list is never filled with your best ideas. That's because when you have a really great idea, you get so excited about it you jump up and want to work on it immediately. Your best ideas are ones that you can't put off until tomorrow. That's how you know it's a great idea. The ideas that go on the idea list are not your best.

3. *Set a lot of goals.* Only five years ago, I had a long list of goals for each year, and I was pretty decent at getting them done (better than 50 percent, at least). Then I experimented with three goals a year, and I was even more focused. Then I did *one goal*, and that was amazing, because it really helped me focus everything I did. Now I do *no goals*, and that's best of all. I let go of future-focused thinking, and focus on what inspires and excites me now. I get even more accomplished, but let go of all the time I used to spend on goal administration (it's more than you might think), and all my mental energy is freed to do what I want to do right now. You might not want to do no goals, but try one goal or three goals.

4. *Be productive when you're waiting.* Lots of people do this— you bring a laptop or mobile device or some papers, to do some work while you're waiting at a doctor's office or at DMV or on the train or in traffic. There's nothing wrong with this, really, except in the philosophy behind it: that

(continued)

(*continued*)

every second should be filled with work, or it's wasted. I object to this. Sitting in a waiting room, doing nothing but sitting in silence or watching other people, is a beautiful way to spend your time. Reading a novel on a train, or taking a nap, is also wonderful. Waiting in line at DMV or the post office and eavesdropping on other human beings, or making conversation with someone, or just soaking in the sounds of humanity, is arguably more important than doing more work or reading work-related documents. Life isn't only about work, and productivity isn't everything. Try some unproductivity instead.

5. *Keep detailed, context to-do lists.* In the early days of *Zen Habits*, back in 2007, I did exactly this—I kept a series of contextual to-do lists for home, work, phone calls, errands, someday, and so on. This became too much work for me, and so instead of organizing, I simplified. I now focus on one or two things to do each day, and if/when I get them done, my day is golden. Everything else I do that day is gravy. And the to-do lists gather dust, which turns out to be a very productive thing for them to do.

Zen Habits blog, September 6, 2011.

How to Say No

Saying no to someone or some project at work just *seems* wrong. We fear that our teammates will accuse us of spelling "team" with an "I." We fear that we'll lose customers or business. We fear that we'll never get that promotion. When you boil it down, avoiding "no" is a very fear-based response.

At the same time, saying no could mean the difference between having a real impact at work and becoming too burned out to be effective at anything. Choosing to do the right things necessitates saying no to everything, and the wrong things. And just in case you have forgotten how juicy and satisfying the word "no" can be from your toddler days (it's a shame we unlearn this), here's a how-to guide for saying no that should help you emerge guilt-free from virtually any situation.

Step 1:   Get clear with yourself about why you are saying no. Though not exhaustive, here is a list of categories that will cover the vast majority of work situations:

- *Priorities*: The request doesn't rise to the top using any of the priority lenses appropriate to your team.

- *Strengths*: The request might be high priority, but it doesn't align well with your strengths, and your shackles meter is buzzing louder than a radar detector on a Georgia highway.

- *Bandwidth*: The request is high priority *and* aligned with your strengths, but your plate is already overflowing with work in these categories.

- *Integrity*: The request falls outside the bounds of what you believe to be ethical behavior or the right thing to do from a compliance standpoint.

Step 2:   Formulate your "no" response. This is very much dependent on which category listed in Step 1 the request falls into. The easiest category is Integrity. Here, you can simply cite the moral reason for your decision and move on. There should be no ambiguity in your answer, and you should feel no guilt; and if the individual making the request persists, you should consider involving HR, legal, or other relevant individuals in the conversation.

If the request comes under Strengths or Bandwidth, the "no" response can include negotiations. For example, if you know that you might have time at the end of the month for a new project, you can offer to delay its start, or offer the option of moving on without you. In the case of Strengths, it helps to know your teammates and who might be an equally well-suited or better person for the task: "I'm not the best person suited for this, but Bill really excels at spreadsheets. Have you asked him? He'll blow through this in half the time." In either case, the bottom-line reason for saying no is that you can't give your full commitment to the request, either because you aren't the best person for the job or because you simply don't have the time at the moment. When you say no in these situations, you save the requestor the potential frustration of delays because you fail to deliver by the deadline. By being open and authentic about your reasons, you can talk it through with the requestor and arrive at an ideal solution for both of you.

In the most difficult category, Priorities, it's important to review the prioritization lenses that are relevant to your team, and discuss the differences of opinion about where work falls in the bigger picture. This is a matter of reconciling disagreements over the importance of the work, whether because individuals are estimating values or costs differently or because of disagreements about urgency. What if you just can't agree? Decide, as a team, which process you will use to resolve the issue. Will you put it to a team vote? Seek consensus? Ask the team lead or product manager to decide? In any case, you should have a clear method that will help the team move past priority disagreements.

When you are juggling myriad requests from different teams, each of which has its own set of prioritization lenses distinct from your own, there is no easy solution. The simple answer is to negotiate. Provide clear insight into your prioritization decisions. Ask each team to help you understand how their requests might weigh against your current set of priorities. Don't be shy about asking that very important question: Why? Share your value and cost estimates. The burden then shifts to the requestors to be clear about the importance of their requests and their potential impact. In many cases, you'll find that others are not clear at all about this. By forcing clarity, which might be painful, you'll be playing a very important part in advancing the Work Revolution.

Step 3:   Practice saying no in innocuous situations. Peter Bregman, in the article "Flexing Your 'No Thanks' Muscle," suggests practicing saying no to all of those pesky requests we encounter once or more daily: [7]

- "Would you like to sign up for a store credit card and receive 10 percent off your purchase today?" No, thanks.

- "Would you like to receive e-mail offers about special store events?" No, thanks.

- "Would you like to donate a dollar to the children's hospital?" (Translated implication: "Would you like to prove that you don't hate children by donating just one little dollar to the children's hospital?") Still, no, thanks. I donate deliberately and much more generously to charities of my choosing.

The danger inherent to these requests is that they seem harmless; but one request piles on top of another, and the next thing you know, you are digging out from under a pile of useless store advertisements in your inbox. The telling sign in these situations is the response on the tip of your tongue: "Why not?" When you can't think of a good reason to say no, but you also aren't leaping out of your skin to say yes, just say "no, thank you." As Bregman puts it:

One thing we can do is recognize that we have a limited amount of space in our minds, and each time we say "why not?" to something—or even *consider* saying "why not?" to something—it takes up room. If we learn to automatically say, "no thanks," to things that seem like a good deal, but don't fit into our main areas of focus, we'll simplify our lives and free our minds to focus.

Step 4:   Just say no, as Nancy Reagan so elegantly put it. Once you know *why* you are saying no, and you have formulated the relevant response, don't serve up your no with a side of apologies. Be direct while still being kind; practice it with your dog if you need to (he is sure to gaze at you with puppy eyes, an excellent metaphor for a coworker who wants your help). The more direct you are about your response, the less likely the requestor will come back for clarification on your decision.

SUMMARY

Saying no to everything so that you can say yes to the right things is the essence of prioritization. There will always be a stream of incoming requests and tasks, and you will rarely have the luxury of working with a static list of items that you can cull and then implement. The items on the list keep moving, shifting, contracting, expanding, so in reality prioritization is more like an ongoing effort that cycles over and over, almost daily. *This* is why the prioritization skill is so important, why it's core to leadership—it's a daily behavior.

The more you push items both to the top and bottom, the better you will become at quickly assessing new work to determine whether it is, in fact, one of the right things. Your right things list should evolve to become more tightly defined and crisply stated, until you're able to track your personal progression in terms of how much value you are contributing to an organization over time. Table 7.4 lays out guidelines to help you do this.

Table 7.4   Summary of the Right Things, Not Everything for Organizations, Leaders, and Individuals

Organizations	Develop a strategy statement that defines what is in and out of scope for the organization.
Leaders	Select and relentlessly communicate prioritization lenses that are relevant to the team.
	Consistently apply prioritization lenses to eliminate the lowest-priority work and elevate the highest-priority work.
	Encourage teamwork to jointly tackle highest-priority projects, to execute and launch them quickly.
Individuals	Apply the "shackles" test to prioritize a list of important work.
	Say no to everything and yes to the right things by relentlessly prioritizing.
	Learn to be a quitter: Quit the wrong things.

CHAPTER 8

Grassroots, Not Top-Down

Experts, no matter how smart, only have limited
amounts of information. They also, like all of us, have
biases. It's very rare that one person can know more
than a large group of people, and almost never does
that same person know more about a whole series of
questions. The other problem in finding an expert is
that it's actually hard to identify true experts. In fact, if
a group is smart enough to find a real expert, it's more
than smart enough not to need one.
—James Surowiecki, *The Wisdom of Crowds*

When I started my career as an instructional designer, I worked
for a company that created high-quality training. Its dedicated
graphic designers and artists developed slick participant guides, polished illustrations and animations, and PowerPoint slides that all
coordinated perfectly. We spent a great deal of time tying pretty little
ribbons around our training products. I personally wrote a 100-plus-
page style guide to govern the look, feel, and every last detail for a
large-scale eLearning program for the Navy. I was proud of it then—
and still am!

When I started at Google, I spent some time adjusting to its culture of *launch and iterate*, which meant getting stuff out there and not
worrying whether it was perfect. There, engineers flat-out distrusted
pretty, polished things; perfection implied that someone had spent far
too much time on it. So it was with this mind-set that I began to work
with a team to develop a leadership program for early-career Googlers.
We didn't have the time, budget, or resources to produce a beautifully

designed leadership program, like I might have in my previous job; and it wouldn't have worked with Google culture anyway. We needed something quick, and we needed to reach the masses—a few thousand Googlers spread across the globe.

We decided to tap into the vast treasure trove of leadership resources that are freely available on the web, such as Harvard's leadership videos on YouTube, articles on leadership from the best management thinkers, even movies depicting leadership concepts in action. We felt that it was utterly unnecessary to suck up all this content, reprocess it, and package it into a traditional course. What we did instead was draft a series of simple e-mails. Throughout the span of five weeks, participants received a few e-mails each week providing some basic context around leadership themes, along with links to the various leadership content pieces. Each e-mail required the learner to spend only a few minutes to read an article or watch a video or answer a few questions—little chunks of time to learn a new concept.

We sprinkled in some exercises using simple Google Forms. We asked participants to think critically about what they had learned, or share a related story or an idea on the form. Upon submitting their answers, they could view the answers from all of the other participants. We also kept participants on track in the course by holding live discussion sessions at the end of each week, to create a sense of community.

To summarize, the course development required little more than finding content; putting it in the right order; and writing e-mails to provide the context, objectives, and big picture of the leadership concepts. We used no fancy binders or shiny interfaces. Despite the lack of frills, the program, which has been running for about two years now, consistently received ratings on par with other highly polished leadership programs. Demand for the program remains strong, and the typically superskeptical and picky software engineers actually liked the program *more* than the sales participants, because it was simple, straightforward, and effective.

This is a great example of a grassroots-style initiative: start small, launch quickly to see if it works, and then build on success. It defies the assumptions we often hold, that bigger is better, and imperfect is bad. Grassroots is the opposite—smaller is better, and imperfection is simply part of the process. When organizations empower individuals through grassroots-style initiatives, great things happen—problems get solved and individuals embrace their freedom to solve them. The principle of *grassroots, not top-down*, is about:

- Starting small and letting things grow
- Tapping into collective intelligence
- Empowering individuals

THE POWER OF SMALL

How does your organization handle ideas? Typically, leaders gather ideas (sometimes in suggestion boxes) and then funnel them through many layers of scrutiny and debate, culling hundreds or perhaps thousands of ideas down to a promising few. They provide resources to develop the chosen ideas through proposals, projections, plans, and more layers of approvals, to mitigate the risks associated with implementing the ideas. Eventually, they build and launch the finalist ideas with great fanfare, where minor changes might be made based on the reception of the ideas in the marketplace. It is easy to see why, in this kind of environment, top-down is a requirement: If everyone ran around implementing their own ideas, there would be a lot of expensive failures, far more than the business likely could sustain. The leaders, understandably, serve as gatekeepers, and fund the best ideas according to levels of acceptable risk.

But let me suggest this: What if the cost of trying something out were almost zero? What if there was little or no risk inherent in failure? Going one step further, what if it was possible to test *every* idea (hard to imagine, given what we know to be true from Chapter 7, "The Right Things, Not Everything")? Rather than trying to predict the success of ideas, it would only require observing which of the ideas were successful.

Let's compare the two approaches, hypothetically. An organization has 100 ideas for a new product. Leaders spend several months debating, judging, and making projections about the ideas. Finally, three are chosen for implementation; resources are not available for more than that. The three ideas are fully built out and then launched, perhaps six months down the road. Of the three ideas, two work out well, and one is a failure. All in all, not bad, right?

Another organization has 100 individuals, all of whom have ideas. The leaders empower each of them to test out his or her idea on a really small scale. If the small-scale test works out, the idea progresses. After two weeks of some more testing, the ideas of 50 individuals are still alive. Each of those 50 individuals further tests his or her idea, one bit at a time, testing for success at various levels of scale; from this test, 15 prove to gain momentum and continue to show promise. After a few months of increasingly rigorous testing, 10 emerge, and the company makes the decision to invest in building them all out. They meet with success in every single case. All in all, spectacular results.

Of course, this sounds like a pipedream. How is it possible to test out 100 different ideas with little or no cost or risk? The answer is, it's easier than you may think. Yes, it requires scrappiness, creativity, and quite a bit of faking it. But most important, it requires starting small.

Think you are starting small? Start even smaller.

The biggest mistake we make in organizations is to start too big and launch initiatives having no idea whether they will actually work. Jim Collins and Morten Hansen, in their book *Great by Choice*, call this "firing uncalibrated cannons."[1] Their research showed that "10X" companies, which beat the comparison companies, took the approach of firing first bullets, and then cannons. The key notion is that bullets are small. If you shoot a bullet and it doesn't connect with a target, the cost is very small—never big enough to have a disproportionate negative financial impact on the company. If, on the other hand, the bullet hits its target, the company fires another bullet to see if it also hits the target; and, perhaps a third, just to make sure. Once the bullets are fully calibrated and aimed directly at the target, the company fires a cannon. That is, they invest heavily and take a big risk on the idea, because it has been shown to work.

IDEO is an organization that has mastered the art of "firing bullets." It states clearly and openly that it has a strong culture of prototyping. In fact, the cruder the prototype, the better. For example, the first prototype for a surgical instrument it designed incorporated a dry-erase marker as the tip of the tool, to demonstrate the ergonomics of it. IDEO prototypes "obsessively and reflexively," according to David Kelley, the company's founder and chairman, testing everything the moment someone thinks up a new idea.

Google is also known for its prototyping culture, so much so that two Google engineers, Alberto Savoia and Patrick Copeland, coined the term *pretotype* to refer to the step *before* prototyping. They define pretotyping as "testing the initial appeal *and* actual usage of a potential new product by simulating its core experience with the *smallest possible investment of time and money*" (italics mine).[2] Their notion of pretotyping is so simple that even you (yes, you) can put one together for a new iPhone app. The recommended pretotyping tool? Sticky notes. Here's how it works:

1. Draw the home screen on the first sticky note. Using a pencil, crayons, or even scented markers (your preference), sketch it quickly, without thinking about straight lines or edges.

2. Use a second sticky note to represent the screen you'd access via a menu or a button on the home screen.

3. Create additional notes for each of the other screens in the app.

Essentially, you can see the full layout of the app on the series of notes and get a pretty good idea about how it would look, what it would do, and how it would flow. Now you are done, right? Wrong. The final step is to carry around the series of notes in your pocket and act as if you are using the app! You pretend. (Incidentally, the term *pretotype* was derived from "pretend-o-type," but that proved to be too big a mouthful.) Yes, it feels silly (and most definitely looks silly, from the perspective of outsiders), but this process resolves the questions of whether you'd think to use the app, when you'd want to use it, how useful it would be, and whether it is *sticky* (i.e., whether you'd continue using it).

Noom, Inc., a start-up founded by former Google engineers, invests heavily in developing easy ways to test things. According to cofounder, Artem Petakov, they don't spend any time debating ideas or arguing over the pros and cons of an idea; they just test them all.

For example, they tested their initial idea for the CardioTrainer app using e-mail as the mechanism. Pretotypes and prototypes enable fast failure. If an idea doesn't work, they can move on without any guilt or regret, given how small the investment was (both emotionally and in resource terms). Fast failure also means more time to test more ideas. And the more ideas they can test, the more likely they will be to find the successful ones (the right ones!). This approach to testing lots and lots of ideas is liberating. It means that anyone can throw out ideas, and anyone can test them. There is no such thing as a bad idea, just an untested idea.

How can you create an environment of starting small and testing?

Think Like Apollo 13 Engineers

Apollo 13 was the ill-fated mission to the moon that was aborted after an oxygen tank exploded in the service module, leaving the cabin of the crippled ship without a proper system to filter out carbon dioxide, thereby rapidly depleting the air left for the astronauts to breathe. Their only hope for a safe return to Earth was if engineers on the ground in Houston could jerry-rig a solution that the astronauts could replicate on board. The engineers gathered together at the control site all of the same materials they knew the astronauts had on board, dumped them onto a table, and challenged themselves to rig together a carbon dioxide filtering solution from those materials. The contraption they came up with was composed of plastic bags, cardboard, parts of a spacesuit, and lots of tape, but the astronauts were able to replicate the solution successfully on board, which literally saved their lives.

Think about any challenge you face as an Apollo 13 challenge. By which I mean: What exists already in your organization that you can use to build new solutions? How scrappy can you be with what you have on hand?

For the leadership program I and my colleagues built at Google, we took advantage of all kinds of content that was freely available on the web, and pieced it together using Google tools and products. The result was a truly novel configuration that yielded a successful self-paced leadership training course.

THE DEMOCRATIZATION OF SOCIAL CHANGE

Marcos Salazar, Social Entrepreneur*

"How much did you have to pay people to organize the event?"

This was the first question my friend asked me after I told him about the success of our most recent Be Social Change event on The Future of Fashion: Merging Style with Sustainable Social Impact. Be Social Change is an online/offline platform helping to empower, connect, and organize the new world of social change being created by social entrepreneurs. As part of our New York hub, my co-leader, Allie Mahler, and I had brought together major sustainable designers, reps from the fashion industry, and a wide variety of social entrepreneurs for a panel discussion about the most innovative, sustainable practices taking place within the world of fashion today. We had over 140 people attend, with 100-plus on the waiting list. The event was jam-packed, filled with insightful information, engaging conversations, and meaningful connections. Participants raved that they couldn't wait until the next one!

When I answered my friend's question—that we didn't hire anyone, that the two of us organized the entire event—he couldn't understand how that was possible. He had been working for a large, bureaucratic nonprofit for the past 10 years, and for him the event conjured images of paperwork to be filled out, approvals to wait for, people in communications, marketing, and events to coordinate with, as well as months of lead time. Allie and I had organized our event in just over a month.

I explained how we used free services like Google Docs to write and edit our messaging; Meetup.com to announce the event to our 1,000-plus community; Eventbrite to handle the ticketing; and Facebook, Twitter, and good old e-mail for promotion. We then connected with Greenspaces to host us for free. We received generous donations from Maine Root soda and Guayaki

(continued)

(*continued*)

Yerba Mate for refreshments, as well as Kopali Organics, which supplied chocolate. Finally, I revealed the total cost: less than $50, which bought name tags and a case of Three Buck Chuck wine from Trader Joe's. My coworker was amazed, and speechless. He knew this could never happen so quickly within his organization.

What this story highlights is the beginning stages of a new trend within the social sector: the democratization of social change. This transformation is similar to what has taken place in other fields over the past decade. For example, just a few years ago, shooting videos and sharing them on the Internet was rare, seen mostly as an art form. Then YouTube came along, along with advances in video cameras and the development of easy-to-use editing software, and before long, anyone could shoot anything and post it on the web. The result: democratization of video production.

This exact same disruption is taking place within the world of social change. Traditional nonprofits used to have a monopoly on "making a difference." But today, the barriers for creating sustainable impact are dramatically lower. Today, young people around the world are no longer waiting for large nonprofits to work through their bureaucracies to get things done. Instead, like Allie and me and the rest of the Be Social Change team, they are leveraging low-cost technology, free services, and the power of community while applying the principles of entrepreneurship to build their own systems, platforms, and organizations to make the world a better place. Social change will never be the same again.

---

*Marcos Salazar is the cofounder of Be Social Change and founder of SocialChange.is, a storytelling platform where social entrepreneurs can share their ideas, knowledge, and experiences in a narrative form and provide aspiring change-makers with the tools and resources they need to create meaningful and sustainable impact.

Use Data, Not Judgment

Rather than trying to guess whether something will work, consult the data to find out if it actually works. Data-driven decision making is objective and fair, and it eliminates politicking. So, in short, measure everything.

Embrace Mistakes and Failure

Rather than trying to avoid failure by picking only the best ideas, embrace failure as part of the process. As the architect and artist Jim Blake says, "If you aren't getting rejected at least once a day, you aren't trying hard enough." As a corollary, mistakes and sloppiness are, by definition, part of the testing process. Prototypes and pretotypes should be embarrassingly messy and crude; if they aren't, you've spent too much time on them. Build out an idea *just far enough* so that you can test it out.

Let's apply this to an example. Assume my organization is interested in implementing a Twitter-like microblogging/status update tool for the enterprise, which employees can access on the company intranet. Now suppose that instead of checking out potential tools, and evaluating their features and technical requirements, I throw together a pretotype to determine: Is this even a good idea? I start with a small team of three. Our first test is to write an update on a sticky note and post it on a board in the office. How often do we write updates? How useful is it to read other updates? Do we think to look at the board? The initial pretotype confirms whether the general acts of writing and reading statuses are useful, and "sticky." We have our answer in one short day.

If this test works well, I expand the experiment to a broader, 20-person team, consisting of several subgroups working on different projects. We pick a board in a common area, a good simulation of the intranet. How many people write status updates? Is it at all useful to read updates from people outside of our immediate teams? Does the board become overcrowded with too much information? The results of this test answer more questions about use cases; it also clarifies the issues around the tool; specifically, which features are important for actual implementation.

E-mail might be the next best step to "fake it." Set up a group and then install a filter to mimic what the updates will look like and how they will be delivered/accessed. By continuing to push the boundaries of the idea, testing it in ever bigger ways, it quickly becomes obvious whether the idea is worth pursuing, as well as what the right solution looks like, far in advance of investing any money.

Starting small and testing often is empowering. It means that everyone can participate in the idea process, and that leaders are no longer solely responsible for failures. Ideas start at the bottom and rise to the top as they test well, enabling a keen sense of grassroots entrepreneurialism throughout the organization. Innovation and agility become the status quo; they are embedded squarely within the culture of testing and fast failures.

The power of small can also be applied to great benefit in other ways, particularly through the mechanism of collective intelligence.

EMPOWERMENT THROUGH COLLECTIVE INTELLIGENCE

Chances are very good, whether you're aware of it or not, that you are contributing to the effort to digitize books, and thus to make printed, archived information accessible to the world. If, for example, you have typed the words from images, to prove you are a human and not a computer, as you completed a web registration form, you might have translated a tiny slice of a book that was illegible to a scanner.

CAPTCHA is the name of the technology that prevents automated bots from navigating a website and potentially generating spam. Those pesky bots are incapable of deciphering the text from distorted images of random words and nonwords. Humans, on the other hand, solve about 200 million CAPTCHAs a day, collectively contributing about 150,000 work hours in the process.[3] The founders of CAPTCHA realized that they could put this time to work for the greater good.

reCAPTCHA is the version of CAPTCHA that presents a word from a book that cannot be deciphered by a computer, along with a test word. If the user deciphers the test word correctly, the chances are high the user is deciphering the unknown word correctly as well. When several users reach consensus—essentially, all provide the same translation—then the unknown word is solved and the translation is plugged back in to the digitized version of the book. In this way, reCAPTCHA is helping to improve, for example, the quality of the *New York Times'* digitized archives and Google Books, which partners with libraries to scan their vast collections.

reCAPTCHA is an example of the power, and magic, of collective intelligence. What would take millions and millions of dollars in labor costs to do these translations gets done for free—at 99.5 percent accuracy—by millions and millions of people as they go about their Internet business (an existing behavioral stream!). The Internet has provided the technology that enables us to tap into the power of collective intelligence, as never before in history, and the examples of this capability are as numerous and breathtaking as the reCAPTCHA example.

James Surowiecki popularized this phenomenon in his book, *The Wisdom of Crowds*, which outlines the necessary elements of collective intelligence, as distinguished from its dangerous cousin, groupthink:[4]

> There are four key qualities that make a crowd smart. It needs to be diverse, so that people are bringing different pieces of information to the table. It needs to be decentralized, so that no one at the top is dictating the crowd's answer. It needs a way of summarizing people's opinions into one collective verdict. And the people in the crowd need to be independent, so that they pay attention mostly to their own information, and not worrying about what everyone around them thinks.

Our organizations are ripe with opportunities to leverage the wisdom of individuals to solve business problems, develop innovations, cut costs, or solve the myriad small issues surfacing every day in our jobs. Let me reiterate, for emphasis, one of Surowiecki's conditions: "*. . . no one at the top is dictating the crowd's answer.*" This is problematic for organizations clinging to hierarchy as the dominant mode of management. Top-down management is directly at odds with the wisdom of crowds.

Empowering individuals to make decisions and solve problems can pay huge dividends, not only to the organization but to the individuals who work in it. Research has emerged showing the connection between physical health and a sense of empowerment at work. Individuals who are given little discretion to make decisions in their work—referred to as *low intellectual discretion*—or have limited freedom to set their schedules, have significantly greater chances of developing cardiovascular disease, and dying of it. That's right—your workplace can literally give you a heart attack.

In today's knowledge economy, we have an incredible opportunity to capture the wisdom and intelligence of our highly educated workforce. While it might be scary to think about putting important decisions into the hands of the hundreds or thousands of people working in organizations around the world, the principles behind collective intelligence actually make this a low-risk prospect. Collective intelligence frees up senior leaders to focus on the important matters; it might even decrease the organization's health insurance costs in the process!

Problem Solving through Collective Intelligence

MIT's Center for Collective Intelligence studied nearly 250 examples of collective intelligence to better understand its mechanisms and variations—essentially, why it works and how to use crowds to solve different kinds of problems. Researchers deconstructed collective intelligence to make it easier to configure an initiative in a way that has the best chance for success.[5]

Collective intelligence can be effectively used for two major purposes: *creation* and *decision making*. Examples of creation include solving a problem, contributing a review, writing documentation or a tutorial, or developing an app or design. The crowd can also be leveraged to make effective decisions. The power in both cases is the diversity of individuals who, in aggregate, act much smarter than any given individual.

Creation   The typical mode in organizations is to break down a goal into tasks and then assign them to teams or individuals, to "own." Collective intelligence provides an alternative: Submit a task to the crowd and solicit their involvement. Creation can take one of two forms:

- *Independent creation*: Individuals independently create their own, stand-alone, solutions. For example, employees submit videos describing their favorite memories from work events.

- *Collaborative creation*: Individuals work together in a collaborative way to develop a solution. For example, employees contribute interdependently to construct a mosaic of images or designs for the new office entryway.

The development of wikis is a blend of the two approaches: Individuals write articles relevant to the organization (independent creation), but then another individual can make edits for accuracy or content (collaborative creation).

A great example of collective creation was the Zappos initiative to articulate the core attributes of the organizational culture. Tony Hsieh, the founder, asked employees the following question: "If you had to describe the Zappos culture in two or three paragraphs, what would you say?"[6] Contributions were purely voluntary, and every contribution was included, without censorship or editing. The result was the "Zappos Culture Book," a comprehensive collection of employee essays detailing the good, the bad, and the ugly parts of the Zappos culture (which, as it turns out, was mostly good). The "Culture Book" is now a yearly tradition, serving as a snapshot of the company's evolving culture, and available for anyone to read.

Creation by collective intelligence is an effective tactic to harness the pockets of knowledge or skills across your organization. For example, rather than hiring an outside vendor to plan and organize a team conference, solicit involvement from the company crowd:

- Hold a contest to find the best venue for the best value.

- Use a voting mechanism to suggest conference topics and determine the most popular ones.

- Solicit volunteers to organize and lead individual conference sessions on topics they are passionate about, or on which they are experts.

Essentially, "outsource" to the crowd any and all of the tasks individuals across your teams would love to do themselves.

Decision Making   We tend to think about decision making in organizations as a leadership responsibility. An individual may recommend a decision, perhaps after soliciting input from a number of people, but a specific point person is charged with making the final call. Individuals also make decisions on a moment-to-moment basis in their jobs—what they will work on, when, how they will get the project done. Collective intelligence decision making is another tool with incredible power to leverage the diversity of perspectives in the organization. In any given situation, a single individual, regardless of how senior he or she is, has a very limited vantage point. Collective intelligence is the perfect tool for situations in which hundreds, or even thousands, of pairs of eyes are far better than one, for peering around corners and into every nook and cranny of organizational wisdom to make the best choices.

I like to think of this as a search task. Let's say you lose a very important notebook somewhere in your office. Let's also say that your office building is *very big*. Is it better for one person to spend hours and hours searching independently for it, or for everyone to take five seconds to look around their small areas for the notebook? The power of leveraging everyone for an insignificant amount of time is huge—and it can be applied to decision making for your organization.

A great example of leveraging collective intelligence for decision making was Google's cost-cutting initiative in 2009, when I was still with the company. Like every other organization on the planet, Google leaders were worried about the economy. It was a time of mass uncertainty, and the depth of the economic troubles for the global economy was still unknown. So Google made the wise decision to take a look at costs and make some cuts.

Now, from an outsider perspective, there were plenty of obvious ways Google could cut costs; surely, one obvious place to start was "The Perks." It would have been easy for an executive to go through the budget, line by line, and start slashing items from it. But what the leadership team did instead—and remains in my mind as one of the most brilliant moves I saw them make—was to ask the employees for input. After all, it was us, the employees, who had the most to lose from the potential cuts, so who better to suggest where to make them? We were the ones traveling, using the copy machines, benefitting from The Perks. The leadership team realized that by asking employees to take stock of their daily work lives, they could identify opportunities to cut costs, and make suggestions that might not have been evident to the leadership team. And in the end, because the cuts would be based on our suggestions, we wouldn't resent them. Thus, in addition, the leaders would achieve instant buy-in.

To enable the process, the leaders set up a Google Moderator vote; we posted our ideas about opportunities to cut costs, and then voted on those we liked most and, conversely, voted down the ones we objected to most strongly. All of us, individually and collectively, began scanning our environments for potential waste, identifying heretofore little-known opportunities for creating efficiencies, and thereby saving ourselves from cutting costs in the areas we most valued. Hundreds of suggestions poured in, and thousands of votes were cast. Sure enough, Patrick Pichette, Google's CFO, was thrilled with the result.

The employee-driven cost-cutting initiative did, in fact, result in efficiencies in some of The Perks, such as shortening café hours. But the effort preserved the perks most precious to employees, those important for work/life balancing or blending. Moreover, we felt empowered; we knew it was fully within our control to make innovative suggestions about how we might do things differently to save money. In this way, Google employees became responsible stewards of the company.

Collective intelligence decisions can be made through voting (as in Google's cost-cutting initiative) or by averaging (such as the way Netflix and Amazon rate movies and books, respectively). Voting works best when the crowd will be committed to the outcome of the decision. Averages are more useful when the decision involves estimating a numerical factor. For example, NASA used collective intelligence to invite amateurs to study photos of the surface of Mars to identify the position of craters. The agency found that the accuracy of the amateur submissions—the averaged coordinates of the crowd—to be just as accurate as those of the experts.[7] Collective intelligence can also be used to guide future decisions made by individuals in a crowd. For example, publishing the names of the most visited company intranet sites, the best-attended training courses, or the most popular medical insurance providers (if the organization offers a choice) exposes the aggregate of hundreds of individual decisions, which implies greater quality through their popularity.

Motivation to Contribute

A major tenet of collective intelligence is that anyone in the prescribed crowd may contribute. It is a choice, not a mandate. And anyone— everyone—is free to make that choice. The implication is, then, that the choice is compelling enough for people to want to contribute; and this is where a collective intelligence initiative is most apt to fail. If, say, you launch a naming contest for your holiday party, make sure, first, that people actually *care* about the name, and, second, recognize the value in suggesting names.

The MIT Center for Collective Intelligence boils down motivational factors into three broad categories (for the sake of simplicity):[8]

- *Money*: Money talks, and so do points, rewards, and other similar mechanisms.

  Example: InnoCentive is an organization that awards large cash prizes to researchers that submit valid solutions to difficult scientific challenges.

- *Love*: Either the task itself is intrinsically enjoyable, or the task contributes to a noble cause.

  Example: Linux developers contribute to the open-source platform because they are passionate about writing software code, and get intrinsic value out of being part of the community.

- *Glory*: Reputation matters, and individual contributions can be recognized for quality; it is quite motivating to learn whether others think that we are smart.

  Example: Threadless is a T-shirt company whose product line is completely sourced from individuals submitting T-shirt designs. The Threadless customer community votes on the best designs, which are then printed and sold. Having *your* design on a widely produced T-shirt? Priceless.

I would add one more category here: Outcome. If the result of a collective intelligence initiative has teeth, or will significantly impact an individual's world, then that can provide a great deal of motivation. I might not care about the name of my company's holiday party, but I would care whether the company chooses to spend the budget on an open bar or floral centerpieces!

A common myth about motivation is that money is the most powerful motivator. In fact, both love and glory—whether individually or in conjunction with one another—can be surprisingly powerful motivators. Tap into people's passion about their work. Let them contribute to the greater good. Enable the crowd to work together to make beautiful designs or devise smart solutions. Empowerment, in and of itself, is enough to mobilize people to take action, and the collective results are greater than the sum of its parts.

LETTING GO OF CONTROL IN ORGANIZATIONS

Without question, collective intelligence mechanisms are emerging as strong organizational tools; but there is a more general application that applies to the management realm. The main theme in the Work Revolution is empowering individuals and letting go of tight-fisted control to allow people the autonomy to do their work in the best way for them. Grassroots management is at the core of this:

- Instead of rules, use guiding principles.
- Push decision making down to the individuals.
- Focus on individual impact, not activities.

All of these are examples of abdicating control and empowering workers. It is not, however, an easy transition to make, and I am not suggesting it can be done overnight.

Organizations accustomed to functioning according to top-down rules and monitoring carefully to ensure compliance, may find it tricky to let go of the reins. But by following grassroots management principles, it is possible to start small with a defined group, implement a grassroots-inspired initiative, and then replicate success over time, with more and larger groups. This is exactly what CSC, a global IT consulting and services company, did at one of its divisions.

CSC Germany experienced a downturn in 2007 and 2008. The initial response of leaders was to further tighten control, from the top. This only caused them to slide behind even further, so they decided to experiment with a completely new management approach, which they called their no-control experiment.[9] In one 60-person department, they explicitly gave employees the freedom to do their work as they thought it should be done. To help them, management implemented peer coaching groups and fostered a strong knowledge culture, among other things. The turnaround of the division was astounding. In 2009, its results rose sharply, and have continued to rise since then.

CSC expanded on this success by rolling out the approach to another 34-person group at CSC Germany; this group, too, showed marked improvement in productivity. CSC continued to introduce the no-control management style across the organization, one group at a time—grassroots style, if you will. According to A.D. Amar, Carsten Hentrich, and Vlatka Hlupic, in their *Harvard Business Review* article "To Be a Better Leader, Give Up Authority":[10]

> Relaxation of control can benefit any knowledge company, but particularly in certain circumstances: when the organization begins to miss opportunities because it can't understand or respond to market demands; when work is impaired because employees feel excessively pressured and harbor dissatisfaction; and when crises imperil the business.

The benefit of giving up control can permeate every corner of the organization. Not only can it empower employees; it can also bring relief to a multitude of support groups throughout the organization. For example, the IT organization might provide self-service tools to empower individual users to troubleshoot issues and install applications. In this way, approvals processes would no longer be necessary, thus reducing the response time for the myriad tasks individuals need to get done (does management really need to approve the purchase of a $10 stapler?).

While I was on Google's Engineering Education team (engEDU), we made the deliberate decision to give up control of our training programs. In a traditional training department, instructional designers work directly with subject matter experts to capture their expertise on a topic. Instructional designers then develop training classes from this knowledge and, using highly trained facilitators, roll them out as required courses to a predefined audience. We threw out that model almost completely.

engEDU still develops courses, but precious few of them from scratch. Most important, there is no such thing as mandatory training—when engineers need to learn something, they sign up for classes. This shift ensured that engEDU focused on only the most relevant topics for engineers; their presence in classes is an indicator of whether their needs are being met. Further, we pushed training down to the engineers themselves, so that they could teach each other. We stopped trying to be the middlemen in the knowledge economy, and instead developed processes and self-service tools to make it easier for the natural educators and experts in the organization to develop classes and market them to other engineers who might be interested in the topics.

Google has evolved into a true learning organization, one where individuals can participate both as teachers and students, offering any class they might dream up—from building a bicycle wheel to front-end engineering. We never vetoed a class; instead, we let collective intelligence do the curation work. We did, however, publish data to report on the most highly rated classes, the best attended classes, and most recommended classes, which naturally provided social motivation (glory) for the engineering "faculty," as we dubbed them.

For any given initiative at Google, the question always was: "How can we push control down to the individual?" We found, almost without fail, that when individuals have the full set of information about a decision, and they are empowered to make it, they will do the right thing.

It's not just at Google where employees are capable of making sound decisions at the individual level. William Abernathy, in his book *The Sin of Wages: Where the Conventional Pay System Has Led Us and How to Find a Way Out*, gives many examples from his work with manufacturing plants and banks that demonstrate the power of pushing decisions to the individual. For example, he describes a bank's transition to a performance-based pay system.[11] Under the new system, bank tellers would be paid based on results, defined as the ratio of expenses to the number of items they processed. *Float* was a significant part of the expense the bank tellers were directly responsible for controlling. However, they had no idea what float was, despite the fact that each of them was an experienced teller; management had never bothered to explain the concept to them! Essentially, float represents the interest banks charge each other to carry debt when a customer cashes a check from another bank. The faster tellers can process deposits, the lesser the expense to the bank. When the bank tellers learned this, they were shocked: "We thought the bank wanted these checks processed quickly just to reduce overtime!"

Within an hour under the new system, the bank tellers had figured out how to prioritize high-dollar checks for processing and how to reroute courier pickups to minimize delays.

Leaders Fostering Diversity

If grassroots management is important to the future of organizations, leaders will play a critical role in starting the trend. The role of the leader is to foster productive conflict, while serving as an active "miner" of individual and collective intelligence.

Leaders as Debate Facilitators   One of the conditions of collective intelligence systems is that the participants be independent and diverse, free from biases that might produce homogenous decisions or opinions. The reason collective intelligence works is because of this diversity. Each individual brings a different set of perspectives, information, and experiences to inform his or her decision, and the aggregate of the diversity results in a hyperinformed decision.

It thus falls to leaders to form teams and hire individuals that are intentionally diverse. As Jonathan Rosenberg, a former Google executive, once said: "If both of us agree, one of us is redundant." The more diversity you have on a team, the more certain you can be that individual members will debate a full spectrum of ideas, which is critical for thinking through all of the implications of a decision.

Of course, on a highly diverse team, by its very definition, members will disagree—a lot. And disagreement is something most of us shy away from. In general, we like harmony and agreement. It makes us feel good. Nevertheless, we have to learn to disagree effectively.

Patrick Lencioni talks about this in his book *The Five Dysfunctions of a Team*. He cites "fear of conflict" as one of the five dysfunctions, which shows up as artificial harmony on a team. As he puts it, "I don't think anyone ever gets completely used to conflict. If it's not a little uncomfortable, then it's not real. The key is to keep doing it anyway."[12] The sign of a healthy team is one in which constructive conflict is not only accepted; it is the norm. When individuals feel free to voice their concerns, ideas, and opinions, you know you've built up a strong team.

The job of the leader is to create a safe, trusting environment, and to encourage individuals to hash things out in a productive and respectful way. As a leader, your role is to condition people to become tolerant of disagreement, by giving them the skills to navigate disagreement constructively. This requires:

- Teaching people to focus on issues, not personalities. It's okay to debate issues. It is not okay to label individuals, in any way— as pig-headed, obstinate, or "wrong." It's the issues, people.

- Encouraging strong individuals to listen more, and more introverted individuals to speak up. Everyone must have a voice.

- Focusing debate so that it moves forward, rather than devolving into an endless cycle of rehashing.

When I managed the "Team team," at Google I would constantly scan everyone in every meeting, looking for signs of frustration or holding back. If I sensed someone had something to say but wasn't saying it, I'd ask for her opinion. If I knew someone disagreed with a statement, I'd ask him to state a counteropinion. If one person responded in anger, or emotionally, to what another person said, I'd ask the first individual to refocus and restate the issue of the disagreement. I didn't so much as lead the meetings as I worked actively to make sure everyone was voicing their opinions and perspectives, to safeguard against getting tripped up on personal issues.

This process takes practice, yes, but if you serve as a leader in any capacity, developing this skill will enable you to build a highly effective team, whose members all are empowered to think critically.

Leaders as Intelligence Multipliers   "There is more intelligence than is visible to the naked eye [in organizations] . . . ; the organizations that can access the *most brains* will win," write Liz Wiseman and Greg McKeown in their book *Multipliers: How the Best Leaders Make Everyone Smarter.*[13] They make the connection between the collective intelligence in our organizations and the leaders who capitalize on it. They also articulate the difference between the leaders who thrive in this context and the ones who insist on wringing every bit of excitement from each and every employee who crosses their path.

Wiseman and McKeown define *multipliers* as the leaders who bring out the genius in each individual, and draw out the wisdom of the crowds from every team. These leaders:

- Attract talented individuals to their teams and maximize their full potential.

- Liberate individuals while simultaneously challenging them to do their best work.

- Drive rigorous debate to arrive at the best decisions (sound familiar?).

- Invest in individuals by giving them ownership and holding them accountable for results.

In short, multipliers do just that—they multiply the intelligence of individuals so the sum is greater than the parts, to the tune of two times. For example, every time I met with Maggie Johnson, the director of Google's engEDU, she challenged me to think at a completely different level; at the same time, she also found ways to validate and draw out my knowledge and expertise. Maintaining this balance should be the ultimate goal for managers.

Diminishers, in contrast, are managers who staunchly believe their employees won't be able to figure things out on their own, without the advanced wisdom and knowledge of "higher-ups." They act as a metaphorical black hole, sucking away the intelligence of the team, by as much as 50 percent. In particular, they:

- Hoard talent, but also manage to underutilize individuals at the same time.

- Create tension in the environment, which serves to diminish people's ability to do their best thinking.

- Act as know-it-alls (which I refer to as KIAs), who manage by handing out directives.

- Make authoritative decisions that lack consistency.

- Micromanage team members, pushing to get results through their direct involvement.

Diminishers are more common in top-down environments, though they certainly can show up in grassroots organizations, as well (where, typically, they don't last long). Multipliers, in stark contrast, embody the definition of leaders who are best suited to head our highly educated workforce. They foster empowerment and autonomy, as well as productive conflict and inspiration, for great performance.

How can you learn to act as a multiplier? The most direct way is to ask a lot of questions. Solicit answers from individuals; challenge them to propose solutions. Ask the right questions to help them get there (remember the "Ask, Don't Tell" management style described in Chapter 4, "Impact, Not Activities"). If a team member asks, "What should we do in X situation?" answer by asking: "What do you think we should do? What are our alternatives? How would you weigh them?" Telling people what to do may be the most direct decision-making route, but asking people what they would do is the most direct route to harnessing collective intelligence.

INDIVIDUALS INSPIRING DIFFERENTIATION

What if you work in a top-down organization? What if your manager is a diminisher? And what if your team is made up of individuals who are afraid to speak up? You still have "response-ability." You still have room to help create an environment in which you can personally thrive. I'm talking about grassroots movements, in which grassroots groups are the new employee unions. Grassroots movements generate excitement, give people an individuated voice, and prompt action to make change.

There is incredible power in being the employee who steps up, even quietly and with the utmost respect, to start a movement. Maybe you attempt to improve the copy machine situation, to end the cycle of it breaking down every two days. You troubleshoot the maintenance issues and, ultimately, convince the vendor to replace the damn thing once and for all. Maybe you lobby for a new coffee supplier, because the current brew is so weak it could be pawned off as drinking water in a third-world country. Maybe you convince management to get rid of the TPS forms because, in reality, they serve no real function except to annoy both managers and employees.

Pick an issue, any issue, about which you are passionate. Then, fix it. It really is that simple.

Grassroots initiatives will achieve several goals at once:

- They will fix problems for which solutions didn't magically appear until this point.

- They will show that you are capable of both ideas and execution; and managers will look at you in a new light—the leadership light.

- They will inspire other individuals to start their own grassroots movements, to, say, fix the toilet that is causing recurring nightmares for everyone.

Think management will shun your efforts? Perhaps. But if you undertake a movement because you really believe in it, and it brings real value to individuals in your organization, it's a win-win situation: You will feel empowered, and you will start to find other ways to make a difference in your personal work situation.

Beyond that, starting small and watching movements grow virally is very twenty-first century. You never know what the reactions will be to your courageous actions; you just might be surprised. The worst-case scenario is that you realize, well ahead of your peers, that you are on a sinking ship and it's time to get off and board a new one.

SUMMARY

Grassroots, not top-down is the principle of empowering individuals at the bottom, rather than dictating to them from the top (see Table 8.1). It involves embracing smallness and imperfection, to create an environment of scrappiness, agility, and innovation. Grassroots initiatives let great ideas take root and then grow organically over time, to become big.

Table 8.1   Summary of Grassroots, Not Top-Down, Guidelines for Organizations, Leaders, and Individuals

Organizations	Empower every individual to contribute and test ideas; pick the best ideas through trial, not judgment.
	Invest in systems that make it easy to test and measure everything.
	Start small—really small—with any new initiative and product.
	Apply collective intelligence to organizational problem solving, decision making, and creation.
Leaders	Build teams to create true diversity of thought and perspective.
	Empower individuals to make decisions by teaching them how the business operates.
	Foster productive debate within teams.
	Act as a multiplier, not a diminisher, of your team's intelligence.
	Ask questions to help solve problems; don't direct the solutions.
Individuals	Find creative ways to test your ideas quickly. Learn the art of pretotyping.
	Kick-start grassroots movements for issues you are passionate about.
	Take initiative to fix what's broken in your organization.
Everyone	Apply the Apollo 13 challenge to organizational problem solving.
	Embrace mistakes, failure, and imperfection.

CHAPTER 9

Conclusion

During my tenure at Google, I facilitated numerous team-building sessions with groups across the organization, to help them become more effective and, ultimately, get along better. Sometimes, we would bump up against a long-standing issue, which became known as the "pink elephant" (the "elephant in the room" being the classic metaphor for an issue that everyone sees clearly but no one talks about). At Google, we colored the elephant pink to emphasize the ridiculousness of ignoring the very thing that was looming large in a team's environment.

True to my organizational development roots, in this book, I have attempted to describe current work environments, paint the ideal future state, and share tactics and strategies to bridge the gap between them. But I, too, have danced around a big pink elephant: fear.

Nothing energizes me like inspiring a conference audience with tales from the Google culture. They sit wide-eyed; incredulous. Of course, they ask a lot of questions, especially about The Perks. Some walk away feeling envious; others, hopeless, realizing there is not a chance on the planet such concepts will fly at their organizations.

I hear their objections and the what-ifs. And not just from the managers or leaders of these organizations, but from the frontline employees, too. Behind all of their objections looms the fear. Everyone is fearful of the unknown, even as much as they fantasize about working in a wonderland like Google. What I have come to realize is these fears are based on a few simple things—which is *not* to say that they are irrational. The fears are real; but they *can* be faced, and managed, which ultimately defuses their power.

FEARS OF LEADERS

In a command-and-control organization, the one crutch leaders can lean on is certainty. Although business results cannot be certain, since they are based on many factors both within and outside of the control of the organization, the path leading toward the results *can* be laid out, inch by inch. That is why leaders detail who will do what, how, and by when, to get expected results. They define when people will show up for work, how many hours they are expected to be there, and when they can leave. They calculate how much sick time and vacation time to deduct from expected productivity. Likewise, they factor in every decision that is made, and forecast results. So for me to suggest that leaders relinquish all of this control is, understandably, not the most welcome advice. When I recommend to leaders to stop telling people what to do, I expect their response will be: "If I don't tell people what to do, then what *do* I do?" Their fear: irrelevance.

To address this fear, let me first clarify what are *not* intended outcomes of the Work Revolution:

- That employees act like prima donnas, showing up to work at random times, doing only the work that fits with their chosen passions, having three-martini lunches, and going home at 4:00.

- That they make conflicting decisions about products or services, or do nothing at all; that their sense of urgency becomes as extinct as the dinosaurs.

- That profits start to swirl down the drain as expense reports flow in, full of outrageous claims employees justify based on their "empowerment."

- That no one is willing to do the grunt work, or jump in to tackle the less glamorous tasks, because they're not in line with anyone's strengths.

Let me be crystal clear: I'm not advocating for anarchy. I say this because, often, when I describe the work practices at Google, many people immediately conjure up images of employees running around dressed like slobs, gobbling the free food, and doing no "real" work at all. Nothing could be further from the truth. My experience at Google and similar organizations is that the freer employees are, the harder they work. And the more accountable they are for their results and impact, the more serious they are about adhering to priorities and meeting the needs of customers/users. Finally, let me say this: Managers are *never* irrelevant.

FEARS OF INDIVIDUALS

It's obvious why organizational leaders might have fears around the Work Revolution. But you might think that individuals in the organization feel they have everything to gain and nothing to lose in the Work Revolution. Right?

Wrong.

Individual contributors are just as fearful as leaders when it comes to making drastic changes. For starters, individuals in a typical command-and-control system tend to homogenize, to become indistinguishable and interchangeable with one another, as Barry Oshry explains in his book, *Seeing Systems: Unlocking the Mysteries of Organizational Life*.[1] The system is such that peers punish any kind of differentiation or individual excellence. They are pressured to band together, work just hard enough (but not too hard), and stick it out as the "Bottoms," which ultimately translates to bargaining power, the only tangible form of power at that level of a hierarchical organization.

Now, just for the sake of argument, let's say that an individual is strong enough to stand up to her peers; she decides to take the initiative to start a grassroots campaign of one sort or another. In this scenario, she is opening herself up to a long list of risks:

- Risk of being seen as insubordinate, by taking action where managers didn't have the will or foresight to do so.

- Risk of stepping on toes, by taking action where another individual dropped his or her responsibilities.

- Risk of making a mistake; if the initiative fails, it's a very public form of failure.

- Risk of being as accused of shirking core job responsibilities; if she is spending time on this initiative, she has to be short-changing her prescribed job responsibilities.

Any individual who asks *why* one too many times, quits a project because he knows it is low-value, insists on work that complements his strengths, or launches a new project because the manager didn't agree with the opportunity, stands to *lose his job*.

That's right—by standing up for a Work Revolution, individuals are potentially putting their livelihood on the line.

It's the System, Stupid

The problem is that people imagine implementing the Work Revolution concepts and principles within their current system. In other words, if you take the *energy, not schedules* principle and plop it in the middle of an organization that retains its command-and-control management practices, I guarantee that their worst fears will be realized. Here are three examples.

Example 1: You choose to launch a survey to capture grassroots sentiment about how employees are feeling, and promise that employee-driven action committees will make changes based on the results.

Result: The survey says that employees are miserable; the action committee votes to enact a set of policies to expand vacation time and eliminate timesheets.

Fallout: Management has the (proper) foresight to understand what a train wreck this will be, so they spend the next year diffusing the tension caused by unleashing the pessimism of the employees, and smoothing over the fact that the employee-driven action committee was disassembled just four weeks after its inception.

Moral: Grassroots initiatives implemented in a system where employees don't understand the mission of the organization, where they are not held accountable for results, and where they have no measures of impact, are bound to fail.

Example 2: Your organization decides to embrace the individual- strengths principle and launches a full campaign to identify strengths, and then empower individuals to find the work that aligns with their strengths and say no to work that doesn't.

> *Result*: Individuals flock to the sexy projects in the organization, dropping critical responsibilities that drive revenue for the company; no one is left to do the grunt work that keeps the organization afloat. Or, everyone quits, because they realize how unfulfilled they are in their current roles.

> *Moral*: The strengths-based work principle only functions when you have people who care deeply about the mission of the organization and are willing to band together to find the *best* fit for responsibilities, given what needs to be done. Start first with the right people, and then figure out how to help them find their best roles in the company.

Any objections to the principles described in this book will be based entirely on a failure to imagine—to conceptualize a different kind of work system. For example, maybe you start by adopting the *strengths, not job slots* principle to get the right people on board, who believe passionately in your organizational mission. Then, if you implement *impact, not activities*, you will set the precedent of caring *most* about results and rewarding individuals who create impact. Next, you can implement systems to support *energy, not schedules*, and *grassroots, not top-down*, once you are sure you have the proper rewards system in place. Finally, everyone will be motivated to do the *right things, not everything*, because they are empowered to balance their own workloads and figure out what is best for the organization. The point is, the Work Revolution principles can't be picked up wholesale and then plopped down into a traditional work system. They must be paired and linked properly, to ensure people are motivated by the right things, and understand what the organization is trying to accomplish overall.

Unfortunately, I cannot state categorically which principle to implement first at any organization. It is very much dependent on each individual organization; which areas in it need the most help. (Refer back to Chapter 2 to help diagnose yours.) What I do recommend is that you find ways to start small—whether as an employee or leader—to implement changes grassroots-style. See what works, and build on success.

TRUST VERSUS FEAR

Trust is the antidote to fear. When you fear, you can't trust. If you fear that employees won't make sound decisions, you won't trust them to do so, and you'll feel the need to check up on every decision they make, thereby undermining any autonomy you might have granted them. If you fear that your employer will take advantage of you at every turn, you won't be generous with your time and contributions. In both of these cases, you can see how the cycle starts and perpetuates. If a leader always second-guesses or checks up on your decisions, you'll mistrust the leader and, over time, begin to take less initiative. When you take less initiative, the leader will label you as a "cruiser"—someone not motivated to step up. And the cycle is put in motion.

The question then becomes: Why can't you trust? Is the fear legitimate? Or is the fear and mistrust based on assumptions you are making that may not be true?

Some Reasons to Trust

You may very well have leaders and coworkers in your organization who should not be trusted, but I will posit that the vast majority are honorable, noble, and eager to do great work. (And for those who are not, why are they still employed at your organization?) My optimism about the good intentions of people isn't unfounded. You don't have to look far to find compelling reasons to trust. Just keep reading.

Reason 1: We can find meaning in just about anything.

Proof: Farmville, Sim City

Relation to Work: For some reason, we have this grand assumption that people can't possibly find meaning from work unless they are doctors saving lives, lawyers getting innocent people out of jail, or teachers helping children learn how to read. Online games such as Farmville or Sim City offer iron-clad proof that *this is not true*. We can find meaning in everything we do; indeed, we subscribe meaning to things that have absolutely no meaning (e.g, superstitious behavior)! So if we take the extra step daily in our roles at work to articulate the meaning of what we are doing, and what we are asking others to do, we are providing instant gratification.

When we shift to focus on the meaning of our jobs and work tasks, we start caring about the details, and we realize that the details matter. And when individuals throughout your organization understand and care about the meaning of what they are doing, they will do everything in their power to harvest crops and gift zebra unicorns to each other.

Reason 2: People like to win, or to root for the winning team.

Proof: Sports of all kinds—football, baseball, basketball, sloshball …

Relation to Work: In the end, business is really about winning. Points are tallied (e.g., stock price), bets are placed (e.g., investments), and payouts are given (e.g., bonuses). Competing organizations are like college football rivalries. People are capable of investing a lot of energy, time, and emotion into sports, so why not generate the same level of energy at work, around our businesses? The problem with our current organizations is that we often hide or disguise the points; we haven't found effective ways of rallying the team; and we've forgotten to have pep talks.

Reason 3: Problem solving and strategizing are fun!

Proof: Board games, scavenger hunts, crossword puzzles, brainteasers, riddles

Relation to Work: Chess wouldn't be nearly as fun if the only thing you could do was move the pieces around on the board according to the instructions of someone standing behind you. People clearly love to solve puzzles, tackle problems, and come up with solutions. It's no coincidence that I've never found a team that dislikes brainstorming. We love thinking about possibilities and imagining a grander vision, as well as how we might go about achieving the vision. We have so much opportunity to engage everyone in our organizations, to solve tangible problems and think about innovative solutions; they are more than eager to do so. After all, browsing Facebook is only interesting for about an hour, before we're ready to do something *real.*

Reason 4: It's not much fun being a parent, but the rewards of being a mother or father are countless.

Proof: We keep having babies.

Relation to Work: We don't have children because we enjoy changing their diapers, disciplining them, or telling them to clean their rooms. We have children because it gives us joy to watch them learn to do things on their own, blossom into their own people, and grow up to do exciting things. We have children because of the relationships we have with them, which continue to grow, and because of the positive impact we hope we can have on their lives.

Similarly, when a leader becomes more of a mentor—someone to help individuals grow, find their strengths, learn new things, and expand their capabilities to contribute—great things happen. It's no fun to show up to work, tell people what to do, and then nag them until they get things done. Fortunately, it doesn't have to be this way; as it turns out, employees are already adults. They don't need parents; they need leaders who care about them as unique individuals, and can see their potential.

What Success Looks Like

When we ditch the old rules and start to conduct business in a new way, what becomes obvious is that we've been torturing ourselves unnecessarily for decades. We've lived under the assumption that since work is a necessity, it must be drudgery. As you have seen in the examples throughout this book, there is a better way.

I choose to believe that people, in the main, are inherently interested in doing a good job and making a powerful and positive impact. Humans are uniquely and remarkably capable of finding meaning in almost anything; so why do we so often think it is impossible for employees to find meaning and happiness in their work?

We all have the opportunity to get this right. In the world I want to create, here's what work looks like:

- We all know what we're working toward, and we each play a unique and distinct role in making that happen. We each feel important, because we are bringing our individual strengths to the table.

- We learn to respond to our natural rhythms. When we feel run down, we take recovery time, and others jump in to help us out. When we are energized and strong, we push hard and put in everything we've got to get the job done.

- Healthy individuals translate to healthy organizations. When individuals take care of themselves, the indisputable result is strong organizational performance.

- We learn to distinguish between what matters and what doesn't, and we get really good at challenging each other to figure this out.

- Our sense of urgency is based on real deadlines, rather than someone's arbitrary project plan. We do work when it *really* needs to be done. If there's no True Urgency, then maybe it's not that important!

- Most important, individuals are rewarded based on the value they bring to an organization. In turn, organizations are successful when they reward the verifiable contributions of individuals.

Beyond this, I envision a world in which rush hour is a relic of the past, because the 9-to-5 workday has been abandoned like a tapped-out gold mine in the middle of the wilderness. I envision prosperity on a global scale, as never before in history, and a world where the boundaries of geographical space and time zones are meaningless. I envision rates of heart disease and addiction plummeting, since they were caused in large part by the learned helplessness of working in hopeless job environments.

Perhaps more simply, I envision a time when we no longer dread Sunday nights, because work is not dreadful anymore, and the weekends no longer serve as the delineation between work and play. When we are all free to volunteer on a Monday morning at our children's school library, or work out on a Wednesday afternoon to train for an upcoming triathlon, all the while knowing we are contributing in our own way and in our own time to create excellence in our organizations, then we will be living the dream of the Work Revolution.

EPILOGUE

When I made the life-changing decision to leave Google, move to New York, start a new job, *and* write a book, I knew it wasn't exactly a "sane" thing to do, that it might lead to "major burnout" and potential "work/life imbalance" (as Chris Farley's *Saturday Night Live* character, Bennett Brauer, might have expressed it). During one of the last conversations I had with Maggie Johnson, my wonderfully supportive manager at Google, who seems to magically handle about a billion responsibilities flawlessly (there aren't enough adjectives to describe her brilliance), she said simply: "I would never let you do this, you know." Of course, she didn't *really* mean she wouldn't let me write the book. She was referring to the fact that I was absolutely nuts to take on so much at one time.

However, I found the challenge to be just what I needed to bring clarity to the concepts in the Work Revolution. If I had any hope of finishing the book, and making it worth the read, I had to live and breathe every one of the principles I was promoting in it, religiously.

To accomplish what I needed to do, I embarked on a continuous process of challenging my assumptions, refining my work relationships, noticing my energy patterns, and making tough choices about how to spend my time. Given I wanted to make a great first impression at my new job, this was especially daunting, as I came face-to-face with all of my demons related to work expectations, both real and perceived. But as I came to realize, my biggest demon was me—the pressure I put on myself and the concern I had about what other people might be thinking (but probably were not).

In the end, I wrote the book (obviously) and I still have my job. But I learned a lot of important lessons along the way, which I share here, in terms of the principles I've "preached" throughout the book.

Grassroots, Not Top-Down

The process of finding a publisher most definitely requires starting small, testing, and letting the ideas grow. I tested my initial ideas for this book on my friends and family, in conversations about Google. I tested it at a gut level, too; I felt the fire of passion burn around the topic, and when I tried to brush away the idea of writing the book, it would inevitably pop back up in one way or another. Ultimately, I couldn't suppress these ideas, so I started speaking about them at conferences, where the audience reaction was hugely positive— another good indicator I was on to something. Finally, I wrote the book proposal—the final test—and floated it by prospective agents and John Wiley & Sons, Inc. I didn't actually start writing the book until I got the contract with Wiley, which was the clearest sign that this book was the right thing for me.

The Right Things, Not Everything

I had to give up a lot to write this book. I couldn't juggle everything I fit in to my normal pre-book life; I had to make hard choices about what was most important to me. I stopped watching TV and movies. I'm at least a full year behind on any subject related to popular culture. During this period, I relied completely on *The Week Magazine* to deliver all of the important national and international news to me; I simply couldn't keep up with it on a daily basis. This proved to be a bit problematic when I moved to New York and had to wait for my forwarded mail to arrive from California. It meant I was receiving *The Week* (and therefore important news) about three weeks behind schedule. Typical conversation at the time:

> Me: Gaddafi is dead?!
> Companion (giving
> me a hard stare):   Seriously? Where have *you* been?

I managed to continue exercising, but I did downgrade my goal of completing a Half Ironman to entering an Olympic distance triathlon. By exercising, I was able to keep up my energy, so doing it was important, even when it felt like it took precious time out of my days.

At work, I focused strictly on the most important projects, and didn't overreach in an attempt to do everything. This was extraordinarily hard for me, since my weakness is to take on too much and do too many things at once, but the book taught me to prioritize ruthlessly.

ENERGY, NOT SCHEDULES

In the first few weeks at my new job, I showed up early and stayed late. I wanted to get a huge jump-start on my work and prove myself. Soon enough however, my energy level crashed; as I said before, I'm one of those people who don't function well before 9:00 AM, unless I trick my body with jet lag by flying to the opposite side of the world. Consequently, I stopped going in to work early and finally settled into a schedule that coordinated with my rivers of energy. I started showing up 10:00-ish and worked however late I needed, to get the work done; and I stopped worrying whether the people around me were judging me.

I also learned that my best book-writing time was on the weekends. I found I couldn't spend a full day at work and still muster the energy to write at night during the week. So I used week nights to exercise, have dinners with friends, and do most of my socializing. This is how I created the recovery cycles I needed, and I felt less inclined to go out on the weekends when I really needed to be writing.

STRENGTHS, NOT JOB SLOTS

I took the job in New York because I really love the people at my company and I believe in the mission. And because I felt a sense of belonging there, I knew it was the right place for me, and that I would somehow figure out how to do my job and keep up with my writing. Sure enough, my manager and teammates embraced the fact I was writing a book, and in time it felt completely natural to be doing both at the same time.

Further, I knew my strengths were perfectly aligned with the role I had accepted; or, more accurately, were well-suited to meet the challenges I was now facing. I knew I would be intrinsically excited about the projects I was asked to take on, which enabled me to tolerate the pressures of the job during the writing process.

On the book-writing front, I took Maggie's advice and got some help. Sarah Bloomfield, whom I once managed at Google (she is a rising superstar in her own right), agreed to take on a role as my thought partner. She served, essentially, as my second brain, expanding my ideas in important ways; and her strengths complemented my own. I was also lucky that my best friend and roommate, Jenny Blake, had published her book the previous year. Jenny's strength is her "big thinking," and was key in helping me move my book from proposal to manuscript and then out to market. Who could complain about having a life coach as a roommate? As a team of one (i.e., a sole author on a book), I learned the importance of reaching out to my network to fill in the holes around my strengths.

IMPACT, NOT ACTIVITIES

I reduced everything in my life down by answering the question: How important is this activity to my sanity/happiness/energy/overall impact? I had no room to cave in to social pressures or to do things that didn't make sense for me. Sometimes, it is a true blessing to be forced to make the hard choices; it creates clarity.

PUTTING IT ALL TOGETHER

The final lesson I learned is that I will never completely figure it all out. My needs will change, my energy cycles will evolve, and I'll learn more about my strengths and what I love most in life. Figuring these things out is a nonstop iterative loop, both for ourselves and for the organizations where we choose to work.

In Joseph Galliano's book *Dear Me: A Letter to My Sixteen-Year-Old Self*, he quotes Hugh Jackman giving his younger self this advice:[1]

Keep writing down one list—and one list only—the 5 things you love to do, and the 5 things you are good at . . . [T]hey will keep changing, but one day they will match up . . . and there is your path. . . . But even then keep writing your list just to make sure you are still on the right track.

I love you.

—From YOU!

P.S. Buy shares in Google when they are invented!!!!!!

The Work Revolution Compendium

This compendium is intended to serve as a summarized reference of all the concrete steps individuals, leaders, and organizations can take to jump-start the Work Revolution. In it I include essential resources, those that shaped my thinking about these ideas and forever changed the way I see the world. I encourage you to use them to learn more about the guiding principles and actions I have laid out in *The Work Revolution: Freedom and Excellence for All*, so that they come to life for you, and in your organization.

UNIVERSAL PRINCIPLES

The Universal Principles represent the underlying philosophical shifts we need to make as prerequisites to starting the Work Revolution. These principles suggest we radically alter our work relationships, and get a new attitude for thinking about how to approach problem solving.

- Focus on the value, and all else will follow.

- Redefine what work looks like.

- Embrace mistakes, failure, and imperfection.

- Be kindly honest, not passive aggressive.

- Apply the Apollo 13 challenge to organizational problem solving.

Organizations

Table A.1　Guiding Principles for Organizations

Principle	Major Idea
Impact, Not Activities	Focus on the impact of individuals and teams; drop all rules, policies, and processes fixated on activities alone.
Energy, Not Schedules	Define True Urgency, and enable teams and individuals to pivot their schedules around this determination, to best suit their energy needs.
Strengths, Not Job Slots	Hire people who belong in your organization, and create fluidity to enable them to find their true home within it.
The Right Things, Not Everything	Define the scope of your organization in terms of which opportunities you will pursue and which you will reject.
Grassroots, Not Top-down	Tap into the collective intelligence of every individual in the organization to solve problems and make decisions.

Lay the Foundation

- Develop a problem-based mission statement.

- Articulate the character of your organizational culture—the personality of the collective; how things get done.

- Develop a strategy statement that defines what is in, and out of, scope for the organization.

- Develop a robust set of guiding principles that inform decision making at every level of the organization.

Build Guideposts and Supporting Infrastructure

- Define measures of success that show the connection between efforts and results.

- Invest in systems that make it easy to test and measure everything.

- Ditch all the policies and rules that focus on activities and are disconnected from results.

- Create workspaces and implement perks that enable individuals to recharge.

- Invest in automation to eliminate repetitive, boring work.

Empower Your Workforce

- Align products and initiatives with natural channels of behavior.

- Eliminate bureaucracy and bad managers.

- Build cultural-belonging assessments into the hiring process.

- Ensure liquidity between roles and teams so that individuals can find their true organizational homes.

- Empower every individual to contribute and test ideas; pick the best ideas through trial, not judgment.

- Start small and stay scrappy as you test any new initiative or product.

- Apply collective intelligence to organizational problem solving, decision making, and creation.

Essential Resources

Books

Good to Great: Why Some Companies Make the Leap—and Others Don't, by Jim Collins (London: Random House Business, 2001). Collins's hedgehog concept is a great place to start to build a problem-based mission statement.

Great by Choice: Uncertainty, Chaos, and Luck—Why Some Thrive Despite Them All, also by Jim Collins and Morten T. Hansen (New York: Harper Business, 2011). His focus on discipline is spot-on; and "fire bullets, then cannons" nails the concept of starting small, grassroots-style.

The Wisdom of Crowds: Why the Many Are Smarter Than the Few, by James Surowiecki (London: Abacus, 2006). The original book to unlock the magic behind collective intelligence.

The Sin of Wages: Where the Conventional Pay System Has Led Us and How to Find a Way Out, by William Abernathy (PerfSys Press, 1996). An eye-opener, chockful of interesting examples and concrete strategies for focusing on impact, not activities.

Oops! 13 Management Practices That Waste Time & Money (and What to Do Instead), by Aubrey Daniels (Atlanta: Performance Management Publications, 2009). Serves as a great tool to uncover bureaucracy in your organizations, and provides alternative strategies focused on impact and results.

Unlock Behavior, Unleash Profits, by Leslie Wilk Braksick (New York: McGraw-Hill, 2007). Provides a framework for identifying behavior channels, as well as actionable models for changing behavior and focusing on results.

Seeing Systems: Unlocking the Mysteries of Organizational Life, by Barry Oshry (San Francisco: Berrett-Koehler Publishers, 2007). Takes you on a journey through the systems at work in our organizations that drive behavior in predictably dysfunctional ways, as well as what you can do about it.

Articles

"Can You Say What Your Strategy Is?" by David Collis and Michael Rukstad (*Harvard Business Review*, April 2008, pg. 82–90). If you read only one article about strategy, let this be the one. It is the canonical how-to for creating a strategy statement. Pure gold.

"Harnessing Crowds: Mapping the Genome of Collective Intelligence," by Thomas Malone, Robert Laubacher, and Chrysanthos Dellarocas (available from http://papers.ssrn.com/sol3/papers.cfm?abstract_id=1381502). Deconstructs collective intelligence to make it an accessible tool for any organization.

Tool

Organizational Culture Assessment Instrument (available at www.ocai-online .com). An online assessment that gives you insight into your current organizational culture. Free for individuals.

Leaders

Table A.2   Guiding Principles for Leaders

Principle	Major Idea
Impact, Not Activities	Set the target, define the measures, and focus the team on impact.
Energy, Not Schedules	Define the truly urgent work, and harness the energy channels of individuals around it.
Strengths, Not Job Slots	Build out teams with a diversity of strengths, and allocate roles that align with individual strengths.
The Right Things, Not Everything	Define the prioritization lenses that are most important to each team.
Grassroots, Not Top-Down	Bring an Apollo 13, test-everything approach to every idea, and let the best ideas win.

Build the Team

- Assess the strengths in your team.

- Fill team roles by focusing on diversity of strengths, thoughts, and perspectives.

Point the Team in the Right Direction and Set Them Free

- Define the vision for the team; specify what you are trying to achieve.

- Ask a lot of questions to figure out *what* to do, then set people free to figure out *how*.

- Select and relentlessly communicate prioritization lenses that are relevant to the team.

- Highlight True Urgency projects and deadlines.

- Allocate work based on strengths alignment.

- Empower workgroups to coordinate the best working schedules for team members.

- Encourage teamwork to tackle highest-priority projects jointly, to execute and launch them quickly.

- Foster constructive debate within teams.

Nurture Independent Thinking

- Teach individuals to think strategically about their work.

- Give frequent feedback on the impact of people's work.

- Empower individuals to make decisions by teaching them how the business operates.

- Act as a multiplier, not a diminisher, of your team's intelligence.

- Ask questions to help solve problems; don't direct the solutions.

Essential Resources

Books

Measure of a Leader: An Actionable Formula for Legendary Leadership, by Aubrey Daniels and James Daniels (Atlanta: Performance Management

Publications, 2005). Tackles the notion of leadership, resulting in a truly pragmatic, operational definition.

Managing Without Supervising: Creating an Organization-wide Performance System, by William Abernathy (PerfSys Press, 2000). Describes a radically different way of management, dubbed the Total Performance System (TPS; not to be confused with TPS reports).

Strengths-Based Leadership: Great Leaders, Teams, and Why People Follow, by Tom Rath and Barry Conchie (New York: Gallup Press, 2008). How do you create diversity in your teams? Using the four quadrants of leadership styles is an excellent way to begin; and the approach aligns nicely with StrengthsFinder 2.0 for individuals.

Multipliers: How the Best Leaders Make Everyone Smarter, by Liz Wiseman and Greg McKeown (New York: HarperBusiness, 2010). There are good managers and bad ones, and this book draws the distinctions in a new way, by looking through the lens of collective intelligence. Better yet, Wiseman and McKeown highlight strategies to help you become a good one.

Bringing Out the Best in People, by Aubrey Daniels (New York: McGraw-Hill, 1999). Yes, another Daniels book; this one is a classic. Lays out, in easily applicable ways, the behavioral science behind effective management.

Quiet Leadership: Six Steps to Transforming Performance at Work, by David Rock (New York: HarperBusiness, 2007). He explains how to nurture independent thinking.

The Five Dysfunctions of a Team: A Leadership Fable, by Patrick Lencioni (San Francisco: Jossey-Bass, 2002). This is absolutely the best depiction of productive conflict; the other four concepts are good, too.

Individuals

Table A.3   Guiding Principles for Individuals

Principle	Major Idea
Impact, Not Activities	Articulate the potential impact of everything you do, and show the impact of your work.
Energy, Not Schedules	Learn your natural cycles of energy and how to work smart within them.
Strengths, Not Job Slots	Highlight your strengths, and seek work that aligns with them.
The Right Things, Not Everything	Consistently apply prioritization lenses to eliminate the lowest-priority work and elevate the highest-priority projects.
Grassroots, Not Top-Down	Initiate change; start grassroots movements for issues you are passionate about.

Define Your Sweet Spots

- Get clear on your energy cycles—when you work best and when you shouldn't work at all.

- Advertise your morning or night "handicap" and negotiate a work schedule that flows with your river of energy.

- Define your strengths through self-observation and assessments.

- Share your strengths with your manager and leads.

Force Clarity around Your Work

- Ask why? Then ask why again? Or ask: "What problem are we trying to solve?"

- Give each other permission to "call bullshit"—question the importance and reason behind everything.

- Pay attention to your gut signals regarding low-value work.

- Use the shackles test to prioritize important work.

Take Control Over Your Work Life

- Say no to everything and yes to the right things by relentlessly prioritizing.

- Learn to be a quitter—to quit the wrong things.

- Take initiative to fix things that are broken in your organization.

- Find creative ways to test your ideas quickly. Learn the art of pretotyping.

- Schedule recovery time after cycles of hard work—each day and for longer-term projects.

- Ditch the guilt around ditching work that doesn't work for you.

Essential Resources

Books

Finding Your Own North Star: How to Claim the Life You Were Meant to Live, by Martha Beck (London: Piatkus, 2001). We all need to relearn who we are, at our core. Reading this is book is the best way to start. If it works for you, then continue on with Beck's *Steering by Starlight*.

Conscious Business: How to Build Value Through Values, by Fred Kofman (Boulder: Sounds True, 2006). I was lucky enough to work in Google's sales organization when Sheryl Sandberg led it, and she insisted that everyone in the organization learn the principles described in this book. It was pure organizational magic; it created a culture of impeccable commitments and "response-ability" like I've never seen before.

StandOut: The Groundbreaking New Strengths Assessment from the Leader of the Strengths Revolution, by Marcus Buckingham (Nashville, TN: Thomas Nelson, 2011). This book/assessment combo, and the related report, lays an excellent foundation for understanding how you are different from your peers. The beauty is in its simplicity.

StrengthsFinder 2.0, by Tom Rath (New York: Gallup Press, 2007). This book/assessment duo served up my first-ever *aha* moment around my strengths, though it is slightly hard to digest given that there are 34 strengths. The free version gives you your top five.

Prototype It, by Alberto Savoia (available in Google Docs format at www.pretotyping.org). The how-to for developing pretotypes, I consider this book (in pretotype format, as of January 2012) the bible of innovation.

Article

"Manage Your Energy, Not Your Time," by Tony Schwartz and Catherine McCarthy (*Harvard Business Review*, available from http://hbr.org/2007/10/manage-your-energy-not-your-time/ar/1). If you are tired of being tired, follow these practical tips to gain control over your work life.

NOTES

CHAPTER 1: INTRODUCTION

1. "Employee Engagement Report: Beyond the Numbers—A Practical Approach for Individuals, Managers, and Executives." Report. Skillman, NJ: BlessingWhite, 2011.
2. Inbox Zero. http://inboxzero.com; accessed January 1, 2012.
3. Hamel, Gary. *The Future of Management.* Boston: Harvard Business School Press, 2007.
4. Csikszentmihalyi, Mihaly. *Flow: The Psychology of Optimal Experience.* New York: Harper Perennial, 2008.
5. Beck, Martha Nibley. *Finding Your Own North Star: How to Claim the Life You Were Meant to Live.* London: Piatkus, 2001.
6. Ibid. *Steering by Starlight: How to Fulfill Your Destiny, No Matter What.* London: Piatkus, 2009.
7. Ibid. *Finding Your Own North Star.*
8. Patterson, Kerry, Joseph Grenny, David Maxfield, and Ron McMillan. *Influencer: The Power to Change Anything.* Highbridge, 2007.
9. Kofman, Fred. *Conscious Business: How to Build Value Through Values.* Boulder, CO: Sounds True, 2006.
10. Blake, Jenny. *Life after College: The Complete Guide to Getting What You Want.* Philadelphia: Running Press, 2011.
11. Hoehn, Charlie. *Recession-Proof Graduate: Charlie Hoehn's Guide to Getting Any Job Within a Year of Finishing College.* Amazon Digital Services.
12. Shatterboxx—Warning: May Cause Designgasm. www.shatterboxx.com; accessed January 1, 2012.
13. Daniels, Aubrey C., and James E. Daniels. *Measure of a Leader: An Actionable Formula for Legendary Leadership.* Atlanta, GA: Performance Management Publications (PMP), 2005.
14. Oshry, Barry. *Seeing Systems: Unlocking the Mysteries of Organizational Life.* San Francisco: Berrett-Koehler Publishers, 2007.
15. Ashworth, Will. "The Average Lifespan of S&P 500 Companies," Investopedia, August 25, 2010. http://stocks.investopedia.com; accessed January 1, 2012.

CHAPTER 3: THE NEW RULES

1. Black, Lewis, comedian. "The Ozone, Sunblock, The Flu, and Nyquil." Recorded June 14, 2005. Stand Up! Records.
2. Crum, Chris. "Solving the Insolvable Problem of Information Overload." WebProNews, January 10, 2011. www.webpronews.com/solving-the-insolvable-problem-of-information-overload-2011–01; accessed January 1, 2012.
3. Ressler, Cali, and Jody Thompson. *Why Work Sucks and How to Fix It: The Results-Only Revolution*. New York: Portfolio/Penguin, 2011.
4. "Work Life Success." Great Place to Work Institute: United States. March 2008. www.greatplacetowork.com; accessed April 2, 2011.
5. Pink, Daniel H. "Netflix Lets Its Staff Take as Much Holiday as They Want, Whenever They Want—and It Works." *The Telegraph*, August 14, 2010. www.telegraph.co.uk/finance/newsbysector/mediatechnologyan dtelecoms/7945719/Netflix-lets-its-staff-take-as-much-holiday-as-they-want-whenever-they-want-and-it-works.html; accessed January 1, 2012.
6. Semler, Ricardo. *The Seven-day Weekend: A Better Way to Work in the 21st Century*. London: Arrow Books, 2007.
7. Hsieh, Tony. *Delivering Happiness: A Path to Profits, Passion, and Purpose*. New York: Business Plus, 2010.

CHAPTER 4: IMPACT, NOT ACTIVITIES

1. Taylor, Frederick Winslow. *The Principles of Scientific Management*. New York: Harper, 1911.
2. Ibid. *Shop Management*. New York: Harper & Brothers, 1911.
3. U.S. National Center for Education Statistics. *Digest of Education Statistics*, 1900–1985. http://nces.ed.gov/programs/digest.; accessed January 1, 2012.
4. Minnesota Population Center, University of Minnesota. Integrated Public Use Microdata Series (IPUMs). http://usa.ipums.org/usa-action/variables/OCCcodes_tab; accessed January 1, 2012.
5. Taylor, Frederick Winslow. *Shop Management*.
6. Clow, Julie. "What Problem Are We Really Trying to Solve?" In *Learning Perspectives 2010*, edited by Nigel Paine and Elliott Masie. Saratoga Springs, NY: MASIE Center & The Learning CONSORTIUM.
7. General Mills. www.generalmills.com/en/Company.aspx; accessed January 1, 2012.

8. Kraft Foods. www.kraftfoodscompany.com/About/index.aspx; accessed January 1, 2012.

9. "Company Mission Statements." Mission Statements. www.mission statements.com/company_mission_statements.html; accessed January 3, 2012.

10. Kourlas, Gia. "Rockettes: Rebooted for a New Era." *New York Times*, November 6, 2011, New York ed., p. AR1.

11. Hsieh, Tony. *Delivering Happiness: A Path to Profits, Passion, and Purpose.* New York: Business Plus, 2010.

12. Abernathy, William B. *The Sin of Wages: Where the Conventional Pay System Has Led Us and How to Find a Way Out.* PerfSys Press, 1996.

13. Ressler, Cali, and Jody Thompson. *Why Work Sucks and How to Fix It: The Results-Only Revolution.* New York: Portfolio/Penguin, 2011.

CHAPTER 5: ENERGY, NOT SCHEDULES

1. Cockburn, Alistair. *Crystal Clear: A Human-Powered Methodology for Small Teams.* Boston: Addison-Wesley, 2005.

2. Loehr, James E., and Tony Schwartz. *The Power of Full Engagement: Managing Energy, Not Time, Is the Key to High Performance and Personal Renewal.* New York: Free Press, 2003.

3. Felton, Mark, and David O. Lyon. "The Post-Reinforcement Pause." *Journal of the Experimental Analysis of Behavior* 9, no. 2 (1966): 131–34. doi:10.1901/jeab.1966.9–131.

4. "Ten Things We Know to Be True." Google. www.google.com/about/corporate/company/tenthings.html; accessed January 1, 2012.

5. Gladwell, Malcolm. *Blink: The Power of Thinking without Thinking.* New York: Little, Brown and, 2005.

6. Skinner, B. F. *Science and Human Behavior.* New York: Macmillan, 1953.

7. Reese, Ellen P., Jane Howard, and T. W. Reese. *Human Behavior: Analysis and Application.* Dubuque, IA: W.C. Brown, 1978.

8. Schoenfeld, William N., and John Farmer. "Reinforcement Schedules and the Behavior Stream." In *The Theory of Reinforcement Schedules*, by William N. Schoenfeld. New York: Appleton-Century-Crofts, 1970.

9. Darlin, Damon. "The Man in the Middle Is Thriving on the Net." *New York Times*, September 25, 2011, New York ed., p. BU4.

10. The President's SAVE Award. www.whitehouse.gov/save-award; accessed January 1, 2012.

11. Goleman, Daniel. *Emotional Intelligence.* New York: Bantam Books, 1995.

CHAPTER 6: STRENGTHS, NOT JOB SLOTS

1. Rath, Tom. *StrengthsFinder 2.0*. New York: Gallup Press, 2007.
2. Peterson, Christopher, and Martin E. P. Seligman. *Character Strengths and Virtues: A Handbook and Classification*. New York: Oxford University Press, 2004.
3. Buckingham, Marcus. *StandOut: The Groundbreaking New Strengths Assessment from the Leader of the Strengths Revolution*. Nashville, TN: Thomas Nelson, 2011.
4. Csikszentmihalyi, Mihaly. *Flow: The Psychology of Optimal Experience*. New York: Harper Perennial, 2008.
5. Hevesi, Dennis. "Betty Skelton, Air and Land Daredevil, Dies at 85." *New York Times*, September 10, 2011. www.nytimes.com/2011/09/11/us/11skelton.html; accessed January 1, 2012.
6. Karsan, Rudy, and Kevin Kruse. *We: How to Increase Performance and Profits through Full Engagement*. Hoboken, NJ: John Wiley & Sons, Inc., 2011.
7. Rath, Tom. *StrengthsFinder 2.0*.
8. Buckingham, Marcus. *StandOut*.
9. Values In Action (VIA) Institute on Character. http://viacharacter.org; accessed January 1, 2012.
10. Narrative Science. www.narrativescience.com; accessed January 1, 2012.
11. Gunn, Tim, and Kate Moloney. *Tim Gunn: A Guide to Quality, Taste, & Style*. New York: Abrams Image, 2007.
12. True Colors International. www.true-colors.com/index.html; accessed January 1, 2012.
13. Rath, Tom, and Barry Conchie. *Strengths-Based Leadership: Great Leaders, Teams, and Why People Follow*. New York: Gallup Press, 2008.
14. Ware, Jim. "Crisis Lessons from Thrivers, Survivors, & Divers: Research on Investment Leadership & Culture." Report, 2010. Focus Consulting Group.
15. Collins, James C. *Good to Great: Why Some Companies Make the Leap—and Others Don't*. London: Random House Business, 2001.
16. Organizational Culture Assessment Instrument (OCAI). www.ocai-online.com; accessed January 1, 2012.
17. Godin, Seth. *Tribes: We Need You to Lead Us*. New York: Portfolio, 2008.
18. Brown, C. Brené. *The Gifts of Imperfection: Let Go of Who You Think You're Supposed to Be and Embrace Who You Are*. Center City, MN: Hazelden, 2010.
19. Hagel, John, John Seely Brown, and Lang Davison. *The Power of Pull: How Small Moves, Smartly Made, Can Set Big Things in Motion*. New York: Basic Books, 2010.

20. Marlar, Jenny. "Seven in 10 U.S. Workers Say Their Jobs Are Ideal." Gallup, March 1, 2010. www.gallup.com/poll/126227/Seven-Workers-Say-Jobs-Ideal.aspx; accessed January 1, 2012.

21. Whyte, David. *The Heart Aroused: Poetry and the Preservation of the Soul in Corporate America*. New York: Currency Doubleday, 1994.

22. Semler, Ricardo. *The Seven-Day Weekend: A Better Way to Work in the 21st Century*. London: Arrow Books, 2007.

23. Welch, Liz. "The Way I Work: Jen Bilik of Knock Knock." *Inc.*, October 2011. www.inc.com/magazine/201110/the-way-i-work-jen-bilik-of-knock-knock.html; accessed January 1, 2012.

24. Erker, Scott. "Hiring Success: The Importance of Culture Fit." *DDI World* audio blog, 2011. www.ddiworld.com/thought-leadership/podcasts/ddi-2011-series/hiring-success-the-importance-of-culture-fit; accessed January 1, 2012.

25. "E3 and Organizational Outcomes." White Paper. Development Dimensions International. Bridgeville, PA, 2004

26. Kasl, Charlotte Sophia. *If the Buddha Dated: Handbook for Finding Love on a Spiritual Path*. New York: Penguin/Arkana, 1999.

27. Buckingham, Marcus. *StandOut*. Nashville, TN: Thomas Nelson, 2011.

28. Branham, Leigh. *Keeping the People Who Keep You in Business: 24 Ways to Hang On to Your Most Valuable Talent*. New York, NY: AMACOM, 2000.

29. Hagel, John III, John Seely Brown, Duleesha Kulasooriya, and Dan Elbert. "Measuring the Forces of Long-Term Change: The 2010 Shift Index." Report. Santa Clara, CA: Deloitte Center for the Edge.

30. Ware, Jim. "Crisis Lessons from Thrivers, Survivors & Divers: Research on Investment Leadership & Culture." Report. Focus Consulting Group.

31. In Edmans, Alex. "Does the Stock Market Fully Value Intangibles? Employee Satisfaction and Equity Prices." *Journal of Financial Economics*, January 20, 2010. http://ssrn.com/abstract=985735; accessed January 1, 2012.

32. In Pattison, Kermit. "Chip Conley Took the Maslow Pyramid, Made It an Employee Pyramid and Saved His Company." *Fast Company*, August 26, 2010. www.fastcompany.com/1685009/chip-conley-wants-your-employees-to-hit-their-peak; accessed January 1, 2012.

33. Terwiesch, Christian, and Karl T. Ulrich. *Innovation Tournaments: Creating and Selecting Exceptional Opportunities*. Boston: Harvard Business Press, 2009.

CHAPTER 7: THE RIGHT THINGS, NOT EVERYTHING

1. "Leadership." *Wikipedia*. http://en.wikipedia.org/wiki/Leadership; accessed January 1, 2012.

2. Ibid.

3. Collis, David J., and Michael G. Rukstad. "Can You Say What Your Strategy Is?" *Harvard Business Review*, p. 82–90, April 2008.

4. Cockburn, Alistair. *Crystal Clear: A Human-Powered Methodology for Small Teams*. Boston: Addison-Wesley, 2005.

5. Beck, Martha Nibley. *Steering by Starlight: How to Fulfill Your Destiny, No Matter What*. London: Piatkus, 2009.

6. Collins, James C., and Morten T. Hansen. *Great by Choice: Uncertainty, Chaos, and Luck—Why Some Thrive Despite Them All*. New York: Harper Business, 2011.

7. Bregman, Peter. "Flexing Your 'No Thanks' Muscle." *Harvard Business Review* blog, July 18, 2011. http://blogs.hbr.org/bregman/2011/07/flexing-your-no-thanks-muscle.html; accessed January 1, 2012.

Chapter 8: Grassroots, Not Top-Down

1. Collins, James C., and Morten T. Hansen. *Great by Choice: Uncertainty, Chaos, and Luck—Why Some Thrive Despite Them All*. New York: Harper Business, 2011.

2. Pretotyping. www.pretotyping.org/home; accessed February 08, 2012.

3. "Duolingo: The Next Chapter in Human Computation." Presentation by Luis Von Ahn, TEDxCMU, April 25, 2011. http://tedxcmu.com/videos/luis-von-ahn; accessed January 1, 2012.

4. Surowiecki, James. *The Wisdom of Crowds: Why the Many Are Smarter Than the Few*. London: Abacus, 2006.

5. Malone, Thomas W., Robert Laubacher, and Chrysanthos Dellarocas. "Harnessing Crowds: Mapping the Genome of Collective Intelligence." MIT Sloan Research Paper No. 4732–09. February 3, 2009. http://ssrn.com/abstract=1381502; accessed January 1, 2012.

6. "The Zappos Insights Culture Book." 2010. www.zapposinsights.com/culture-book; accessed January 1, 2012.

7. Malone, Thomas et al. *Harnessing Crowds*.

8. Ibid.

9. In Amar, A.D., Carsten Hentrich, and Vlatka Hlupic. "To Be a Better Leader, Give Up Authority." *Harvard Business Review*, December 2009. http://hbr.org/2009/12/to-be-a-better-leader-give-up-authority/ar/1; accessed January 1, 2012.

10. Ibid.

11. Abernathy, William B. *The Sin of Wages: Where the Conventional Pay System Has Led Us and How to Find a Way Out*. PerfSys Press, 1996.

12. Lencioni, Patrick. *The Five Dysfunctions of a Team: A Leadership Fable.* San Francisco: Jossey-Bass, 2002.
13. Wiseman, Liz, and Greg McKeown. *Multipliers: How the Best Leaders Make Everyone Smarter.* New York: HarperBusiness, 2010.

CHAPTER 9: CONCLUSION

1. Oshry, Barry. *Seeing Systems: Unlocking the Mysteries of Organizational Life.* San Francisco: Berrett-Koehler Publishers, 2007.

EPILOGUE

1. In Galliano, Joseph. *Dear Me: A Letter to My Sixteen-Year-Old Self.* New York: Atria Books, 2011.

ACKNOWLEDGMENTS

I must start by acknowledging the people who shaped my early steps along the path to writing this book. In graduate school, the juxtaposition of my two co-chairmen, Thomas Critchfield and Roger Blashfield, contributed to my ability to think outside of the bounds of the status quo. Thanks to both of you, for challenging me intellectually and encouraging me to finish the program—by being scrappy, when necessary. I never did publish my major area paper. Will this suffice?

Thank you, Mary Hekl, for convincing me to "take the leap of faith" and join Google. That was where this book idea first took root; it then grew, for five years, before becoming a reality.

Thanks to Bill Baker for the dinner conversation and the Dolores Park brainstorming session, which underscored my belief in the book and inspired me to take it seriously. Your notion of "high-impact junkies" is important. You still need to write your book.

My book goal officially took off at my thirty-sixth birthday dinner in New York, perhaps one of the most inspiring dinners of my life, followed by the Creative Day of Genius on New Year's Eve 2011. I have two people to thank for this:

Michele Assad: From our crib sessions as babies to our phone sessions halfway around the world from each other today, I could not have navigated life without you. You are audacious, brave, smart, savvy, beautiful, strong, and tenacious—essentially everything I could possibly want in a big sister. You paved the road for me to think big, and you made it very easy to follow in your footsteps. I am forever grateful, and proud to call you my big sister.

Jenny Blake: My New York Yellow Brick Road fellow traveler, IP partner, HFF buddy, yoga guru, live-in life coach, and big-dream co-pilot—I cannot possibly express the depth of my appreciation for all of the little ways you make life more fun and the roller-coaster rides less scary. I will forever love our fun life-coach games.

Thanks, as well, to Kevin Kruse, Matt Holt, Shannon Vargo, and Sarah Lazin, for the chain of events, introductions, and advocacy you each provided, which made winning a book contract look easy. I was very lucky. Thanks also to Elana Schulman, for patiently guiding me through the publishing process.

I owe huge thanks, too, to the following individuals, who directly contributed to the content of this book:

Sarah Bloomfield: Your editing, opinions, guidance, enthusiasm, and encouragement helped me find my voice, untangle my thoughts, and trust in my ideas to produce something that really does represent *me*. You are an amazing colleague, and this manuscript would not have been what it is without your help. One day, I hope to return the favor.

Barry Stern: You restored my faith in the value of networking. After our first fortuitous meeting at the conference, followed by deep, poolside conversation over margaritas (the circle of trust!), I knew you'd forever be a good friend and thought partner. Your insight, experience, and perspective have shaped my ideas; and your generosity in reviewing the manuscript has been overwhelming. Thank you.

Brian Lanier: Your sharp eye and design sense saved me. I loved working again with my favorite art director. You will forever feel like home, and be able to make me laugh. Thank you, also, for saving my Christmas.

Chris Lopez: I have always respected your brilliance. Your work with teams is magical, even if you cringe at such a characterization. Thank you for your sharp insight and keen attention to details. I owe Chapter 7, "The Right Things, Not Everything" to your wisdom. I hope I got it half right.

Elisa Doucette, Jenny Blake, and Michele Assad: Thank you for reading early versions of the chapters and the book flap cover text, and for all other random assistance at critical moments. And most of all, thank you for the accountability e-mails, e-cards, phone calls, shopping trips, tweets, and hugs, all of which literally pulled me through this process. You were there when I needed you most!

My deep gratitude goes out to all of the writers who contributed their insightful articles and blog posts for inclusion in *The Work Revolution*: Sarah Bloomfield, Barry Stern, Marcos Salazar, Jessica Lawrence, Joe McCarthy, Chris Crum, Jenny Blake, and Leo Babauta. Your contributions provided the missing puzzle pieces that made the picture complete.

My heart, and thanks, goes out to all my work buddies throughout my career who made the workplace feel a little bit more like home: DeAnna Selva, Jennifer Yench, Jennifer Muntean, Brian Lanier, Sheily Chhabria, Jenny Blake, Candice Reimers (whom I'd also like to thank for the eight-hour bike rides that taught me perseverance, among *many* other things), Josh Kenitzer, Stephanie Chiang, Sarah Bloomfield, Kelsey Ruescher, Susan Maron, and Emily Sobel.

To my managers and mentors, who inspired me and served as models for my ideas about great leaders: Maggie Johnson, Jonni Kanerva, Ann Ruble, and Kannan Pashupathy. You all contributed greatly to my development—thank you.

Big hugs to my friends who encouraged me in important ways throughout the book project: Lance Dublin, Laurance Alvarado, Jenya Denissova, Sally Williams, Kevin Coady (for keeping me on track with my training, despite it all), Nate Cooper, and JK. And huge thanks to the amazing NY Creative Interns for helping me launch the book with a bang.

Unbelievable to me, the Wolveri entered my life in just the nick of time to provide neverending support, wisdom, ideas, and hugs to carry me over the finish line: Allie Mahler, Jenny Blake, Nicholas Reese, Willie F. Jackson, Nicky Hajal, Michael Hrostoski, Kyle Durand, Dan Jarvis, Sean Ogle, and Karol Gajda—I love you all. You reminded me to have fun, play, and be *me* in the most critical of moments.

Dad and Crystal, thank you for your neverending support. Your prayers lifted me up in critical moments, and your belief in what I can do keeps me humble and gracious.

Finally, thank you Danielle. You are the best daughter I could ever have. That you feel proud of me as your momma makes me glow. I am proud of *you* for figuring out what you love, for exploring your strengths, and for persevering through difficult times to follow your own North Star. May this book contribute to making a better world of work for you, and may you find happiness in your own work life.

ABOUT THE AUTHOR

Julie Clow earned her PhD in psychology—experimental analysis of behavior, with an emphasis on organizational behavior management—from Auburn University in 2000, at the age of 25. She started her career as an independent consultant, and subsequently joined a small woman-owned business, Carley Corporation, in Orlando, Florida, to produce custom training solutions for large-scale clients, such as such as the U.S. Navy and Marine Corps, Asia-Pacific Economic Community, BellSouth, and SunTrust Bank. She quickly rose to become the Chief Learning Officer at Carley Corporation, where she won and then managed several multimillion-dollar contracts. In 2006, Julie joined Google, where she spent five years focusing on team effectiveness, leadership and management, and organizational culture, primarily for engineers. During her tenure there, she discovered the power of freedom and autonomy to transform organizations into a thriving place to work. She now serves as the Vice President of Learning and Development for an equally inspired investment management company.

In her free time, Julie enjoys a wide range of outdoor activities, including triathlons, road biking, hiking, and surfing. She resides in New York, New York.

You can connect with Julie on Twitter at @clowjul, or by visiting www.theworkrevolutionbook.com.

Index

ABC Model, 115–117
Abernathy, William, 81, 199–200
Activities
    focus on impact vs., 57, 75–77,
        90, 220
    identification of low-value, 110
    roots of management of, 63–68
Adhocracy culture, 142
Amar, A. D., 198
Amiel, Henri-Fréderic, 127
Analytical thinking, 110–111
Anchoring phenomenon, 94
Antecedents, 114, 115
Apollo 13, 186
Apple, 73–74
Assembly lines, 63
Automation, 68, 69
Averaging, 195

Babauta, Leo, 174–176
Beck, Martha, 8, 15, 39, 172
Behavior
    analysis of, 114–118
    explanation of, 114
    leveraging channels of, 118–120
Be Social Change, 187–188
Best Buy, 48–50, 86
Bilik, Jen, 146
Black, Lewis, 41
Blake, Jenny, 11, 101–103
Blake, Jim, 189
Bloomfield, Sarah, 87–89

Bregman, Peter, 178–179
Brown, Brené, 143
Brown, John Seely, 144
Buckingham, Marcus, 127–128,
    151
Bureaucracy, 121–122

Call centers, 49–50
CAPTCHA, 190–191
Career counseling, 125
Career-life bull's-eye, 130
Carroll, Lewis, 62
Cater2.me, 118–119
Center for Collective Intelligence
    (Massachusetts Institute of
    Technology), 192, 196
Change. *See also* Organizational
    change
    nature of, 8–9
    resistance to, 47
Clan culture, 142
Collaboration
    cross-team, 153–154
    work-hour flexibility and, 48
Collaborative creation, 193
Collective intelligence
    creation by, 192–194
    decision making by, 194–196
    elements of, 191
    empowerment though, 190–192
    motivation to contribute to,
        196–197

Collins, Jim, 140–141, 173, 184

Collis, David, 163, 164

Communication information, 42–43

Conchie, Barry, 139

Conformity, 143–145

Conley, Chip, 152

Conscious Business (Kofman), 9

Consequences, 114–115

Copeland, Patrick, 185

Coworkers, 25–26

Creation, forms of, 193

Credit Acceptance, 49–50, 104

Crum, Chris, 44

CSC, 198

Csikszentmihaly, Mihalyi, 128

Culture. *See* Organizational culture

Customer service
  activity-focused, 75–77
  impact-focused, 77, 79

Daniels, Aubrey, 13

Daniels, Jamie, 13

Davison, Lang, 144

Dead-end mission statements, 72

Dear Me: A Letter to My Sixteen-Year-Old Self (Galliano), 220–221

Decision making
  creative intelligence and, 194–196
  data-driven, 189
  energy of, 110–113

Delivering Happiness: A Path to Profits, Passion, and Purpose (Hsieh), 77

Deluxe Job-Shove-It Quiz
  guiding principles analysis of answers to, 31–37
  organizational layers analysis of answers to, 28–31
  questions in, 20–28

Democratization of social change, 187–188

Development Dimensions International (DDI), 146, 147

Diminishers, 202–203

Discretionary performance, 54

Diversity, on teams, 200–201

Dostoevsky, Fyodor, 47

Dress codes, 51–52, 83

Economic crisis of 2008, 140

Educational attainment, 64–66

Edward Jones, 163–164

E-mail, processing of, 4, 43

Employee benefits, 3, 53–54

Employee engagement, 151–154

Employee Engagement Report (BlessingWhite) (2011), 2–3

Employees. *See* Individuals

Employee turnover, 48–49

Empowerment
  environment for, 58, 197
  lack of employee, 3
  of teams, 135
  though collective intelligence, 190–197
  of workforce, 225

Energy
  channels of behavior and, 118–120
  of decision making, 110–113
  eliminating bad, 120–124
  of individuals, 97–107

knowledge of your personal, 130

in organizations, 96

schedules and focus of, 58,
98–100, 219

tips to manage your, 101–105

of value, 107–120

workplace as charger of,
105–107

Energy suckers

bad managers as, 123–124

bureaucracy as, 121–122

passive aggression as, 122–123

Engagement, lack of, 2–4

engEDU (Google), 199, 202

Erickson, Tammy, 69

Failure, 189–190

Fears

of individuals, 209–210

of leaders, 208–209

trust vs., 212

Feedback, role of, 78–79

Finding Your Own North Star
(Beck), 8, 39

The Five Dysfunctions of a Team
(Lencioni), 201

Fixed-schedule rule, 49–50

Fixed schedules of reinforcement,
106

Flexibility

in dress code, 51–52

in establishing new, 57–59

processes, 56–57

self-management, 55–56

in sick days and vacation time,
50–51

in work hours, 48–49

in work schedules, 49–50

Flow, 8, 128

Fluidity

strategies to achieve, 152–154

use of common language for,
154

Focus Consulting Group, 140

40-hour workweek rule, 48–49

Galliano, Joseph, 220–221

General Mills, 71

*The Gifts of Imperfection: Let Go of
Who You Think You're Supposed
to be and Embrace Who You Are*
(Brown), 143–144

Gladwell, Malcolm, 112

Globalization, realities of, 41–42

Godin, Seth, 142

*Good to Great: Why Some Companies
Make the Leap—and Others
Don't* (Collins), 140–141

Google

cost-cutting initiative at,
194–195

engEDU at, 199, 202

fluidity at, 152–154

focus on strategy at, 163

innovative practices at, 5, 6, 16,
106–107, 207, 209

leadership program at, 181–182,
186

as learning organization, 199

perks and benefits at, 3, 53–54

Personal Development Plan at,
113–114, 117–118

prototyping culture at, 185, 186

teams at, 133–137, 201–202, 207

training program decisions at,
199

Grant, Bud, 151
Grassroots initiatives
empowerment through
collective intelligence and,
190–197
explanation of, 182–183
function of, 197–200
goals of, 204–205
leaders and, 200–203
power of small and, 183–186,
189–190
*Great by Choice: Uncertainty, Chaos,
and Luck—Why Some Thrive
Despite Them All* (Collins and
Hansen), 173, 184
Guiding principles
development of, 78
for individuals, 228–229
Job-Shove-It Quiz and,
31–37
for leaders, 226–227
for organizations, 74–78,
224–225
rules vs., 74
Gunn, Tim, 137

Haberman, Linda, 74
Hagel, John, 144
Hansen, Morten, 173, 184
*The Heart Aroused: Poetry and the
Preservation of the Soul in
Corporate America* (Whyte),
145
Hentrich, Carsten, 198
Hierarchical culture, 142
Hiring
with organizational culture in
mind, 146–149

process of, 125–126
for specific job slots, 126
Hlupic, Vlatka, 198
Hoehn, Charlie, 11
Hsieh, Tony, 77, 193

Idea lists, 175
IDEO, 5, 105, 184–185
If Buddha Dated (Kasl), 147
Impact
focus on, 57, 77, 90, 220
of individuals, 81–87, 91
of leaders, 91
manager's role of sharing, 80–81
of organizations, 91
problems related to, 67–68
Inbox Zero, 4
Independent creation, 193
Individuals
bonding between, 147–149
differentiation inspired by,
203–205
energy of, 97–107
engagement of, 2–4
fears of, 209–210
guiding principles for, 228–229
impact of, 81–87, 91
as instigators, 81–87
recognizing differences among,
44–45
role in change, 10–13
role of, 26–27
Industrial Revolution, 63
*Influencer: The Power to Change
Anything* (Patterson et al.), 9
Information
accessing and processing, 3–4,
42–43

forms of, 42
overload of, 43–44
Innovation, at Google, 5, 6
Internal transfers, 126
Intuition, relying on, 111–113

Job slots
   flexibility in, 55–56
   focus on strengths vs., 58,
      219–220
   hiring for specific, 126
   rigidity of, 134
Johnson, Maggie, 202, 217
Joie de Vivre hotel chain, 152

Kanerva, Jonni, 6
Karsan, Rudy, 130
Kasl, Charlotte, 147
Kelly, Tom, 105
Knock Knock, 146
Knowledge work
   energy of individuals and, 97
   nature of, 69
   nineteenth-century shift to, 64
Kofman, Fred, 9, 10
Kraft, 71
Kruse, Kevin, 130

Lawrence, Jessica, 6–8
Leaders
   as debate facilitators, 200–202
   fears of, 208–209
   function of, 91, 201
   guiding principles for, 226–227
   as intelligence multipliers,
      202–203
   prioritizing by, 164–165
   role in change, 13–14

Leadership
   Deluxe Job-Shove-It Quiz on,
      23–25, 29–30
   explanation of, 13–14,
      160–161
   strengths-based, 133
Leadership development
   function of, 160–161
   at Google, 181–182, 186
   prioritization and, 161
Learning information, 42
Lencioni, Patrick, 157, 201
Life After College: The Complete
      Guide to Getting What You
      Want (Blake), 11, 102, 103
Lopez, Chris, 169–170
Low intelligence discretion, 192

Mahler, Allie, 187, 188
Management
   of activities, 63–68
   Scientific, 63–65, 68
   top-down, 191, 197, 203
Management style
   activity-focused, 75–77
   impact-focused, 77, 79
Managers
   Ask, Don't Tell role of, 79–80
   effects of bad, 123–124
   sharing impact as role of,
      80–81
Market culture, 142
McCarthy, Joe, 143–145
McCord, Patty, 51
McKeown, Greg, 202
Measure of a Leader (Daniels and
      Daniels), 13, 14
Micromanagement, 69

Mission statements
  construction of, 73–74
  dead-end, 72
  function of, 71–72
  problem-based, 72, 74
Moloney, Kate, 137
Motivation, 196–197
Multipliers, intelligence, 202–203
Multipliers: How the Best Leaders Make Everyone Smarter (Wiseman and McKeown), 202

Narrative Science, 136
NASA, 195
Netflix, 50–51
Networking, 137
News from Martha Beck Inc. (Beck), 15
No, learning to say, 176–179
Noom, Inc., 186–187

Obama, Barack, 122
Occupational codes, 66
Occupations, nineteenth-century, 70
Organizational behavior channels, 118–120
Organizational change
  channels of, 9–15
  difficulties in facilitating, 39–40
  nature of, 8–9
  role of employees in, 10–13
  role of leaders in, 13–14
  role of organizations in, 14–15
Organizational culture
  clash of current and aspirational, 149–151

finding people that fit into, 146–149
individual strengths and, 140–142
types of, 142
Organizational Culture Assessment Instrument (OCAI), 142
Organizations
  building strengths-based, 139–142, 146–149, 151–154
  change in, 14–15, 69–70
  conformity and, 144–145
  dimensions of bonding in, 147–149
  employee's role in, 26–27, 30–31
  guiding principles for, 74–78, 224–225
  harnessing energy in, 96
  impact of, 91
  leadership in, 23–25, 29–30
  letting go of control in, 197–200
  management approaches to fit types of, 45–46
  measures of success of, 78–79
  mission statements for, 70–74
  philosophy of, 20–22, 28–29
  power of small in, 183–186, 189–190
  as problem statements, 69–79
  recognizing need for flexibility in, 46–47
  rules of, 22–23, 29
  strategy of, 161–164
  teams and coworkers in, 25, 26, 30
  top-down, 191, 197, 203
Oshry, Barry, 14, 209

Passive aggression, 122–123
Perks, 53–54
Petakov, Artem, 186
Peterson, Christopher, 127
Pichette, Patrick, 195
PIC/NIC Analysis, 115–118
Planning fallacy, 93–94
Players, 10
Post-reinforcement pause, 106
The Power of Full Engagement
    (Schwartz), 102
*The Power of Pull: Institutions as
    Platforms for Individual Growth*
    (Hagel et al.), 144
Pretotypes, 185, 189
Prioritization
    to capitalize on personal
        strengths, 172–174
    determining mission worthiness
        and, 165–166
    leadership and, 164–165
    learning to say "no" and,
        176–179
    process of ranking in, 167–168
    putting it all together in,
        168–169
    role of, 58, 161–164
    role of elimination in, 166
    strategies for, 172–174
    on teams, 169–171, 178
Problem-based mission statements,
    72, 74
Problem solving
    shift to, 68
    through collective intelligence,
        192–196
Problem statements, 84–85
Processes, flexibility in, 56–57

Productivity
    Scientific Management and,
        63, 68
    strategies for, 174–176
    work-hour flexibility and, 48
    work schedules and, 99, 100
Project management, 169–170
Prototyping culture, 185–186, 189

Questioning, in workplace, 82–83
Quitting, 173–174

Rath, Tom, 127, 139
Reagan, Nancy, 179
reCAPTCHA, 190–191
Recession-Proof Graduate
    (Hoehn), 11
Reinforcement, fixed schedules
    of, 106
Resources
    for individuals, 228–230
    for leaders, 227–228
    for organizations, 225–226
Results, focus on, 57–58
Rockettes, 74
Roles, strengths-based, 134
Rosenberg, Jonathan, 200
Rukstad, Michael, 163, 164
Rules
    Deluxe Job-Shove-It Quiz on
        organization, 22–23, 29
    dress code, 51–52, 83
    fear of breaking old, 47
    fixed-schedule, 49–50
    40-hour workweek, 48–49
    guiding principles vs., 74
    job slot, 55–56
    offering challenges to, 83

Rules (*continued*)
  perks and benefits, 53–54
  principles for establishing
    flexible, 57–59
  vacation and sick time, 50–51
  well-defined processes, 56–57

Salazar, Marcos, 187–188
SAVE Award, 122
Savoia, Alberto, 185
Schedules. *See also* Work hours
  fixed-work, 98–99
  flexibility in, 49–50
  focus on energy vs., 58, 98–100,
    219
  natural-energy, 99–100
  true urgency and, 103–104
Schwartz, Tony, 102
Scientific Management (Taylor),
    63–65, 68
Search engines, 67–68
*Seeing Systems: Unlocking the
    Mysteries of Organizational Life*
    (Oshry), 14, 209
Self-management, 55–56
Seligman, Martin, 127
Semco, 55–56, 146
Semler, Ricardo, 56
Shatterboxx, 11
Shop Management (Taylor), 63, 64
Sick days, 50–51
*The Sin of Wages: Where the
    Conventional Pay System Has
    Led Us and How to Find a Way
    Out* (Abernathy), 81, 199–200
Skelton, Betty, 129
Skinner, B. F., 114
Social change, 187–188

Social media
  age and adoption of, 11, 12
  promotion using, 187
Southwest Airlines, 142
Start-ups
  background and culture of, 6–8
  role of investors in, 7
  success of, 4–5
*Steering by Starlight: How to Fulfill
    Your Destiny, No Matter What*
    (Beck), 8, 172
Stern, Barry, 151
Strategy
  explanation of, 161–162
  role in organizations, 161–163
*Strength-Based Leadership: Great
    Leaders, Teams, and Why People
    Follow* (Rath and Conchie),
    139
Strengths
  applications for personal, 129
  assessment of your, 131–132
  building organizations on,
    139–142, 146–149, 151–154
  knowledge of your, 128–131
  learning to say "no" and,
    176–179
  prioritizing to capitalize on
    personal, 172–174
  of teams, 132–139
  terms and definitions for,
    127–128
Strengths-based organizations
  employee engagement in, 151
  explanation of, 151
  fluidity in, 152–154
  organizational culture fit and,
    139–142, 146–149

Strengths-based roles, 134
Surowiecki, James, 181, 191

Talent, 127
Taylor, Frederick, 63–65, 67
Teams
  defining vision and goals
    of, 135
  Deluxe Job-Shove-It Quiz on,
    25–26
  development process on,
    169–171
  diversity on, 200–201
  empowerment of, 135
  filling in gaps in, 135–138
  interactions between, 153–154
  in organizations, 25, 26, 30
  prioritization on, 169–171,
    178
  recruiting new members to,
    138–139
  role of leaders of, 227
  strengths of, 132–135, 137
Technology, 41–42
Testing, 189–190
Thin-slice judgments, 111
Time
  manage energy not, 102–105
  problems causes by obsession
    with, 93–95
Tim Gunn: A Guide to Quality,
  Tastes, and Style (Gunn and
  Moloney), 137
To-do lists, 176
Top-down organizations, 191,
  197, 203
Tribes, 142
True Colors assessment, 138–139

Trust
  fear vs., 212
  reasons to, 212–214

Unconditional responsibility, 9–10
Universal Principles, 223

Vacation time, 50–51
Value
  discovering organizational
    channels of, 113–120
  energy of, 107–113
  role of individuals in finding,
    107–113
Varon, Jamie, 11
Victims, 9–10
Virgin America, 142
Vision, for teams, 135
Voting, 195

We: How to Increase Performance and
  Profits through Full Engagement
  (Karsan and Kruse), 130
Whyte, David, 145
Wikis, 193
The Wisdom of Crowds (Surowiecki),
  191
Wiseman, Liz, 202
W.L. Gore, 5
Work
  allocation of, 133–135
  changing entire world of, 6
  engagement in, 130
  evolution of, 1, 2
  focus on, 81
  popular culture on, 2
  signals of low-value, 109–110
  ways to think about, 87–88

Workforce
  educational attainment of,
    64–66
  empowerment of, 225
Work hours. *See also* Schedules
  flexibility in, 48–49
  problems related to traditional,
    46, 98–99
Workplace
  freedom in, 5
  as individual energy charger,
    105–107
  role of questioning in,
    82–83
  visions of success in, 214–216

Work practices, 88–89
Work Revolution
  change in all organizations as
    strategy for, 5–6, 10
  following easy path as strategy
    for, 8–9
  guidelines for success in, 15
  implementation of, 210–212
  manifesto for, 4–5
  role of individuals in, 10–13
  role of leaders in, 13–14
  role of organizations in, 14–15

Zappos, 56–57, 77, 79, 193
Zen Habits, 174